Wandering Architects

Detmar Blow
(portrait by Neville Lytton, 1910)

WANDERING ARCHITECTS

In Pursuit of an Arts and Crafts Ideal

MICHAEL DRURY

SHAUN TYAS
STAMFORD
2000

Typeset and designed using the disc of the author by the publisher

Published by

SHAUN TYAS (an imprint of 'Paul Watkins')
18 Adelaide Street
Stamford
Lincolnshire
PE9 2EN

ISBN

1 900289 13 X

Printed and bound in the United Kingdom by the Alden Group, Oxford.

This book is dedicated to the memory of H. Dalton Clifford who introduced me to the work of Detmar Blow, of which he had been aware since writing for *Country Life* in the 1950s. He met Harold Falkner and Philip Tilden at that time too, helping Tilden complete and publish his autobiography. Without him, the work of these accomplished architects might have remained in obscurity longer than their talents deserved.

CONTENTS

ACKNOWLEDGMENTS

This book would not have been possible without the help and co-operation of the owners of the houses and the other buildings it describes. I would like to acknowledge too the advice and encouragement given by Tony Clifford, Jane Fawcett, Margaret Richardson, and Andrew Saint when I first became interested in Detmar Blow's early career in 1984. Subsequently the response to enquiries on a broader front has been greatly appreciated. In particular I would like to thank Detmar Blow's daughter and son-in-law, Lucilla & Philip Warre-Cornish; Blow's grandchildren: Detmar Blow, Simon Blow and Mary Rose Blacker; the late Roger Powell and his daughter, Mrs Thompson-Lewis, for the use of family archive material about Alfred Powell; Mrs Rosamund Caffrey for memories of her father, Hugh Fairfax-Cholmeley; Ian Allan and Pam Phillips, Herbert North's granddaughter; Nicholas Mander for his help on Norman Jewson; Donald Gimson; Mrs Edward Barnsley and Allan Lupton; Annette Carruthers and Mary Greensted from Cheltenham Museum; Charles Keighley and Lynne Walker for information relating to Randall Wells; Mrs Farrow, her friends, neighbours and associates in the Farnham Society for their help on the work of Harold Falkner; James Bettley for advice on Philip Tilden and Alan Crawford for his extracts from the Ashbee diaries relating to Tilden and for his help throughout; Reginald Snell for his help on William Weir; Miss Greenhill, the librarian at the SPAB and Jane for putting up with all this plus three under five at the outset.

PICTURE ACKNOWLEDGEMENTS

The author is grateful to the following for permission to reproduce illustrations: The Architectural Association; Mary Rose Blacker; Detmar and Isabella Blow; Simon Blow; The British Architectural Library; Cheltenham Art Gallery and Museums; Country Life Picture Library; Miles D'Arcy Irvine, Antony Feltham-King; Roger Levin (fig. 63); Nicholas Mander; Alan H. Martin (fig. 101); The Metropolitan Museum of Art; National Monuments Record; The National Trust; Reginald Snell; The Society for the Protection of Ancient Buildings; Daniel Sykes at Bedales School; Mrs Thompson-Lewis; Lucilla and Philip Warre Cornish; The William Morris Gallery (fig. 19); and Wiltshire Archaeological and Natural History Society.

1. Mareuil, near Abbeville (from *The Architect*, April 4th, 1890).

INTRODUCTION

This book is about a group of Arts and Crafts architects who worked with their own hands on site. They travelled from building to building, often living far from home and this lifestyle characterises the group, referred to collectively as the Wandering Architects. As such it was they who came closest to fulfilling architecturally the ideals of the Arts and Crafts movement, as propounded by John Ruskin who had suggested that, to inject new life into architecture, building and design should be brought together under the direct control of a single mind – better still under the control of a single hand.

William Morris, having decided to take up architecture after reading Ruskin as an undergraduate, turned to other things because, as his friend Philip Webb said: 'He found he could not get into close contact with it; it had to be done at second hand.'[1] The Wandering Architects set out, and succeeded to a greater or lesser degree, to follow the path Morris had turned from. Their guide was Philip Webb. Forsaking a conventional architectural career in a London office for a closer involvement in the building process on site, they proved that the teaching of the Arts and Crafts, founded upon a direct relationship between the artist and his work, could be applied successfully even to architecture.

Because they built with their own hands and because building is time-consuming work, their output was small. As a result they have tended to be overlooked by historians, in contrast to the better known and more prolific architects of the Arts and Crafts movement. But if the movement was about a direct relationship between a man and his art, then many of the more well-known men fell short of the mark. Lutyens, Voysey and Mackintosh all depended upon the agency of others to see their designs built. And although others like Lethaby, Prior and Gimson were deeply committed to a direct relationship between designer and builder, none were to realise their own creations at first hand. It was only the Wandering Architects who succeeded in achieving this ideal.

In assessing their achievement and attempting to redress the historical balance, it should be remembered that the Arts and Crafts movement was an attempt to re-establish a way of working that allowed the creative process its proper place in daily life. In architecture, Ruskin and Morris believed such a process to have been integral to the medieval way of working but they feared it

[1] W. R. Lethaby, *Philip Webb and His Work* (1935), p. 122.

to have been lost long since in the highly developed contractual methods commonly used in the post industrial era. Through the itinerant lifestyle that they were often obliged to adopt, the Wandering Architects rediscovered the footsteps of their medieval forebears. To those who strove towards an integration of lifestyle and working methods, architecture was to be judged not just in terms of the buildings that resulted but in terms also of the opportunities it presented to reintroduce a hand crafted basis to the building process.

Some, like Morris, went further. To them, the Arts and Crafts movement became political. So deep rooted were the issues that cultural and economic aspects could not be separated. So what were these issues? The attributes that the Wandering Architects shared, the attributes that made them a collective group, reflect these issues directly. By working with their own hands, they epitomised an anti-industrial stance. Their crafted approach was a reaction to the value system of late Victorian commercial manufacture. They were the architectural wing of an industrial counter-revolution that sprang directly from Morris's involvement in the evolution of the socialist movement in this country.

Some of the Wandering Architects undoubtedly saw themselves in such a light. Others less so, if at all. Were they then a cohesive group? Did they have anything in common other than a shared working method? There are inter-relationships that clearly indicate that they did. They spring from a common background in the architectural practices that were still, late in the nineteenth century and long after his most influential work, well steeped in the teaching of Ruskin. These practices are also, hardly coincidentally, those closest to the influence of William Morris. Several of the Wandering Architects shared a formative period in such practices but many also served their time directly with Morris, most frequently through his Society for the Protection of Ancient Buildings.

As the principal architect member of the SPAB in its early days, Philip Webb became as important to the group in question, perhaps more so in many instances, than Morris himself. Certainly Webb was more instrumental in its architectural development on a day to day basis for, although he took exception to the system of articled pupillage, he went out of his way to ensure that the younger architects associated with the SPAB were not only fully equipped to deal with the repair of ancient buildings but also had a true understanding, as Webb and Morris saw it, at least, of the medieval way of thinking that had resulted in the creation of such buildings in the first instance. In this way the school of Wandering Architects was essentially within the Gothic Revival tradition, but it was to stand for no pale imitations, no scholarly reconstructions of medieval work. Instead it was to regenerate architecture from the same standpoint as our medieval forebears. Its proponents were to put themselves into the same way of thinking about their art as their medieval counterparts and then, from this position of understanding, attempt to create new buildings relevant to their time.

It will be clear by now that, if a study of the Wandering Architects is to be relevant when assessed within their own terms of reference, it must dwell as much on lifestyle as it does on architectural style. So this book concentrates on the architects and their lives as well as their output. It was never their intention to make grandiloquent architectural statements in terms of built form but the ideologically fastidious way they went about realising their architecture impresses in a quite different way and should not be undervalued.

Despite their common goals and their often intertwined careers, some aspects of the Wandering Architects are difficult to study collectively. As a result this book is organised as a series of related studies, each dealing with the career, or the relevant part of the career, of one particular member of the group. These studies are arranged in an interconnected way, as suggested by the relationships between the group members but because it is a book about many people it may appear disjointed in places. There is, nevertheless, a single thread which runs through it and that thread is the career of Detmar Blow. Taught in turn by Ruskin, Morris and Webb, he knew Lethaby and Gimson, working closely with the latter in an architectural endeavour that covered the last five years of the nineteenth century. It was never a partnership; nor was his association with Alfred Powell, at about the same time, despite their shared office accommodation at one stage. Blow worked too with Basil Stallybrass, another Wandering Architect, this time on a more clearly defined basis, for Stallybrass was part of the itinerant team Blow assembled during this period, a team whose achievements characterise, perhaps better than any other, the ideals of the Wandering Architect's method of building at first hand. The threads of Blow's career become intertwined with other key members of the group to such an extent that the narrative returns to him regularly throughout the book.

A point should perhaps be made on the use of source material. If Blow's career indicates the difficulties inherent in squaring an itinerant medieval lifestyle with the demands of a twentieth-century architectural practice, it is the original source material that offers the truest flavour of the Wandering Architects, their contemporaries and their times. For this reason primary sources are quoted wherever possible to give as direct an insight into the architects' thinking and into the thinking of their contemporaries.

In conclusion one should not dwell too long on the fate that befell Detmar Blow. In many ways his life story is too neat a parable, for it is the story of a man who started his career as a disciple of Ruskin and Morris, only to end it as a

WANDERING ARCHITECTS

The Offices of Philip Webb, Norman Shaw and John Sedding

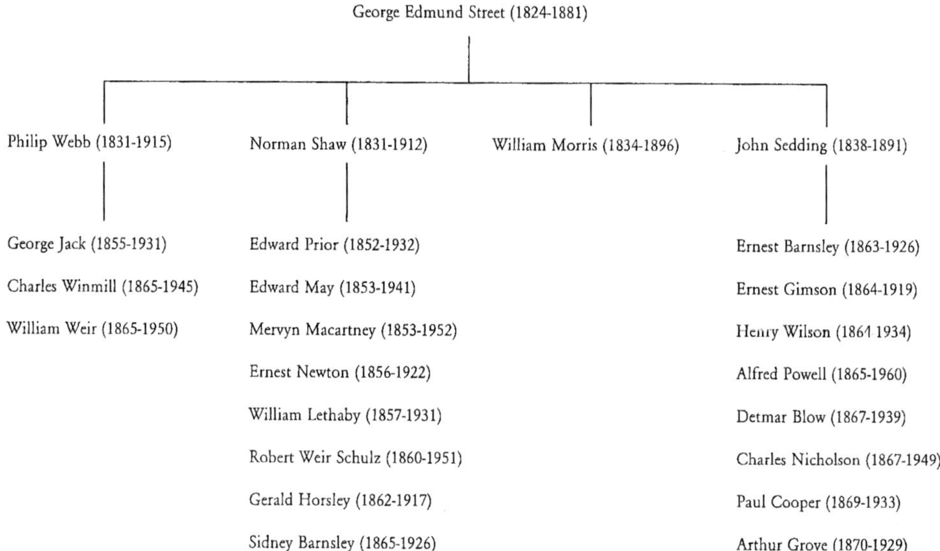

broken man, cast aside when agent to the richest man in England. But the achievements of the Wandering Architects might have been better appreciated earlier had things ended otherwise for Blow, for although successful as a society architect, his career is not a success story. Perhaps, however, in the final judgement the achievement of Blow and the other Wandering Architects will be valued as a significant contribution to the architectural history of the twentieth century. The link between William Morris and the Modern Movement is one that has been pursued by architectural historians over the last fifty years and more. That there is a link is clear but the Morris centenary, celebrated in 1996, has shown that his influence on twentieth-century architecture, although significant, has been broad and diffuse. His influence on the Wandering Architects, however, had neither of these characteristics. They represent Morrisian architecture directly and without compromise and may usefully serve as an indicator of how his teaching could lead to a way of building that was neither historically derivative nor stylistically eclectic. If not the forerunners of the Modern Movement, they may well have been the last progressive movement to precede it.

Chapter 1
STARTING POINTS
Cockerell's Connections

The painter should grind his own colours; the architect work in the mason's yard with his men.

John Ruskin, *The Stones of Venice*

According to Detmar Blow the rolls and coffee, even more than the fine architecture, were why John Ruskin so loved France.[1] So it is fitting that this story starts, on Sunday, 24 June 1888, with Ruskin's breakfast at the Tête de Boeuf in Abbeville. His arrival came as a shock to Sydney Cockerell, a young man at the other end of the dining room,[2] for Cockerell had been told by Ruskin only a few weeks earlier that continuing poor health and state of mind had caused plans for such a trip to be shelved.[3] Ruskin came over, perhaps somewhat embarrassed, and introduced his companion Arthur Severn. Cockerell in turn introduced his, Detmar Blow, who was travelling on a scholarship won from the Architectural Association in London. He was heading for Beauvais and had persuaded Cockerell to join him.

After breakfast Severn took Blow sketching while Ruskin and Cockerell went out to walk the streets of the old town. Later they all drove along the riverside to see the Romanesque church at Mareuil (1). For Blow this chance meeting with Ruskin was to wreck the plans he had made for his travelling scholarship but in their place it substituted a six month period of travel with Ruskin that was to fundamentally influence his career. For Ruskin (1819–1900) the trip was also significant for it was to be his last, marking only a temporary reemergence from a self-imposed exile in the Lake District. Already he was becoming a remote figure, a whole generation of young architects having grown up since he had written *The Stones of Venice* thirty-five years before.

1 The Hon Neville Lytton, 'The Art of Detmar Blow', *English Life* (June 1925), pp. 56–9.

2 Sydney Cockerell's Diaries, the Cockerell Papers, British Museum Manuscripts Collection. Quotations in the text followed in brackets by a date that includes the day of the week, i.e. [Sunday 24 June 1888], are from Sydney Cockerell's diaries.

3 Sydney Carlisle Cockerell, *Friends of a Lifetime*, ed Viola Meynell (London: Jonathan Cape, 1940), pp. 48–9.

Ruskin's teaching, used and abused by the Gothic Revivalists, compromised in the Battle of the Styles, was becoming buried in the increasing professionalism of architecture that followed in the last decades of the century. But to Ruskin architecture was an art, not a profession and his last disciple, Detmar Blow (1867–1939), typified a small group of architects who struggled through the 1890s towards an architecture that cared less about style and more about the nature of building itself, as Ruskin had advocated in mid-century.

Their achievement must be set in context from the outset if it is to be appreciated. That John Ruskin had made a great impact upon the previous generation there is no doubt. Nonetheless much of what he wrote proved hard to reconcile with an architecture which reflected Victorian society in the second half of the 19th century. For Ruskin architecture was not something that could be produced on the factory floor. It had to be a true reflection of the spirit of mankind, expressing all its failings as well as its triumphs of individuality. Ruskin instigated the true Gothic Revival in the 1850s with his *Seven Lamps of Architecture* but did so by talking of architecture in terms of life and truth rather than in terms of Early or Middle Pointed and the niceties of Gothic style. He raged against the products of an industrialized building industry and held up the Lamp of Sacrifice – the sweat and torment of individual creativity – in place of machine-made ornament. He held up the Lamp of Memory – a reverence for the historical continuum – in place of manufacturers' catalogue art. Any beauty achieved by man in building was, for him, due to man's very vitality:

> There is not a cluster of weeds growing in any cranny of ruin which has not a beauty ... in some respects ... superior to that of the most elaborate sculpture of its stones. The carved work, though tenfold less rich than the knots of grass beside it ... a thousandfold less delicate ... a millionfold less admirable, it is admirable nonetheless as the work of poor clumsy, toilsome man.[4]

Such a philosophy posed considerable problems for the architect. These problems are well illustrated by the difficulties experienced in architecture by the greatest exponent of the Arts and Crafts movement, William Morris (1834–96). As undergraduates at Oxford he and his friend Edward Burne-Jones had read *The Stones of Venice* and it determined the direction of their careers; that of Morris initially to architecture, and that of Burne-Jones to painting. In 1856 Morris took articles in the office of George Edmund Street (1824–81) but it was to be a short-lived excursion. Ruskin had preached a direct and personal involvement in the creative process and Morris found he could not realize this in a conventional architectural practice. He concluded that if new life were to be

[4] John Ruskin, *The Seven Lamps of Architecture*, 4th edn (Orpington: George Allen, 1883) [first published in 1849], p. 53.

injected into architecture the architect himself needed to change. But it was not until much later, in fact in 1888, the year Blow met Ruskin, that Morris was to write of Ruskin's influence as follows:

> The essence of what Ruskin taught us was simple enough ... it was really nothing more recondite than this, that the art of any epoch must of necessity be an expression of its social life and that the social life of the Middle Ages allowed the workman freedom of individual expression, which on the other hand our social life forbids him.[5]

Although architecture as practiced in the 1850s in Street's Oxford office may not have suited Morris, the three architects who were to prove most influential on the Arts and Crafts generation that followed them all trained there. These three were Philip Webb (1831–1915), Norman Shaw (1831–1912) and John Dando Sedding (1838–91). Of the three it was Philip Webb's rational interpretation of traditional craftsmanship that was perhaps the most cogent influence. By 1888 Webb had already produced thirty years of uncompromising domestic architecture, since building the Red House for Morris. But Webb took no pupils himself on principle and the most prolific seed beds for the Arts and Crafts movement were the offices of the other two, Shaw and Sedding. A grounding in the Old English and Queen Anne styles of the former and an awareness of craftsmanship and artistic detail as exemplified by the latter was thought by many to be the best architectural education available at the time.

The pupils and followers of Webb, Shaw and Sedding formed the architectural backbone of the Arts and Crafts movement (2). One of the first to emerge from Shaw's office was Ernest Newton (1856–1922) who left in 1879. He had to work assiduously through the 1880s, landing his first important commission, Bullers Wood, at the end of the decade. In 1888, when Blow met Ruskin, Newton was thirty-two and at that date perhaps the most successful of Shaw's pupils. Amongst others Edward Prior (1852–1932), then thirty-six, had left in 1880. Despite being the oldest he had still to fully develop his own distinctive style. Mervyn Macartney (1853–1932) and E. J. May (1853–1941), both a year younger, were also working hard to make a name for themselves in their master's shadow. William Richard Lethaby (1857–1931) was thirty-one and about to leave Shaw, having joined him to replace Newton as senior assistant ten years before.

In 1888 Shaw was building New Scotland Yard on the Thames Embankment. The practice was at its peak and many talented young men were still attracted to it. Of those completing their training with him at about that

[5] William Morris, 'The Revival of Architecture', Lecture, 1888, in *The Collected Works of William Morris*, 24 vols (London: Longman, Green & Co., 1910–15), XXII, p. 323.

time, several travelled abroad before settling down. Sidney Barnsley (1865–1926), only twenty-three, left that year for Greece to study Byzantine architecture with Robert Weir Schultz (1861–1951) who had spent a couple of years with Shaw to 1886. Gerald Horsley (1862–1917), another of that office's outstanding pupils, was also abroad in 1888, having won the Owen Jones Travelling Studentship from the Royal Institute of British Architects. He was in Sicily drawing at La Zisa in Palermo that year.

In the late 1880s travel occupied the minds of the younger pupils who passed through the office of John Sedding also. While Sidney Barnsley trained with Shaw, his elder brother Ernest was articled to Sedding thus forming a link between the two offices. Making his move in 1887, Ernest Barnsley (1863–1926) left to travel in France and Italy that summer with Ernest Gimson (1864–1919), before setting up practice in Birmingham. Gimson, who had joined Sedding on the recommendation of William Morris, did not finally leave until the following year when he returned to the continent for a second time. In 1889 two other Sedding pupils, Henry Wilson (1864–1934) and Alfred Powell (1865–1960), set off for Northern France to follow, as Powell records, in the footsteps of Blow and Ruskin the previous year, even sketching the same church at Abbeville (see 7):

> We are in the middle of a big sketch of the church of St Wulfran from the window of a cafe which is in a beautiful position for the view and also recommends itself as being the room in which Mr Ruskin has sat 'plusieurs fois' for the same purpose.[6]

Of this group of aspiring young architects Detmar Blow was the youngest. Twenty-one years old when he travelled with Ruskin, he was still living with his family in Croydon, not far from where he was born. Like his friend Sydney Cockerell, he was the son of a city merchant. His architectural education started at the South Kensington School of Art (now the Royal College of Art) in 1883 where he met Edwin Lutyens (1869–1944). Lutyens claimed to have recognised in Blow another precocious talent: 'Between us we could transform the world',[7] he said later and the two men remained in friendly rivalry throughout their careers. According to Blow's own records, he was articled for a four-year period from about 1885 to the firm of Wieson, Son and Aldwinckle[8] but, like Lutyens,

6 Unpublished letter from Alfred Powell to his mother, dated Monday 23 September 1889 from Abbeville, in 'Autographed Letters, etc, by Alfred Hoare Powell and Some Others, Written at Home and Abroad, AD MDCCCLXXIX to MDCCCCXII, Bound 1914 (by Edgar Powell)', p. 106, amongst the Powell papers in the possession of Mrs Thompson-Lewis, Petersfield, Hants.

7 Christopher Hussey, *The Life of Sir Edwin Lutyens* (London: Country Life, 1950), p. 6.

he made little of his formal architectural training in later life. Nonetheless, from 1887 he attended the Architectural Association evening classes, as did Lutyens who followed him in the next year, finding Blow already winning the prizes against stiff competition.

In November 1887, the month of his twentieth birthday, Blow achieved Exceptional Merit in the Class of Design and in January 1888 his student project for 'A Country Mansion to Cost £18,000 pounds' is described in the

3. 'A country mansion to cost £18,000. Perspective sketch by D. J. Blow'. A design exercise published in *Architectural Association Notes*, January 1888.

Architectural Association Notes[9] (3). In February the subject was a fountain and his work was illustrated again[10] – an early indication of Blow's tendency towards the romance of an earlier age (4). The heroes and their deeds are set up as an examplar for passing children who clamber over the monument and swim in its lower basin.[11] That March Blow made a sketching trip to Barfreston in Kent with a colleague, Allen Starling. It seems to have been a great adventure, if the record in Blow's sketchbook (5 & 6) is anything to go by and in June he was

8 Blow refers to his articled pupillage in an application for RIBA Fellowship (RIBA Fellowship Nomination Papers, vol. 17). Although Aldwinckle was an architect of some stature professionally, the firm's work was solid rather than spectacular. Typical amongst its output was Lewisham municipal baths 'with three gothic arches and a jolly water tower' (Nikolaus Pevsner, *London II: South,* Buildings of England (Harmondsworth: Penguin Books, 1983), p. 112).

9 Twenty-two designs were sent in of which Blow's was one of two illustrated. The other was by Charles Canning Winmill.

10 'Notes on Class of Design', *Architectural Association Notes*, II, no. 11 (February 1888), p. 210.

11 The critique was by R. Phene Spiers. April's design subject was an upright piano. It was reviewed by W. D. Caröe who praised Blow in the *A.A. Notes* for 'The most delicate and appropriate late gothic design, altogether pleasing...', *Notes on Class of Design*, II, no. 13 (April 1888), p. 251.

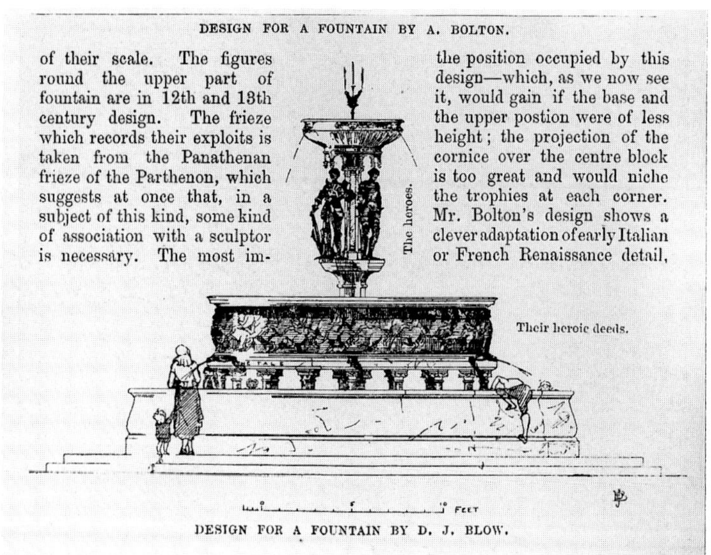
DESIGN FOR A FOUNTAIN BY A. BOLTON.

of their scale. The figures round the upper part of fountain are in 12th and 13th century design. The frieze which records their exploits is taken from the Panathenan frieze of the Parthenon, which suggests at once that, in a subject of this kind, some kind of association with a sculptor is necessary. The most im-

the position occupied by this design—which, as we now see it, would gain if the base and the upper postion were of less height; the projection of the cornice over the centre block is too great and would niche the trophies at each corner. Mr. Bolton's design shows a clever adaptation of early Italian or French Renaissance detail,

DESIGN FOR A FOUNTAIN BY D. J. BLOW.

awarded the A.A. Travelling Studentship, enabling him to set off for France with Cockerell. In November, while he was away, he was awarded first prize in the Class of Design. Lutyens, still attending the Architectural Association evening classes while working in the office of Ernest George was honourably mentioned in this category also.[12]

Ruskin diverted Blow from the project he had planned for his travelling studentship, measuring and drawing the choir of Beauvais cathedral. Blow tells how he was persuaded to travel further afield:

> Owing to the happiest and most delightful circumstances, I was obliged to leave last June the then but shortly commenced pleasures of this studentship and was not able to recommence that same work at Beauvais Cathedral until [the following] March.[13]

But Blow had plenty of other drawing work to do with Ruskin, as Cockerell's diary reveals. The day after they met Ruskin, he 'obtained the loan of The Old Post Office for facility in drawing the west front of St Wulfran's (7). Stayed there nearly all day. R. came up in morning and afternoon and superintended [Detmar's] work in the kindest way. Mr Severn drawing from another window ...' [Monday, 25 June 1888][14]

12 Blow featured in the *Architectural Association Notes* for the last time in the month of August 1888, on the honours list as a probationer at the Royal Academy Architectural School (vol. II, no. 17, p. 317).

13 'A Travelling Student's Notes: A paper by Mr D. J. Blow, Travelling Student of the Architectural Association, read by him at the meeting of that body on the 17th inst.', reported in *The Architect* (24 May 1889), pp. 295–6 and *The Builder* (28 May 1889), pp. 394–6.

14 Sydney Cockerell's Diaries, the Cockerell Papers, British Museum Manuscripts

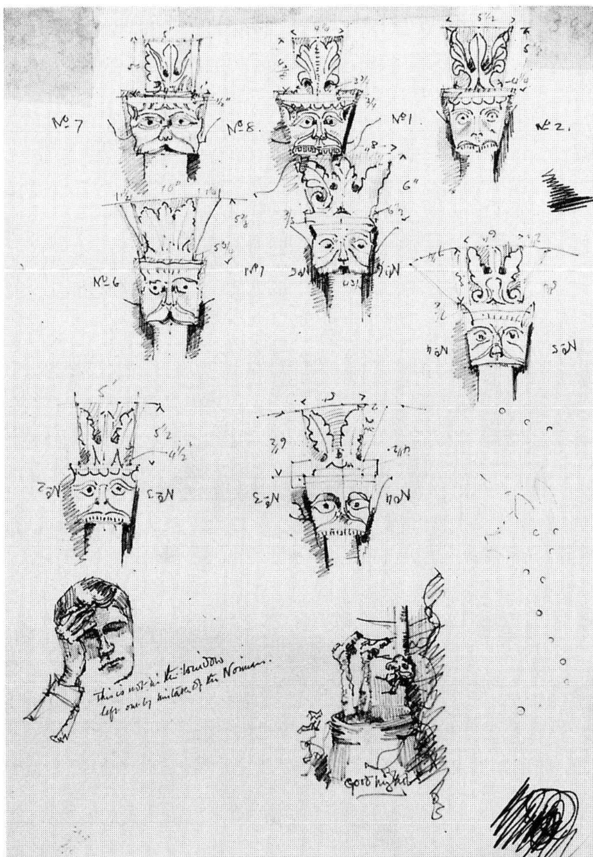

4 (opposite page). 'Design for a Fountain by D. J. Blow'. Published in *Architectural Association Notes*, February 1888.

5 (above). 'We start on our way with our necessary implements', Monday, March 19th, 1888. A drawing by Detmar Blow, made on a sketching trip to Barfreston, Kent, with Allen Walker Starling (British Architectural Library).

6 (left). Sketch showing carved corbels at Barfreston church, Kent, by Detmar Blow, March 1888. The exhausted figure with his head in his hands is captioned 'This is not in the window, left out by mistake of the Normans'; that upside down in the water barrel is inscribed 'Good Night' (BAL).

7. St Wulfran's, Abbeville, sketched by Detmar Blow in February 1889, on his return to France. Blow's earlier drawing, produced under Ruskin's supervision in 1888, does not survive.

From Abbeville they rowed up the Somme, visited the battlefield at Crécy and walked through fields 'red and blue with poppies and corn flowers' [Sunday, 1 July 1888]. Then they travelled on to Beauvais together, the young men getting up early to explore with Ruskin: 'Climbed to the topmost parapet of the ... [cathedral] and looked down upon the sublime poising of the flying buttresses. Amazed by the majesty of the apse. ... Drove to the hill, saw vines growing, lay for long in a hay field and had altogether the delightfullest day since we started. R. in splendid spirits and full of vigour' [Friday, 6 July 1888].

Cockerell had to return home. He had already extended his holiday by a week and was very envious of Blow who reported in a letter, later partly burned in a fire that destroyed so many of the Blow family papers:

> Mr R. wishes to make a special study of a glacier ... He says I shall ... [burned] ... in making drawings and illustrations for him for which he will pay me, which money is to go towards paying my expenses. Oh C. it is really too delightful. I only wish you were here with us ... I am now busy measuring in the cathedral ... I hope you are settling down at your work. Poor C – I do pity you so – all among the coals – if only they were stones.[15]

Collection. Quotations similarly annotated later are from the same source.

Poor Cockerell indeed. He had returned to work on his twenty-first birthday and didn't much like his job; but he took his responsibilities seriously and applied himself to the family coal business – 'Forsaking Ruskin for coal' became a Blow family adage.[16]

Detmar's mother joined him in Beauvais to help sort out his change of plan. Her youngest son, Sydney, came with her and later described his first impressions of Ruskin: 'A delightful smile, a fine forehead, high cheek bones, a fresh complexion like a schoolgirl's, light chestnut hair and a long beard. The beard intrigued me. It completely hid the opening at the top of the waistcoat and I remember wondering whether or not Ruskin ever wore a tie underneath it.'[17] Mrs Blow and young Sydney stayed ten days, first at Beauvais and then at Amiens:

> We would present ourselves at the door of the great man's sitting room every morning at nine o'clock when he would deliver a lecture on some particular architectural feature of the cathedral. The lecture, given by Ruskin sitting at a desk and delivered with as much ceremony as though he were addressing a packed hall of people, would be followed by dishes of wild strawberries and cream. After that we would proceed to the cathedral for practical illustration of the lecture we had had. Ruskin, amazingly active, would take us up to the triforium, the clerestorey and the roof. We would clamber everywhere.[18]

The arrangements made, Detmar and Ruskin set off but for Blow the problems of looking after a sick old man probably proved as demanding, if not more so, than the drawing work. Ruskin found him up to the combined task, it seems: 'Detmar is good as gold',[19] he wrote to Mrs Severn. 'Detmar sketched a Jura Cottage and I painted it for him yesterday at St Laurent' [from Morez, Jura, 2 September 1888].[20] 'The gentians I sent you a day or two ago were gathered by Detmar, higher than I can climb now ...' [Merligen, 11 November 1888].[21] In return Ruskin taught him to draw as the following report, relating to

15 Unpublished letter from Detmar Blow to Sydney Cockerell, 24 July 1888, amongst the Blow family papers at Hilles.

16 Recalled by Lucilla Warre-Cornish, Detmar Blow's younger daughter, in a conversation with the author.

17 Sydney Blow, *The Ghost Walks on Fridays* (Heath Cranton, 1935), p. 24.

18 Ibid., p. 24.

19 Letter from Ruskin to Mrs Severn quoted in *Friends of a Lifetime*, ed. Viola Meynell (London: Jonathan Cape, 1940), p. 49.

20 References from Ruskin's diary quoted by E. T. Cook in *The Life of John Ruskin*, 29 vols (Allen, 1911), pp. 525–7.

21 Ibid.

his address to the Architectural Association on the subject of his travelling scholarship, indicates:

> ... [Blow] had been brought up to draw with the usual hard line, only admired, as William Burgess said, by 'parents, guardians and idiots'. Professor Ruskin had shown him that a more artistic method of drawing would not be less but more architecturally correct as might be witnessed in the inimitable drawings of old Prout. [Blow] not only thought ... that one must design in perspective, but that one must design in light and shade also. One could not design in light and shade until one had learnt to draw in light and shade .... [Blow] advised his fellow students not to content themselves in only sketching architecture. Let them occasionally go to nature and draw a leaf or a flower; they would be all the better for it, and would put more feeling into their work.[22]

Blow may have learnt to draw but research suggests he was never the best of correspondents: 'Can't think why Detmar doesn't write to me', wrote Cockerell in his diary [Fri. 7 Sept 1888]. Having forsaken Ruskin for coal, he longed for news. 'Heard from Detmar (Padua) for the first time in two months, on his way to Venice from Bassano' [Mon. 8 Oct 1888]. But Blow was not having an easy time. He had his hands full with Ruskin's bouts of depression and was terrified of getting in the way. Although Ruskin found him 'a perfect creature in goodness and strength of character', he declared that 'if he has a fault, it's his way of always begging my pardon when I run against him. The other day, just to see how earnestly apologetic he would be, I had two minds to push him into the Lake of Thun.'[23] But by December Ruskin's condition had deteriorated, as Cockerell records: 'Long letter from Mr R. enclosed in one from Detmar. Sparkling fun with sad intervals. D. reports that he [Ruskin] is in very low spirits. Has just arrived in Paris where Mrs Severn joins him today. Had dinner at Voyseys in Streatham and spent delightful evening in talk about Art, etc.' [Mon. 3 Dec 1888]. A week later Blow returned with Mrs Severn and Ruskin ('still very poorly') to Herne Hill. So ended Ruskin's last trip abroad.

Having accompanied Ruskin to Coniston, Blow returned to London where he worked briefly with Arthur Collie, a Bond Street art dealer of Cockerell's aquaintance,[24] but his head was full of Ruskin and he soon found his way into

22 *The Builder*, loc. cit. 25 May 1889, pp. 394–6. A. B. Pite described Blow's work as having obviously been made 'con amore'.

23 Derrick Leon, *Ruskin – The Great Victorian* (London: Routledge & Kegan Paul, 1949), p. 558.

24 Arthur Leslie Collie was publishing small bronzes by contemporary sculptors in limited and numbered issues. The first of the series, a reduction of Hamo Thornycroft's 'Gordon', appeared in 1889; see Susan Beattie, *The New Sculpture*

8. 'Part of S: Side of nave and S: Chancel Aisle: Grantham Ch: Aug 21: 73', a sketch by John Sedding (BAL).

the company of John Sedding and the young architects in his office round the corner in Oxford Street. Blow still had some work to finish abroad however and, encouraged by Sedding,[25] he returned to his studies, reaching Beauvais in March 1889. Blow is said to have been employed by Sedding at some stage,[26] perhaps on his final return from Beauvais at the end of the year,[27] and in Detmar

---

(Yale, New Haven and London, 1983), p. 187. The venture attracted considerable interest [see *Saturday Review* (31 May 1890) p. 672; *The Studio*, vol. 25 (May 1902), pp. 275–6], but was never Collie's sole source of income. He shared premises at 39B Old Bond Street with Thomas Agnew and in 1893 was listed as 'Decorator' and offered 'Old English Furniture, Brasses and Metalwork, Old Delft, Mirrors, Clocks, Wallpapers, Paintings, All Furniture Materials, Velvets, Chintzes, Etc.' (from heading used in an unpublished letter from Collie to John Tweed, 21 Dec. 1893, in the Tweed Papers, Reading Borough Council: Leisure Services, Museum and Art Gallery).

25 Cockerell describes how Blow was 'very grateful for some encouragement, very kindly given from Mr Sedding' (Cockerell Diary, Friday, 1 March 1889).

26 Sydney Blow, *The Ghost Walks on Fridays*, p. 28.

27 Blow introduced Cockerell to Sedding early in 1891 at a lecture by Sedding on 'Crafts in the Middle Ages' at the Whitechapel Crafts School [Monday, 12 January 1891]. But Sedding died later that year, so if Blow worked at Sedding's office during his lifetime it could only have been for a short period, probably in 1890. He made

Blow Sedding must have seen himself at an earlier age, for he too had turned to Ruskin to learn to draw (8). Ruskin had helped him in other ways too, warning him that: 'Modern so-called architects are merely employers of workmen on commission and if you would be a real architect, you must always have either a pencil or a chisel in your own hand.'[28] Sedding followed Ruskin's advice, trying his hand at stone carving and ironwork and later encouraging his own pupils to follow suit: 'The real architect of a building is something different to the distant dictator who uses the agency of post and telegram to communicate his wishes, who draws the plans, writes the specification and looks in occasionally at the works in progress. He must be his own clerk of works, his own carver, his own director; he must be the familiar spirit of the structure as it rises from the ground, must be ready at hand to meet the passing emergency of site, or crooked wall or awkward chimney ... and generally to make the most of the site and the building as applied to it.'[29]

These words perhaps better than any other epitomise the philosophical essence of the wandering architect. So that which Blow learned from Ruskin was reinforced by Sedding as he encouraged Blow to return to his studies in Beauvais. Here we find Blow, as did Cockerell and Arthur Collie who visited him that Easter, 'located with the sacristan in a room quite close to the cathedral' [Good Friday, 19 April 1889]. Together the three friends watched the great Easter fete from the cathedral parapet, visited Paris and made excursions out into the surrounding countryside.[30]

---

no reference to it himself in later years and there is a possibility that his associations with the office at 447 Oxford St were mostly after Sedding's death, when Henry Wilson continued to run a practice from the same address. Certainly Blow used this address when in London later, writing from there on at least one occasion on business for the Society for the Protection of Ancient Buildings (unpublished letter headed 447 Oxford St from Blow to Thackeray Turner, SPAB secretary, 6 Feb 1896, concerning repairs at the Old Post Office, Tintagel. SPAB Archive, Tintagel file).

28 W. R. Lethaby, *Philip Webb & His Work* (Oxford, 1935), p.79.

29 John Dando Sedding, 'Architecture: Old and New', *British Architect*, XV (1881), p. 229, quoted in Margaret Richardson, *Architects of the Arts and Crafts Movement* (London, Trefoil, 1983), p. 72.

30 '7.15 train with D. to Hermes. Norman church in the claws of the architect. ... Walked to the next village of Heilles-Mouchy ... [where they saw the thirteenth century church] ivy creeping through the crevices and stretching over the altar ... pleasant family gave us cider and showed us their cellar built by the monks ages ago – very pretty dark haired girl rang bell at midday – lovely picture!' (Cockerell's diary entry for Wednesday 24 April 1889).

9. 'Leproserie de Saint Lazare, Allone, Oise, France', etching from a sketch made by Detmar Blow in July 1889. Reproduced in *The Architect*, 4 April 1890.

Blow broke this stay to make his address to fellow students at the Architectural Association in May, already quoted (see note 13) Cockerell went along and heard his plea for a return to Ruskinian values. It was well received but Blow had to confess his work at Beauvais was still incomplete: 'With vain and foolish calculation, I had hoped to finish part of the apse by now, but practice soon showed me the absurdity of my speculation, so I have broken the thread of my work for a few days, to show and tell you the little I as yet know...'[31] Blow worked on in France (9), returning again in early August to set up a house for his brother Jellings who married that September. He went back to Beauvais for the last time in November 1889 and finally completed his work.[32] On his return he set about a drawing of part of the triforium at Westminster Abbey with the intention of taking the Royal Academy entrance examination, but his future career was by no means clear to him. He made frequent sketching trips with anyone he could persuade to accompany him, a typical one being with Cockerell to Rochester Cathedral, climbing the castle walls with 'Pigeons flying everywhere and nesting in all the crevices.' [Tues. 21 January 1890] Seeking the company of other artists, Cockerell, always well connected, introduced him to T. M. Rooke, a pupil of Burne-Jones and engaged by Ruskin earlier in his career to make drawings of old buildings. Rooke was a

31 *The Builder*, loc. cit. (25 May 1889), pp. 394–6.

32 The completion of the Beauvais drawings is confirmed by Blow's daughter Lucilla who recalls them still hanging, faint and delicate, after the fire that almost destroyed Blow's house, Hilles. Few of his early drawings survived.

talented cellist and Blow, brought up in a musical family, found a shared interest here too.

In the spring of 1890 Blow returned to Coniston, this time circuitously, meeting Cockerell at Peterborough where they found the cathedral in the process of 'Being scraped and improved by Pearson' [Thurs. 10 April 1890][33] After another couple of days at Lincoln Cathedral 'separating St Hugh's work from that of his successors' [Sun. 13 April 1890], they travelled on to Sheffield where, putting up at the Albany ('An admirable temperance hotel fitted with electric light and every most modern convenience' [Mon. 14 April 1890]), they rose early to attend the opening of the new Ruskin Museum. There were speeches (though 'nothing particularly stirring or interesting said') and faces both familiar and famous. A party of seven, including Cockerell's sister Olive, then continued to Coniston.

Staying near Ambleside,[34] the two young men spent a couple of days walking and climbing before visiting Brantwood to see Ruskin. Having rowed across Coniston Water Cockerell was disappointed to find 'The dear professor, alas! not well enough to see us' [Sat. 19 April 1890]. Blow, an old hand at looking after Ruskin, stayed at Brantwood anyway but Cockerell was obliged to return to Ambleside and ten days later, after an energetic but fundamentally unfulfilled holiday with 'No news yet from that rascally Detmar', he and Olive returned to London. Here he found 'A letter from him at last with news of his interviews with J.R.'

Despite such setbacks Cockerell had not entirely forsaken Ruskin for coal. Back in London he still found time for a variety of interests and shortly before the Coniston trip had attended his first meeting at William Morris' Society for the Protection of Ancient Buildings (SPAB). Later that year Cockerell became a committee member. He had met Morris before at the Hammersmith branch of the Socialist League but his introduction to the SPAB came through Emery Walker, at that time discussing a partnership with Morris in what was later to become the Kelmscott Press. Soon Cockerell, sharing a love of beautiful books with them both, left the family firm to catalogue Morris's library at Kelmscott House. Eventually it was Cockerell who went into partnership with Walker; his

33 In 1895 William Morris and the SPAB became involved in a national campaign to prevent the Dean and Chapter at Peterborough from carrying out Pearson's programme of rebuilding to the west front of the cathedral. It culminated in a report in early 1897, signed by Blow, Philip Webb, W. R. Lethaby, J. T. Micklethwaite and Thackeray Turner (the SPAB secretary), calling for repair from the inside outwards, leaving the external stonework in place. Although Pearson proceeded, the SPAB's actions concentrated attention upon the project and probably helped to retain much of the medieval fabric.

34 With Albert Flemming, see references in Cockerell's diaries.

knowledge of medieval manuscripts, founded at this time, leading in the end to his directorship of the Fitzwilliam Museum in Cambridge and a subsequent knighthood.

In Blow's absence at Coniston, Cockerell had planned a trip for them to visit Ightham Mote with Rooke [Sunday 4th May 1890]. By chance, walking through Knole Park from Sevenoaks station, they met two other young architects, W. R. Lethaby and Ernest Gimson. Blow knew them, presumably through his connection with Sedding's office where he may then have been working. All four became life-long friends, getting to know each other well through their shared enthusiasm for the SPAB. Blow attended his first meeting of the Society the following week when he and Cockerell heard 'Morris and Webb rant ... against the clergy' [Thurs. 8 May 1890], presumably in connection with a proposed medieval church restoration.[35] Gimson had already joined the SPAB the previous year, referring to it always as 'Anti-Scrape', the name by which it had been known since its inception in 1877 when Morris started his campaign against the re-facing of venerable old buildings in the name of 'restoration'. Gimson described his early attendances thus: 'I have joined the Anti-Scrape Society. Morris was good enough to propose me as a member. I attend committee meetings every Thursday afternoon. Morris, Philip Webb and other interesting people are always there. After the meeting we all adjourn to Gatti's for tea and half an hours talk of which, of course, Morris is the life and soul.'[36]

Lethaby was introduced by Gimson in 1891 and his description of the meetings, in a similar vein, are well known:

> The society itself was a remarkable teaching body. Dealing as it did with the common facts of traditional building in scores and hundreds of examples, it became under the technical guidance of Philip Webb ... the real school of practical building, architecture with all the whims which we usually call 'design' left out... . it is a curious fact that this society, engaged in intense study of antiquity, became a school of rational builders and modern building ... For a time, a great time to me, we attended the meetings, from five to seven, and then went across the Strand to Gatti's for an evening meal: Morris often, Webb always and two or three of a number of lesser people, Gimson, Emery Walker, Sydney Cockerell, Detmar Blow and myself; here were stories, jokes, and real talk.[37]

[35] At Gatti's restaurant, after the meeting, Cockerell talked about Ruskin to Philip Webb, to be told that: 'Mr W. avoided J.R. as he did not think he would get on with him, but admired him greatly.'

[36] Letter from Ernest Gimson to W. R. Butler dated 22 June 1890, Leicestershire Museums Service. Referred to by Mary Comino in her *Gimson and the Barnsleys* (London, Evans, 1980), Chapter 3, Note 1, p. 213.

Gimson and Cockerell attended over thirty of the weekly SPAB meetings together in 1891, campaigning hard on the society's behalf. A typical entry from Cockerell's diary tells how they left London 'dark with fog like midnight' [Saturday, 7 Feb 1891] to visit a threatened tithe barn at Burroughbury, near Peterborough.[38] Both attended the 1891 annual general meeting where they met Lutyens and Collie. Webb was in the chair and Morris one of the speakers. For Cockerell, teas at Gatti's after the SPAB committees continued almost every Thursday evening for ten years. His usual, poached eggs on toast and a pot of tea,[39] does not sound like a great attraction (although sometimes a special triumph was celebrated with a bottle of cheap claret) but what kept these young men coming was the company. And over the years it was most especially the company of Philip Webb that was important.

If the SPAB was one important meeting place for young Arts and Crafts architects, the Art Workers' Guild was another. The Guild was formed in the Shaw office and Lethaby was a founder member. He in turn introduced Gimson who described how, with W. R. Butler from the Sedding office and Lethaby and Robert Weir Schultz from Shaw's, he heard Morris speak there: 'Lethaby, Schultz and Butler were in their element, applauding his socialism to the echo.'[40] On 1 April 1892 Detmar Blow was elected to the membership. To give him moral support Gimson brought along Cockerell although the Guild was usually full of their mutual friends anyway - the previous month Gimson and Cockerell, Blow, Lethaby, Wilson, Sidney Barnsley, Collie, Schultz and John Tweed (a sculptor friend of Collie & Blow) had all gathered to hear Morris speak on 'London Improvements'. Such 'Improvements' were almost as much of a red rag to Morris as the 'Restorations' that had inspired the formation of the SPAB. He raged against the architectural establishment on both subjects and this, combined with his fury against the work of so many of the leading establishment architects, began to polarise them collectively into a radical architectural grouping

At the same time they were drawn by Morris' interest in the decorative arts and this resulted in the first of their communal ventures. In June 1890 Gimson wrote to W. R. Butler: 'Lethaby, Blow and I are joining together in a little business. We are going to take a shop in Bloomsbury for the sale of furniture of

37 W. R. Lethaby, A. H. Powell & F. L. Griggs, *Ernest Gimson, His Life & Work* (Stratford on Avon, Shakespeare Head Press, 1924), pp. 2–4.

38 The same year they campaigned together on the SPAB's behalf to protect the Saxon timber church at Greensted in Essex.

39 Wilfrid Blunt, 'Cockerell' (Hamilton, 1964), p. 47.

40 Letter from Ernest Grimson to Ernest Barnsley, 19 Feb 1888, Leicestershire Museums Service, quoted in Comino, op. cit., pp. 50–1.

our own design and make, besides, other things such as plaster friezes, lead, needlework, etc.'[41] Sidney Barnsley was asked to join the group too but he was in Greece with Schultz and although Gimson wrote to him early in the summer of 1890 he got no reply until late autumn: 'I heard from Sidney on Monday. The last letter from me evidently did not reach him. It was full of rejoicing that he was going to make one of the quartet.'[42] By the end of 1890 Reginald Blomfield (1856–1942) and Mervyn Macartney had also joined Kenton & Co., as the firm became known. Older men, both were already in practice. Macartney knew Lethaby from Shaw's office, whereas Blomfield had attended the Royal Academy school before entering the office of his uncle A. W. Blomfield. The presence in the group of these two slightly older men may have stifled the younger men's aspirations for a more communal enterprise. According to Gimson they were 'to have bedrooms and offices in the same building and share expenses.'[43] This never happened. Lethaby described their earliest plans for 'a sort of architect's shop, something outside the deathly dreariness of respectable offices',[44] but this too proved a pipe dream. As the group expanded there were other differences within the group too and this may explain Kenton & Co's relatively short duration. Blomfield for example was less than whole-hearted about Ruskin. He had the opportunity to attend Ruskin's lectures at Oxford but mass adulation put him off: 'Ruskin was a beautiful draughtsman in his own way but I sometimes wish he had painted more and written less on architecture. I attended some of Ruskin's lectures, but I heard so much about Ruskin and so little about anybody else that I gave him up.'[45]

Blomfield enthused about Kenton & Co nonetheless:

> We took an excellent work-shop over some stables at the back of Bedford Row, employed four or five of the best workmen we could get and bought our own materials. We used to meet in each other's rooms and undertake designs of our own choice and invention, more or less in turn ... each man was responsible solely for his own design and it's execution ... Lethaby's and Gimson's inventions ran to simple

41 Unpublished letter from Ernest Gimson to W. R. Butler, 22 June 1890, Leicestershire Museums Service, quoted in Comino, *Gimson and the Barnsleys*, pp. 50–1.

42 Letter from Ernest Gimson to Ernest Barnsley, 1 Oct 1890, Leicestershire Museums Service, quoted in Comino, *Gimson and the Barnsleys*, p. 51.

43 Letter from Ernest Gimson to W. R. Butler, 22 June 1890, Leicestershire Museums Service, quoted in Comino, *Gimson and the Barnsleys*, p. 51.

44 W. R. Lethaby, A. H. Powell & F. L. Griggs, *Ernest Gimson, His Life & Work* (Stratford on Avon, Shakespeare Head Press, 1924), p. 8.

45 Sir Reginald Blomfield, *Memoirs of an Architect* (London: MacMillan & Co., 1932), p. 27.

10. Chair in mahogany with drop-in rush seat, designed by Ernest Gimson and made by Bowen at Kenton & Co. in about 1890. The chairs were originally a set of six and belonged to Gimson's mother in Leicester (Cheltenham Art Gallery & Museums).

> designs of admirable form in oak [see plate 10]. I recollect a mirror frame, rather Persian in design, inlaid with mother-of-pearl, by Sidney Barnsley and much admired.[46]

Cockerell refers to Kenton & Co. as a going concern early in 1891 and visited the workshops in May. They held an exhibition that July, to mark their first year and Cockerell met Collie and Lutyens there. Although it was a success the firm was disbanded in 1892. For many of them, architectural work had left insufficient time for such a venture. Both Lethaby and Sidney Barnsley had substantial projects on site – Lethaby at Avon Tyrell in Hampshire, where he was building a house for Lord Manners and Barnsley at Kingswood, Surrey, where his Byzantine 'Church of the Wisdom of God' was dedicated that July. The two men had set up their practices close to each other near Philip Webb's office at No.1 Raymond Buildings, Grays Inn. This circle, with Webb as its focal point, included Lutyens who was already in practice round the corner in Grays Inn Square and Robert Weir Schultz who also shared an office with Francis Troup (1859–1941) in Grays Inn. Sidney Barnsley had in fact taken rooms at No.3 Raymond Buildings next door to Webb, sharing premises with Gimson from the beginning of 1891. Amongst their earliest and most frequent visitors were Cockerell and Blow but it was another of their friends, Alfred Powell who described the hospitality there:

> It was wonderful in old smoky London to find yourself in those fresh clean rooms, furnished with good oak furniture and a trestle table that at seasonable hours surrendered its drawing boards to a good English meal, in which figured, if I remember right, at least on guest nights, a great stone jar of the best ale.[47]

46 Ibid., p. 76.

47 Lethaby, Powell and Griggs, *Ernest Gimson, His Life & Work*, p. 15.

Throughout the Kenton & Co. episode their continuing involvement with the SPAB and Philip Webb had always been there to remind the founder members of the firm that architecture was the discipline on which the decorative arts depended. This is not to say that Webb discouraged such diversification. Far from it. He encouraged them to involve themselves not only in the arts relating to architecture but also in the practice of the craft skills on which Arts and Crafts architecture depended. Gimson taught himself hand-moulded plasterwork and in another instance Webb suggested to their friend Alfred Powell:

> It would be good fortune for you if you could so arrange things as to have a year's continuous work carpentering ... as you would be keeping your eyes open to all collateral things, you would pick up much general knowledge of various other crafts connected with building and would gain much more help to your after work than in any other way.[48]

Morris' example had shown Webb that not all those who took an interest in architecture were temperamentally suited to the way it was generally practiced at the time, so Webb offered Ernest Gimson and Sidney Barnsley support in their plans for a rural craft community. Gimson had been 'Scouring the country from Yorkshire to the South Downs'[49] for the right location, but it was not until the next spring that he and Barnsley finally made a move to the Cotswolds, persuading Sidney's brother Ernest to join them from Birmingham. Cockerell visited them all in July with Schultz and Francis Troup (who had both studied with the Barnsley brothers at the Royal Academy's architectural school in the mid-1880s):

> Went by excursion train with Schultz and Troup to see Gimson and Barnsley at Ewen near Cirencester. After nice dinner and chat in their pretty garden, walked ... to Pinbury where they have taken (from next spring) a beautiful house looking into the Golden Valley of the Cotswold Hills.' (11) [Sunday 9 July 1893]

Cockerell inherited the rooms at Raymond Buildings[50] vacated by Gimson and Sidney Barnsley although both returned to visit when in London, apparently bringing a breath of the country with them. One evening Lethaby and Cockerell, returning there from the SPAB via Gatti's, 'Found two jugs full of exquisite Fritillaries from Gimson and Barnsley.' [Thursday 20 April 1893]

48 Letter from Philip Webb to Alfred Powell, dated 17 March 1894, quoted in Lethaby, *Philip Webb & His Work* (Oxford, 1935), pp. 123–4.

49 Lethaby, Powell and Griggs, *Ernest Gimson, His Life & Work*, p. 15.

50 Cockerell moved in on 2 April with Harry (W. H.) Cowlishaw, a young architect articled to Thackeray Turner, the SPAB Secretary.

11. 'Ernest Gimson's Cottage at Pinbury Park', from a drawing by F. L. Griggs, 1923.

Lethaby followed Webb's advice in a different way. Whilst others may have turned to the crafts, Lethaby set out to follow Webb's example in architecture, trying to avoid 'the framed perspectives on the wall and clerks slaving in the background'.[51] Like Webb he was self-disciplined and determined to accept the rigours of an uncompromising architecture that encompassed the highest ideals of both art and craftsmanship. 'Art is the expression of man's pleasure in labour' Webb told Lethaby, passing on Morris' interpretation of Ruskin's Nature of Gothic.[52] At Kenton & Co. Lethaby certainly intended at the outset to put such a philosophy into practice, each partner executing his own designs when possible. They never managed it and although Webb's own involvement at Morris & Co. was based upon similar principles, in fact Webb never managed to work with his own hands more than a little,[53] at least on site. Nonetheless he admired those that did, telling Lethaby how the best architects learned their craft in the builder's yard. It had not escaped Webb's notice that

51 W. R. Lethaby, A. H. Powell & F. L. Griggs, *Ernest Gimson, His Life & Work*, p. 8.

52 W. Morris, 'Art Under Plutocracy', 1883, in M. Morris (ed.), *The Collected Works of William Morris,* 24 vols, (London, Longman, Green & Co., 1910–15), vol. 23, p. 173.

53 Webb's account books tell how he worked on the decoration of church roofs for Morris & Co at Brighton and Scarborough in the early 1860s. There is, however, little further evidence of Webb's hand on site.

A. W. Pugin's training included work as a carpenter at Covent Garden nor that Bentley, whose work in the Byzantine style at Westminster Cathedral they were both to much admire later, served as an apprentice to a firm of London builders. William Butterfield too was, Webb told Lethaby, bound to Thomas Arber, builder, of Horseferry Road, Middlesex, to 'learn the art, trade or business of a builder, decorator and furniture maker.'[54]

Kenton & Co. made little impact on the career of Detmar Blow and no designs by him for the firm survive. Blow was still concentrating on architectural drawing work, exhibiting at the SPAB Annual General Meeting in 1890. The subject of his work was Barfreston church, a favourite of his since the visit in 1888 when at the Architectural Association[55] (see plates 5 & 6, above). In the autumn of 1890 Blow and Cockerell made another drawing trip to France, this time with the Rookes, A. Sassoon and Frank Randal (another artist formerly in Ruskin's employ). Blow stayed for six weeks, taking a room opposite the Hotel de France in Troyes at twelve francs a month. Although he and Rooke spent much of the time drawing they found time to visit the fair with Cockerell who distinguished himself at the shies 'demolishing a great many tobacco pipes' [Fri. 19 Sept 1890]. They clambered all over the cathedral, rowed on the river and attended a socialist meeting at the Salon de Mars which was 'very much like an English meeting, except that the speakers were more heated, the arguments being the same' [Sunday 21 Sept 1890].

Blow came home at the end of October uncertain about his future. He had written from France telling how he had discussed with his father the possibility of accepting an offer of work from Ruskin.[56] Earlier in the summer he had designed an addition to Brantwood for Ruskin, showing a model to Cockerell who found it 'plain and satisfactory' [Thurs. 10 July 1890]. Unbuilt, the design does not survive but it was not an architectural commission from Ruskin that Cockerell discussed with him at Gatti's after an SPAB meeting in November: 'Talked for some time about his prospects, D. being anxious to begin making a living as soon as possible. Urged him not to offer himself for the Ruskin

54 W. R. Lethaby, *Philip Webb & His Work*, pp. 67–8.

55 He visited with Allen Walker Starling in March 1888. His sketch books from this trip are the earliest that survive and the first entry shows two young men 'on our way with our necessary implements'. Laden down, they are shown battling against the elements as if their goal were the Eiger rather than the hopfields of Kent (5). The sketches that follow show the Romanesque work in all its detail, interspersed with doodles such as the young man, exhausted by his labours, captioned 'This is not in the window. Left out by mistake of the Normans' (6).

56 Unpublished letter from Detmar Blow to Sydney Cockerell, 12 September 1890, amongst Blow family papers at Hilles.

secretaryship ... D. to see Webb on Saturday and to seek his advice' [Thurs. 20 November 1890].

Four days later Cockerell recorded 'PW was kinder than ever and had given him [Blow] a great deal of advice and encouragement'. As a result Blow's career begins to change direction as Webb's guidance takes over from Ruskin's. Blow starts to take a more positive approach towards architecture rather than drawing alone. For almost certainly Webb would have been concerned about Blow's concentration on drawing for its own sake if he was to pursue a career in architecture. Webb reinterpreted Ruskin's teaching, encouraging Blow to work with his own hands to give form to his architecture. From a later entry in one of Blow's notebooks (marked '1 Raymond Buildings' - Webb's address) it is clear that this message got through: 'Ruskin's teaching was to show that all the means at hand today lead to no result... first have an idea and then find means to express it.' Blow had come to the conclusion that in architecture the concept and its realisation are parts of the same process. That he realised that the architect needed to be equally adept in both spheres is illustrated by his next entry, for he continues:

> One man wishes to go to London but has not a boot to walk in, another wishes to go nowhere in particular as long as he can manage to wear out his many boots in the year.[57]

Detmar Blow had worked out where he wanted to go and Philip Webb, happy that Blow's boots were now well broken in, helped him on his way.

[57] Manuscript notes dated Friday 7 Dec 1893, Detmar Blow Sketchbooks, RIBA Drawings Collection: 1987:55, Sketchbook No. 5, pp. 4–10.

Chapter 2
SETTING OUT
Detmar Blow's Early Excursions, 1891–6

> What, then, is an architect? Simply a master-builder, a chief craftsman. Of old he lived at the building and worked on it with his own hands, generally a mason and sculptor; but though a master-worker he remained a handy craftsman as well as a designer, and in this lay the secret of his art.
>
> Sir T. G. Jackson from 'Architecture, A Profession or an Art'

Philip Webb was like a godfather to Detmar Blow. So said Hugh Fairfax-Cholmeley, the client to whom Webb introduced Blow in 1891, thus offering him his first opportunity to become involved in the building process at first hand.[1] Blow first visited Fairfax-Cholmeley at Brandsby in North Yorkshire that summer and was to spend a considerable proportion of his time there over the next two years. Educated at Oxford, Fairfax-Cholmeley had worked with the Guild of Handicraft with C. R. Ashbee at the Toynbee Hall settlement when, despite having almost been disowned for his socialism, he inherited the Brandsby Estate in 1889. The Guild was well known to Sydney Cockerell and his circle at the SPAB, Cockerel himself visiting twice that year.[2] Set up in a deliberate attempt to promote social integration, the settlement at Toynbee Hall typified a number of similar organisations established at about this time. A group of educated, mainly professional, young men they later moved to new premises in Beaumont Square, part of 'that portion of London which is essentially the workmans quarter'.[3] Fairfax-Cholmeley then left

1 Hugh Fairfax-Cholmeley, unpublished autobiographical notes, private collection.

2 The Sydney Cockerell Diaries, 10/10/1889, 12/11/1889, British Museum Manuscripts Collection. Fairfax-Cholmeley attended SPAB meetings at least twice, met Cockerell and went with him to hear the Cavalliera Rusticana: 'Fairfax Cholmeley spent the evening with us and talked about socialism, landlordism, philanthropy, etc, an interesting enthusiast' [Tuesday 17th May 1892]. Blow proposed Cholmeley for membership of the SPAB on 9 June 1892 and Gimson seconded the motion. Fairfax-Cholmeley later became Master of Ruskin's Guild of St George.

3 From an address given by C. R. Ashbee, Guild of Handicrafts, Craftmans Club,

Ashbee for the Whitechapel Craft School, founded by Hubert Llewellyn Smith and served on its first committee, determining to set up his own idealist venture back in Yorkshire.

The Brandsby estate had previously been run from Gilling Castle and it was here, at the Lodge with Hugh Fairfax-Cholmeley's mother, that Blow first stayed. Hugh founded the Brandsby Dairy Association Ltd, one of the earliest co-operative farming organisations[4] and had no wish to make Gilling Castle his home. He asked Blow to build him a house more fitting to his socialist ideals. On 2 September 1891 Cockerell 'walked along the embankment to Chelsea in the evening, a glorious sunset before me all the way, and dined with the Blow's. Detmar still in Yorkshire. Met Collie, Tweed and Lutyens there.' The Blow family had moved to 96 Cheyne Walk, Chelsea early in 1891 and this became a focus for Detmar's social circle even when he was away, as he was that autumn. He was already involved at Brandsby on work to estate cottages[5] and was working on the design for Mill Hill, as Fairfax-Cholmeley's new house was to be called. Cockerell described how Blow developed socialist views under Fairfax-Cholmeley's influence and saw the new house plans at Cheyne Walk just after Christmas, finding them admirable.[6]

Work started in 1892 and Blow was up for substantial periods of time, at one stage with Arthur Collie who helped with furnishings when the house was finished.[7] Hugh Fairfax-Cholmeley took great pride in Blow's work but he recognised the help and influence of Blow's friends and mentors, considering Webb, Sedding, Gimson, Barnsley, Lethaby and Powell all to have been influential.[8] It was Webb for example who recommended John Ward, a mason from Saltburn, for the stonework and it is typical of Fairfax-Cholmeley's way of working that after Mill Hill was completed a pair of cottages was built nearby,

---

May 1889. Quoted by Alan Crawford in *C. R. Ashbee, Architect and Romantic Socialist* (Yale, London and New Have, 1985), p. 39.

4 E. A. Pratt, *The Transition in Agriculture* (undated), pp. 180–6.

5 It is said that Blow was responsible for panelling the staircase at Bank House where the local carrier, Mr White, lived. Blow stayed at Bank House subsequently when working in Brandsby (Hugh Fairfax-Cholmeley, unpublished autobiographical notes, in the private collection of Mrs Rosamund Caffrey, Hugh Fairfax Cholmeley's daughter).

6 'to the Blow's ... a man named Paul Cooper from Sedding's office also there ... saw ... also plans for the house he is going to build in Yorkshire for Cholmeley. Admirable as far as I was able to judge.' [Sunday 27 Dec 1891].

7 'Hoping to get Cholmeley's full account paid this week' (unpublished letter from A. L. Collie to John Tweed 21 December 1893. Tweed papers, Reading Borough Council: Leisure Services, Museum and Art Gallery).

8 Hugh Fairfax-Cholmeley, unpublished autobiographical notes, private collection.

12. Mill Hill, Brandsby, Yorkshire. The garden front. Arched openings to the left hand part of the elevation at ground floor level were the carriage shed and stable as originally built by Blow. They were later infilled when the house was enlarged by Alfred Powell. Powell's work formed a new entrance front, seen here beyond Blow's gable elevation on the left.

one for Ward, the mason and another for the joiner.[9]

Mill Hill sits on the edge of the escarpment at Brandsby, facing south across the plain to York Minster fifteen miles away on the horizon. Despite its grand setting it was the most modest of buildings. One room deep, it had no communicating passages and ran, as a simple sequence of rooms, below an uninterrupted ridge line (12). At one end, to the east, was the Hall, entered via a vestigial screens passage below a gallery. The only other significant ground floor accommodation, besides a tiny library, was stabling and a cart shed. The bedrooms above led one to another. Later Fairfax-Cholmeley married his gardener's daughter and at her insistence enlarged the house with the help of Alfred Powell (13). This later work contains exquisite craftmanship (14) but detracts from the stark simplicity of the original building, the qualities of which were simply those of unadorned local materials and building techniques. Blow's house, like many of his that followed, is solid and substantial – it was never his intention to impress by architectural showmanship. It is ideologically fastidious in its simplicity and expressed in a built form many of the qualities that his client was striving towards in other ways.

By the summmer of 1893 Mill Hill was almost finished. Friends came to stay, lodging in the unfinished attic and Blow and Fairfax-Cholmeley celebrated with a trip to Whitby and Staithes. Despite such enthusiasm from his client,

[9] They were later converted to a single house and are now known as Barfield House. Ward's daughter-in-law still lived in Brandsby in 1988.

13. Mill Hill. The entrance elevation by Powell, added to Blow's original work.

Blow's uncompromising traditional construction was not accepted unquestioningly. Draughty when first completed, Mill Hill had been built with open bearings around beam ends to insure against rot. Even for such an upholder of the simple life as Fairfax-Cholmeley, newspaper had to be stuffed into the voids to make the draughts bearable. Blow allowed little elaboration and the joiners considered the work unfinished by their standards; but Blow had his admirers nonetheless, one being Fairfax-Cholmeley's future sister-in-law.[10] Her admiration may not have had much to do with his architectural ability however, and to assume that she shared all Blow's ideals would be presumptuous. Blow glorified hard labour but the sisters were Brandsby girls and certainly Cholmeley's wife-to-be did not revel in the deliberate sacrifice of basic creature comforts. When it was suggested that water be drawn from the well she took a dim view and had a pump installed.

Compared to other more typical new small country houses of its time, Hugh Fairfax-Cholmeley's certainly reflected a certain amount of self-inflicted hardship. No doubt he thought it demonstrated his affiliation to the working man. But curiously such attempts at breaking down barriers between the social classes were often associated, not just at Mill Hill but at other of the more radical new Arts and Crafts houses with a way of working that imposed hardships upon the working men who built them. In some instances such a

[10] Cholmeley recalled that his architect found a kindred spirit in the smith also, a man called Granger from Searsby nearby. His great-grandson was making furniture in Brandsby in 1988.

14. Carved newel at Mill Hill, dating from Powell's alterations.

thought process could sentence two men to hours of hard labour in the saw pit in order that roof beams should show the marks of honest endeavour. What may have been a necessity in earlier times had to be emulated in the days of the power saw because Morrisian socialism had become inextricably mixed with an idealized traditional, pre-industrial lifestyle. No doubt Fairfax-Cholmeley, Blow and their friends thought such honest toil added dignity and meaning to the endeavour of all concerned but there is no doubt that in some instances such attitudes did not assist integration between those who saw life from the bottom of the saw pit and those towards the top of the social ladder.

Blow was not a theorist however, preferring practical involvement to a polemic. At Brandsby he began to work with his own hands. The last of his projects there was the construction of stabling at Low Farm, near Mill Hill and Fairfax-Cholmeley recorded that Blow worked with the masons for experience[11] although Fairfax-Cholmeley himself did not. Though at this stage both men had

11 Fairfax-Cholmeley used to talk of an ambition to live in the wilds of Canada, unfulfilled because of his inablity to fend for himself. His achievements were not of the hand-made variety but were considerable nonetheless. When he set up the Brandsby Dairy Association the idea of cooperation for such purposes was virtually unknown to the farming community but from small beginnings this early Cooperative Society grew until, by 1905, it had its own mill and provided motor wagons to transport goods to and from its own warehouse at the neighbouring railway station. (E. A. Pratt, *The Transition in Agriculture*, pp. 180–6.).

become involved with the debate, then current, concerning model plans for labourers cottages, Blow had other things in mind once Low Farm was finished and had to suggest to Fairfax-Cholmeley that someone else complete his building programme. Blow recommended G. P. Bankart, better known as one of the leading exponents, together with Ernest Gimson, of hand-moulded Arts and Crafts plasterwork. As a result there are small decorative panels above Blow's Hall at Mill Hill that represent Bankart's earliest essays in this material.[12] Later Fairfax-Cholmeley continued to work with others from Blow's circle, as Alfred Powell's subsequent involvement in the enlargement of Mill Hill indicates. Blow himself continued to take an interest in developments on the estate and drawings by him relating to Brandsby survive dated as late as 1912.[13]

Although Blow's work at Brandsby had kept him away from London for long periods, he still found time for other things. Early in 1892 he won the RIBA Pugin Scholarship with his drawings of Beauvais and Barfreston. Charles Nicholson and C. R. Mackintosh were runners up, as Blow had been the previous year.[14] Cockerell heard the news while Blow was away but he was among those to congratulate him at the Art Workers' Guild when Blow came home: 'met Detmar for first times since his return from the north. Collie, Barnsley, Lethaby, Voysey ... [were present]' [Friday 5 February 1892]. Typically Webb immediately found a way of turning Blow's success as a draftsman to a practical use. The previous summer Webb had advised the incumbent at St Mary's, East Knoyle, in Wiltshire concerning the condition of the church tower (15) and had suggested a measured survey by a capable architectural student under his direction prior to a detailed structural report. Blow carried out the survey which was submitted in May.

The church at East Knoyle stands within a short walk of Clouds, one of the most highly regarded new country houses of the time. Among Webb's finest architectural achievements, it also typifies his total commitment to a project. By 1892 he had been working there for fifteen years. A three year design period had been followed by seven on site, only for the greater part of the house to be

12 Lawrence Weaver, 'Lesser Country Houses of Today - Mill Hill', *Country Life* (22 May 1915), p. 2* (at this time the magazine included a supplement paginated thus).

13 Fairfax-Cholmeley had entrusted much of his work to Alfred Powell by this date. His association with Powell was a long-standing one, Powell helping him build another house called Swathgill at Coulton near Gilling village in 1926. Traditional in form, it was apparently only recently realised that Swathgill was predominantly a house of the twentieth century. Their association developed into friendship and Cholmeley's daughter Rosamund recalls visits to the Powells in the Cotswolds as a child (recalled by Mrs Rosamund Caffrey, Hugh Fairfax-Cholmeley's daughter, in a telephone conversation with the author, 17 Sept 1988).

14 An even earlier entry in 1890 had gained him an honourable mention.

15. The tower at St Mary's church, East Knoyle, in Wiltshire.

gutted by fire just two years later. It took another three years to rebuild. Webb stuck it out and his approach to conservation work was equally painstaking. Like Morris he had no time for the 'restorations' typical of the time. As he confided to a fellow SPAB committee member:

> I have some considerable experience of the little care modern architects have for buildings, proper: and no knowledge or aptitude for meeting difficulties as they arise, also, it does not 'pay', and one could not become 'eminent' in that way. Where is the love and sincere appreciation of building? Anyone who could do such work, with pleasure in the doing, could do it easily and well ... You can safely say that the greater number of old buildings condemned and pulled down need not be so destroyed. Modern architects could not afford to spend the time over the work, even if they had the wits to set about it and carry on. Then the fatal ignorance of what to do, and the mischief of depending for intelligence on a regulation clerk of work, and expensive builder, has lead to most of our cathedrals being ruined: but there is a worse evil: the rascal clergy will have their architects make a recognisable splash.[15]

Webb's views were well known amongst his clients, most of whom became members of the SPAB. At Clouds the Hon. Percy Wyndham, a Conservative MP, was no exception. Well indoctrinated by Webb, Wyndham offered to pay

[15] Unpublished letter from Philip Webb to G. Y. Wardle, 9 May 1899, SPAB Archive, East Knoyle file.

half the cost if the nearby church tower could be stabilised rather than re-built. Nonetheless its condition was such that it:

> was considered by all who saw it as a hopeless wreck: It was cracked, the core of the walls loose and running out through the cracks, the great arch to the nave had sunk ... and the wall above the arch had dropped with it, disclosing a huge triangular fissure.[16]

Armed with Blow's measured survey, Webb submitted his detailed report in August and when this was accepted, persuaded Blow to supervise repairs on site. Blow wrote enthusiastically to Webb that he was: 'Most anxious to start, fingers burning'[17] and work commenced on 1 September 1892. Webb made it clear to Blow from the start that they were not going to approach the repair of St Mary's in the usual way: 'I would not have undertaken the work without your help, but having done so, we, together, must manage the work so that it shall be done in quite different ways to those perfunctorily performed on precious pieces of antiquity.'[18] Webb described the work to a fellow SPAB committee member later:

> The tower ... was in a bad state and the rector, church warden, bell ringers, etc believed it was not safe and must be pulled down. On examination, I concluded that the foundations had not given way ... the tower had serious cracks in it from the top to nearly the floor of the church: the cracks were developed by bell ringing, as they opened and closed with the swaying: the consequence was, dust of the disturbed core descended and acted as a wedge to the fractures ... I made another, and more close survey with a young architect who was anxious to learn of structural work: and I gave him instructions, and a builder to supply him with three or four capable all-round handy mason/bricklayers.[19] Drawings, plumbings, levels, etc were got done. I ordered the young fellow to set up some scaffolding and begin.[20]

Having tried unsuccessfully to grout the weakened core of the tower walls, Webb realised that they would have to physically rebuild much of it. So Blow

16 Paper to SPAB Annual Meeting, June 1899, SPAB Annual Report, pp. 33–4.

17 Quoted by Rory Spence, 'Theory & Practice in the Early Work of the Society for the Protection of Ancient Buildings', in the catalogue for an exhibition concerning the history and development of the SPAB, entitled *A School of Rational Builders*, 1982, p. 7.

18 Ibid., p. 7.

19 Provided by Albert Estcourt of Gloucester, one of Webb's most trusted builders and the contractor for Clouds. At least two of these men worked for Blow again later (see chapter 5).

20 Unpublished letter from Philip Webb to G. Y. Wardle, 9 May 1899, SPAB Archive, East Knoyle file.

and his men dismantled the inner skin of the tower and working their way upwards rebuilt the cracked areas from the inside. Sometimes their excavations took them so far into the wall thickness they could see daylight through the joints of the facing stones externally. Where the stair turret abutted the tower the walls were enormously thick and material had to be passed into the workmen with what Webb described as a kind of pele-stick (the long handled implement used by bakers to load bread deep into their brick ovens). Webb's description, written six years after the job was finished, continues:

> Of course we had to change our ways of meeting difficulties as the work went on and I am bound to say the men became very handy at their work and as it was fresh to them, they took to it with real enthusiasm and the young architect picked up a lot of useful knowledge, truth to tell for once, so did I. The backbone of such work is personally watching it, with real considering cap on all the while. The young architect used to send for me when he was puzzled and together, with the good workmen, we made the walling sound ... The cost was between £800 and £900. If the tower had been pulled down and rebuilt it could not have cost less than £1,600 or £2,000 and then it would have been a new tower ... Young Detmar Blow, the architect who acted throughout as clerk of works, using his own hands meanwhile, has done some good work in the same way since, but I have not seen it. His good qualities are several. His worst his rashness. He has taken some of these men about the country with him.[21]

Webb's remarks about Blow's impetuosity probably refer to his later involvement at Clare church in Suffolk where the SPAB had difficulties with the Rector, due in part at least to Blow's commitments in too many places at once. The episode is described in Chapter 5. At Clare, as at Knoyle only very limited repairs were carried out externally and new pointing was kept to a minimum, the facing stones being grouted in behind where possible. Blow wrote to Webb concerning the matter at Knoyle in November 1892: 'and what would Mr Webb like, as to any pointing outside the tower? I have said he leaves that to the Almighty, but there are places where we might help the Almighty to keep the devil out.' The repairs were complete by June 1893 when Webb wrote to the rector: 'I have had considerable experience in repairs to churches, but I never saw work done so well and yet with so little disturbance or injury to ancient fabric.' In a letter to Wyndham he says 'I am bound to bear testimony to the invaluable assistance of Detmar Blow: to whom, I am convinced, any success obtained has been chiefly due.'

The work at Knoyle ran in parallel with that at Brandsby, the completion of the church tower being followed by Blow's last summer in Yorkshire.

21 Ibid.

Cockerell saw him at Cheyne Walk when he returned: 'in evening to Chelsea ... Detmar just up from Yorkshire ... [his] beard and moustache quite Holbeinesque, as Webb says' [Saturday 11 November 1893]. Next day they met again in Webb's rooms and Cockerell, by then living in Gimson's old chambers next door, invited Blow to tea: 'Detmar, Lethaby, Fleming, Douglas and the little Rookes came to tea ... Detmar and Lethaby sat up until 11.30pm talking about architecture, etc. We thought we might go to Wells at Christmas time' [Sunday 26 November 1893]. There is no record of such a trip and although the experience Blow gained at Brandsby and Knoyle was considerable, the Webb school of practical training was a long course and early in 1894 Blow left London to spend almost a year learning the craft of a mason. The arrangements were made through Webb but although the details are unclear, an apprenticeship is confirmed by an entry in Webb's address book.[22] The facts are that Blow was away from London for considerable lengths of time from March 1894 until March 1895, spending much of the time in the North East.[23] At the end of this period he was initiated (as Brother D. Blow) into the Friendly Society of Stone Masons, Newcastle Lodge.[24]

The period was interrupted by financial difficulties. Cockerell, visiting Cheyne Walk one day, found no one at home except Detmar's father. The Blow family business had run into trouble and Cockerell was told by Mr Blow the story of his bankruptcy: 'Very sad I found it, ... they will have to leave the house and sell all their furniture I fear, our oldest friends to whom we owe so many kindnesses' [Sunday, 2 September 1894].[25] Detmar, home over the New

22 In fact Blow's RIBA Fellowship Nomination Papers in the British Architectural Library, in his own hand, suggest a stonemasonry apprenticeship during 1891 and 1892 but this was clearly not the case.

23 In July 1894 Blow had been sketching at Corbridge, west of Newcastle, and other locations in his sketch books around this time indicate a prolonged spell in the area (Detmar Blow Sketchbooks, RIBA Drawings Collection: 1987. 55, Sketchbook No. 4, p. 28). In late 1894 and early 1895 the SPAB were corresponding with Blow concerning the tower of St. Nicholas Church, Newcastle. Blow prepared a report on it, in conjunction with C. C. Winmill, another young SPAB architect who studied with Blow at the Architectural Association and later developed under Webb's guidance. Winmill gives Blow's address at the time as 272 West Gate Road, Newcastle (C. C. Winmill, Report on St. Nicholas Church, Newcastle, Sept 1894. SPAB Archive, St Nicholas, Newcastle file).

24 Initiation and Contribution Card for the Friendly Society of Stonemasons, Newcastle Lodge, dated 25 March 1895, amongst the Blow family papers at Hilles.

25 Ever since the move to Cheyne Walk Detmar's father had been in trouble. In 1892 he had been very ill and Cockerell had visited, fearing he had not long to live. He survived but financial difficulties forced them to leave the house (Cockerell Diaries).

Year, tried to put a brave face on it, reassuring Cockerell that the family 'had enough capital at their disposal to keep the wolf from the door for three years at least' [1 January 1895]. Nonetheless the Blows moved to Sussex later in 1895. Cockerell went to visit, staying with them at the Malt House, Graffham, near Petworth on 26 October and next day being shown Westlands, a house they had just taken nearby: 'A picturesque place but needing much repair.' Both Detmar and Sydney Blow, his younger brother, were at home and they walked with Cockerell over the South Downs. Sydney Blow, who at this stage was attempting to follow in Detmar's footsteps, told Cockerell of his apprenticeship as a bricklayer with Lutyens.[26]

Detmar must have felt he needed to be close to home for a while and Webb tried to put a local commission his way. In March 1895 an art teacher in Chichester had written to the SPAB warning them: 'the restoration fiend is to be let loose in Chichester ... the beautiful Market Cross will be his prey'[27](16). Webb tried to contact Blow and a message found him on a brief visit to London from the North East. Thackeray Turner, the SPAB secretary, lent him a tape and a rod for the survey, Blow's being still in Newcastle. Blow advised the SPAB Committee that a repair technique similar to that used at East Knoyle might be adopted. Work would be undertaken internally, filling the interstices of the old fabric with rubble concrete and stitching courses of hard paving

26 Sydney Blow was taken away from Westminster School because he spent too much time at the theatre. He was sent to Bedales, a pioneer co-educational school firmly based on Ruskinian principles, then only in its second term (see also chapters 8 & 9 for further references to Bedales). When he left he found himself placed under Detmar's guidance: 'To be a real architect one most know a building from its foundation upwards' he was told. 'Also I mustn't waste time writing plays. So I became a mortar puddler on one of Lutyens' buildings in Surrey. Twelve shillings and two pence a week I earned, mixing mortar for humorous but illiterate bricklayers. In time I was promoted to trowel but the more I handled bricks the more I realised that they and I had no real affinity' (Sydney Blow, *The Ghost Walks on Fridays* (London, Heath Cranton, 1935), p. 35). Sydney Blow counted Lutyens as a friend from an early age. He tells how, in 1891 when he was thirteen, he would pay to entertain a group of friends all much older than himself, selling old postage stamps from his mother's love letters to pay the bill. The group comprised John Tweed, the sculptor and Arthur Collie, the Bond Street art dealer, as well as Lutyens: 'It was quite a regular occurence for me on Saturdays to leave Westminster School at one o'clock and proceed to Waterloo (via the stamp shop) and there meet Tweed and Collie. Down we used to go to Witley near Hindhead, where we would stay at "The Cricketers" to be joined later in the afternoon by Ned Lutyens whose home was at Thursley nearby' (Sydney Blow, *The Ghost Walks on Fridays*, pp. 37–8).

27 Unpublished letter from Herbert Catt to the SPAB, March 1895. SPAB Archive: Chichester Market Cross file.

16. The market cross at Chichester, drawn by Hedley Fitton for the *Daily Chronicle* and published March 20, 1896 (SPAB archive).

'The restoration fiend is to be let loose in Chichester ... the beautiful Market Cross will be his prey'.

bricks around the structure internally to tie it together. His estimate of cost, at £542 14*s*. 6*d*. allowed himself £80 for sixteen weeks work which clearly bears out Webb's reflections on such repairs and their lack of appeal to 'Modern architects who could not afford to spend the time over the work.'[28] By contrast, Lutyens was working hard at this time to make his name as a society architect and to win the hand of Emily Lytton by impressing her family with his bank balance. After overheads, Lutyens estimated his annual profit then at £945 10*s*. 0*d*. Although over £500 of this was still owing to him, it represents about four times the weekly rate charged by Blow who, conversely was worried he might be charging too much, telling Webb: 'I don't wish to overdo it but have to allow for 'no pay times' in between jobs.'[29] Back in the north again, Blow sent

[28] Unpublished letter from Philip Webb to G. Y. Wardle, 9 May 1899, SPAB Archive, East Knoyle file.

[29] Unpublished letter from Detmar Blow to Philip Webb dated 17 July 1895. SPAB Archive: Chichester Market Cross file.

his report to Webb in July from Ruthwell on the Solway Firth, telling him in passing about the problems he was having getting local stone for his work there at Cowlongon Castle for Johnstone Douglas:

> We are into our second week of work and at a builders yard in the village. Carter, who was at the Newcastle job is working with me, an excellent mason, and we lodge in regular Scotch one-storeyed cot close by with a view across the Solway Firth to the Cumberland Hills on the south and away to Criffell, Kirkcudbright, through the squint window on the west. What with peat fires, and smoke, brose, kale and oat cake, plenty of fun and a bed large enough for four with only two in it, we are doing very well, as I hope are you.[30]

Chichester came to nothing[31] and there was concern amongst Blow's friends when he returned to London that summer with no prospect of work. Arthur Collie, working for Cecil Rhodes in Cape Town, wrote from Groot Schurr to John Tweed the sculptor: 'I was awfully glad to know of Detmar being back in town ... I hope you'll keep him from Newcastle and within reach now. If he is not better employed when I get back – I think I shall have some work he might care to take up.'[32] Blow remained based in the south east for a little while but in the end it was the SPAB again and not Collie who found him work. It was to take him further afield once more but this time south west, to Cornwall.

The Old Post Office at Tintagel was sold at auction on 12 September 1895 (17). Although still known by the same name today, it is in fact a small medieval manor house and a rare survival of early domestic architecture in Cornwall. Over the centuries its enormously heavy slates had bent the rafters to give a wildly uneven roof most fitting to this wild and even more uneven coastline. Arthurian romanticism, popularised by the poetry of Alfred Lord Tennyson,

30 Ibid.

31 The matter became political. The city council favoured Blow's approach but were short of funds. Local elections were to be held and the bishop, favouring comprehensive restoration rather than Blow's conservative repair, had offers of donations almost double Blow's requirements. Blow was concerned that the initiative might be lost if the city did not authorize the work immediately: 'The bishop made inquiries as to the architect's capabilities, no doubt a popular name would have been a greater help to the society. Should the society be able to secure the sympathy of these gentlemen it would be well done at once' (unpublished letter from Detmar Blow to Thackeray Turner dated 18 Sept 1895. SPAB Archive: Chichester Market Cross file). Although the debate continued for another nine months and made national news (14), in the end neither faction succeeded in putting their proposals into practice.

32 Unpublished letter from A. L. Collie to John Tweed dated 22 July 1895. Tweed Papers, Reading Borough Council: Leisure Services, Museum and Art Gallery.

17. The Old Post Office, Tintagel in 1895, prior to the rescue campaign and Blow's repairs.

Algernon Swinburne and William Morris, had already engulfed Tintagel, now reeling in its aftermath with boarding houses, shops and hotels springing up to trade upon it. King Arthur's Arms had appeared in 1873 although the King Arthur's Castle Hotel, an enormous and scenically disruptive cliff-top giant, was not open until 1899. Its 'Excali Bar' still trades on the legends of the past today.

To make way for tourism the old cottages had to go but fortunately the campaigners who rescued the Old Post Office preferred their legends less commercialized. A painter called Constance Phillott alerted the SPAB, hearing that bidders for the Old Post Office were likely to pull it down and redevelop. In fact it went to a Miss Johns, who cared passionately about its continued well-being but bought the house knowing she was unable to pay for its repair. Constance Phillott lobbied her artist friends, many of whom knew the building from painting excursions to Tintagel and a good number were pursuaded to donate pictures to raise money.[33] Thackeray Turner, Secretary to the SPAB, accepted the post of treasurer to the fund thus set up and recommended Detmar Blow to undertake the repairs.

Blow wrote to Turner in February 1896 from Sedding's old office at 447, Oxford Street, now run by Henry Wilson, accepting the work and stating his charges. An inspection and report could be done at one pound per day plus expenses. If the work were to proceed he would charge three pounds a week on site. Miss Phillott agreed the rates and Blow made his first visit whilst the

33 They included Walter Langley of the Newlyn School, T. R. Lamont, Birket Foster, S. P. Jackson, C. Davidson and many others.

18. The Old Post Office. Tintagel, in 1985.

picture sale was being held and funds raised. Miss Johns, the owner, wished to extend the building at the same time and was prepared to pay £100 for such work and this, together with £150 from the pictures, gave Blow a budget of £250. On 14 March he wrote to Thackeray Turner from Abinger Hammer, near Dorking, where he was staying with Alfred Powell, under the misapprehension that: 'I am now to work out the repairs and any addition to the amount of £350 to include all expenses.' Thackeray Turner did not take his responsibilties as treasurer for the fund lightly and forcefully informed Blow of his mathematical error, a postcard coming back from Abinger blaming Powell's handwriting when passing on the message.[34]

Perhaps because he was already commited to work with Powell in Surrey himself, Blow nominated Herbert North, a pupil articled to Henry Wilson, to supervise the work on site at Tintagel in his place. All went well and by November Miss Phillot could write to Thackeray Turner expressing her satisfaction at the completed job:

> It must be a great pleasure to all artists who have admired it in its former condition to see it now, not looking new but in a sound, safe state with all its picturesque character ... and the ferns and mosses on the roof, and the ivy on its walls ... quite un-hurt by the workmen. The improvement of the interior by the removal of modern rubbish and restoration of the old central hall and spiral staircase is of course immense. The thanks of all artists who take pleasure in such buildings

[34] SPAB Archive: The Old Post Office, Tintagel file.

> are due to you and to Mr Detmar Blow who has bestowed such skill, time and patience on the charming old place.[35] (18)

Blow reported to the SPAB Committee a total expenditure of £256 11*s.* 6½*d.*[36] Soon after Miss Johns made an arrangement whereby the Old Post Office became the property of the recently formed National Trust when she died; it can still be seen today, more or less as Blow left it.[37]

Whilst Blow was in the country, Cockerell was still in town but he had at last given up coal, if not for Ruskin then at least for Morris. He had moved from Gimson's old rooms in Raymond Buildings to lodgings near Richmond Park and was working at Kelmscott House in Hammersmith. Cruelly for Cockerell his employment as Morris' secretary was short lived for, as Blow had been to Ruskin, so Cockerell was to be to Morris as the great man's health deteriorated. By February 1896, when Blow was first getting involved at Tintagel, Morris was no longer able to attend meetings at the SPAB. Concern grew and on 18 August, returning from Norway on a sea cruise taken for his health, he collapsed. He was diagnosed as tubercular and Cockerell, fearing for the worst, took his turn at night watching. On 25 September Blow, who had visited Cockerell in Richmond with his arm in a sling after putting his hand through a pane of glass, joined the group attending the failing Morris: 'W. M. wandered a good deal but recognised us, he was very restless. Detmar, Walker and I stayed with him at night. He thought he was on the Garonne [the ship on which he had sailed to Norway] at sea' [Wednesday, 30 September 1896].

That Thursday Blow took the night watch with Miss De Morgan, sister of William the potter and was at his side again two nights later when Morris died. Cockerell records:

> Lady Burne-Jones, Mrs Morris, May, Detmar and Miss De Morgan were in the room. Miss De Morgan and Walker started off to Kelmscott to tell Jenny. Carruthers, Price, Philip Webb and Murray called. Murray made two drawings, one of which he gave to me. I had never seen a dead man before and I was startled to see how little he resembled the living Morris. [Saturday, 3 October 1896]

35 Unpublished letter from Constance Phillot to Thackeray Turner dated 23 Nov 1896 in the SPAB Archive: The Old Post Office, Tintagel file.

36 SPAB Agenda Book, 19 Nov 1896.

37 Later the Trust sought Blow's opinion concerning a proposed addition to the Old Post Office. He did not approve: 'I venture to think nothing but a hovel or one-storeyed out-house should be built on the ground adjoining ... plans shown me did not come within these limits' (unpublished letter from Detmar Blow to John Kent, acting SPAB secretary, dated 11 Jan 1900. SPAB Archive: The Old Post Office, Tintagel file).

Blow is said to have made a death bed drawing too, later lost in the same fire that destroyed so many of his papers.[38] An entry in Cockerell's diary [Sunday 4th October] may have referred to it: 'W. B. Richmond and Murray came in the morning and made drawings, Detmar and Philip Webb at lunch – Theodore Watts and others in the afternoon.' Next day it was Blow who went to Kelmscott, to make arrangements for the funeral which was to take place on the morrow. There were crowds at Hammersmith and Paddington as the coffin set off with the mourners for Lechlade, arriving about noon, as Cockerell describes:

> 'Detmar had decked out a yellow cart with willows and vine leaves (19). The coffin was placed in this and the mourners followed in ten carriages. Burne-Jones, Lethaby and about forty from London. Raining still. After the interment went to the house and stayed the night. Miss De Morgan, May, Jenny, Mrs Morris, Sparling, Miss Roberts and Detmar there' [Tuesday, 6 October 1896].

Amongst those present during the day was George Bernard Shaw who described Blow's funeral arrangements later: 'The poet's body was carried to the grave not in a hearse but in a great harvest wagon, driven by Detmar Blow, the architect in a wagoner's smock.'[39]

19

38 Recalled by Lucilla Warre-Cornish, Detmar Blow's younger daughter, in a conversation with the author.

39 Dan H. Laurence (ed.), *Collected Letters of George Bernard Shaw*, 4 vols (Max Reinhardt, 1965–88), letter from GBS to Frances Dillon, 22 November 1908.

Chapter 3
A HARD ROAD
Alfred Powell's Career before 1900

> It would be good fortune for you if you could so arrange things as to have a year's continuous work at carpentering in its various kinds... . you would pick up much general knowledge of the various other crafts connected with building and would gain much more help to your after work than in any other way ...
>
> Philip Webb to Alfred Hoare Powell, 17 March 1894

Early in 1897, soon after Morris' funeral, Detmar Blow set up in practice in rented rooms at 21 Old Buildings, Lincolns Inn.[1] He shared the premises with Alfred Powell, one of the group of young architects from J. D. Sedding's old office. Their careers prior to that date had followed a similar pattern and so it continued as both became itinerant architects in the last few years of the nineteenth century. For Powell, however, the path proved a hard one to follow.

Alfred Hoare Powell (1865–1960), a vicar's son and the eighth of ten children, was educated at Uppingham. After three years in which he studied at the Slade and was articled as a pupil to the architect W. O. Milne he joined Sedding in 1887. Here he met Ernest Gimson, Ernest Barnsley, Arthur Grove, Charles Nicholson, John Paul Cooper and Henry Wilson. His travels with Wilson in Northern France in 1889, following in the footsteps of Blow and Ruskin the year before, have been mentioned already. When Sedding died in 1891 Powell was still in his employment and Powell's watercolour of that year, showing Sedding's design for the rood screen at the church of St Mary, Stamford, Lincolnshire was a tribute to the talents of both the master and the pupil (20). At the time of Sedding's death Powell was working at the Trinity College Mission in the Camberwell Road and lived on the job:

1 Cockerell visited them for the first time on 16 February (Cockerell Diaries). Quotations found in the text of this chapter followed in brackets by a date that includes the day of the week, i.e. [Sunday 24 June 1888], are from Sydney Cockerell's diaries. These are to be found amongst the Cockerell Papers in the British Museum Manuscripts Collection.

20 (opposite). Design for the rood screen at the church of St Mary, Stamford, Lincs, 1891, drawn by Alfred H. Powell for J. D. Sedding (BAL).

> I generally get up and have an hour in the garden before breakfast and see how the bricklayers are getting on. They take some persuading to follow what I wish and not their own rather parrotical [sic] habits but it is all going on well and is a most interesting occupation for me. I watch them as I am dressing and can throw the soap at them if they do it wrong![2]

Henry Wilson took over the office and Grove, Cooper, Nicholson and Powell all continued to work together initially. Carrying on in the same vein as Sedding, Wilson worked in the decorative arts as well as architecture and both he and John Paul Cooper later became well known as art metalworkers, jewellers and silversmiths. The others began to find their own way where they could although they remained a cohesive group and worked collectively on certain projects. Powell continued his work for Trinity College in his own right and watched as his colleagues took their own first steps away from the Sedding office:

> Grove ... has taken lodgings with his brother just close here in Elm Place which will be great fun for us both. I found him the rooms quite accidentally... . My friend Blow has got the Pugin Studentship (under 25) which has pleased us all immensely and Nicholson in our office was second with a medal of merit. We have not heard about the Victoria Cath. yet. Let us hope ours is going across the sea in the company of the favoured three![3]

After 1895 only Arthur Grove remained with Wilson[4] but of them all it was perhaps Nicholson, more than any other, who continued the architectural tradition Sedding had inherited from G. E. Street. Street's muscular Gothic,

[2] Unpublished letter from Alfred Powell to his father, dated 3 Sept 1891, in 'Autographed Letters, etc. by Alfred Hoare Powell and Some Others. Written at Home and Abroad, AD MDCCCLXXIX to MDCCCCXII. Bound 1914' (by Edgar Powell), p. 106; amongst the Powell papers in the possession of Mrs Thompson-Lewis, Petersfield, Hants.

[3] Unpublished letter from Alfred Powell to his mother, dated 22 Jan 1892 from Selwood Place, in 'Autographed Letters, Etc. ... ', pp. 112–3. See also chapter 2 for reference to Blow's Pugin Scholarship. The reference to 'the Victoria Cath.' suggests that Powell and others from Sedding's office may have put forward designs for Westminster Cathedral, the commission for which Bentley did not receive until 1894.

[4] Margaret Richardson, 'Architects of the Arts and Crafts Movement' (London, Trefoil, 1983), p. 73. L. MacDonald Gill, the younger brother of Eric Gill had joined them. Later he went on to work with Charles Nicholson, who had left Wilson in 1893. When Wilson's practice eventually moved from the old Sedding office he sub-let from E. S. Prior with whom Grove later collaborated.

tempered by Sedding's sensitivity and craftsmanship evolved a stage further in Nicholson's work and he kept the tradition alive until his death in 1949. H. S. Goodhart-Rendel, a pupil of Nicholson's, said of him:

> He was the most remarkable architect who ever lived. He had an extraordinary facility for drawing anything. He designed two Cathedrals, Portsmouth and Sheffield, and some forty churches. He did not care much for publicity. The number of things he has done without anyone noticing is simply incredible. His ecclesiastical career kept him rather apart. Also he was violently anti-academic and looked on architecture as an Art.[5]

Goodhart Rendel's summary of Nicholson's achievements is, remarkably, something of an understatement. His proposals for Liverpool Cathedral were amongst the most exciting of the designs short-listed in the final stage of the competition won by Giles Gilbert Scott. Nonetheless his work can be seen in no less than eighteen other English cathedrals and his enlargement of parish churches to form the parish church cathedrals of the 1920s and 1930s would have made him famous had any achieved their full realisation.[6] Portsmouth and Sheffield, Chelmsford and Bradford Cathedrals would all have been substantial buildings of considerable merit had his designs been implemented.

Alfred Powell's own architectural career was less spectacular. In May 1892 he started work at the church in Barrington, Cambridgeshire, staying there until September (apart from a fortnight's holiday with John Paul Cooper to visit Lacock, Wells and Bristol). He repaired the roof and attended to some masonry too. It gave him his first opportunity to try such things with his own hands, as he told his father:

> I am modelling a cross for the gable of the south porch here and am going to be rash enough to try and carve it in stone ... We went an expedition on bicycles the other day to see one of the many fallen church towers hereabout - Great Chishill in Essex and we rode to it along the watershed of the Cam on our right and the dear Thames on our left ... The tower is the sixth in a few years that has fallen and presents a gruesome appearance ... The tower was all built of flints and had an iron band all round it which the vicar and churchwardens agreed in thinking very unsightly and so removed it!! with such

5 Nikolaus Pevsner, 'Goodhart-Rendel's Roll-Call', *Architectural Review*, 138, no. 824 (October 1965), p. 263. H. S. Goodhart-Rendel worked for Nicholson and continued the tradition Nicholson inherited. He died in 1959.

6 Michael Drury, 'Sir Charles Nicholson - Portsmouth's First Cathedral Architect', in *Forever Building - Essays to Mark the Completion of the Cathedral Church of St Thomas of Canterbury, Portsmouth*, ed. Sarah Quail and Alan Wilkinson (Portsmouth Cathedral Council, 1995), pp. 121–42.

21. Fallen church tower at Great Chishill, Essex. Extract from Alfred Powell's letter to his father, 18 August 1892, in a private collection: 'The tower is the 6th in a few years that has fallen and presents a gruesome appearance...'

Barrington Vicarage.
Aug. 18. 1892.

My dear Father,
Thank you so much for your letter & its contents which were very welcome as I was run out all but a little. I am sorry to have let two posts go by without your having an answer, but as the post goes immediately after tea & as I always forget till tea time that there is a post & as we always have someone to tea – it is rather a difficult matter to get off any letters at all! You say little about the Grange people which sounds rather exciting – Edwd. Hodgkin told me

we went an expedition on bicycles the other day to see one of the many fallen church towers hereabout – Gt. Chishill in Essex & we rode to it along the watershed of the Cam on our right & the dear Thames on our left & as it was raining I thought of sending you a message that way but I fear it would not have got to the river your side of London! The tower is the 6th in a few years that has fallen & presents a gruesome appearance – It stands finely on a hill top (the whole blds [illegible] much) with a very pretty village

consequences (21). Cooper is coming here for Sunday did I tell you? ... I hope you will hear of somebody who wants a house built soon as I shall be ready for another job before long.[7]

In another letter to his mother about the gable cross a week later he added:

> Woolard, the mason here, and a delightful man expects me to be 'getting on nicely with it about Christmastime'! but I hope it will not be as bad as that. I am more afraid of splitting the stone than taking four months.

His fears were groundless and within a fortnight Powell was down at the blacksmith's, trying his hand at forge work:

> The last fortnight here I have been very busy making a pair of wrought iron hinges for a new door for the north porch. The blacksmith (in the village) is very much alarmed at the drawing I brought him, having never made anything much more elaborate than a horseshoe and was almost unwilling to take it in hand till I took off my coat and made him begin. (I don't mean to say I knocked him down first.) It has been the talk of the village the whole fortnight and I am regarded as a very wonderful sort of person. It was most exciting work and a good deal of it very troublesome but though rude they are finished and strong and will I hope look well. We are also making the

[7] Unpublished letter from Alfred Powell to his father, dated 18 Aug 1892 from Barrington Vicarage, in 'Autographed Letters, etc. ...', pp. 122–5, amongst the Powell papers.

22. 'Scorpion on our bedroom wall, September 24, 1893, Verona', from Alfred Powell's sketchbook (BAL).

> door in church, of oak. And I am learning how to carpenter by so doing and have actually learnt how to sharpen a plane, which looked at from a distance has always seemed a matter of great difficulty and risk! I hope all will be finished by the weekend though I am most loth to go away ... but I must get on with my drawings or I shan't get them done by Christmas. Mr Coneybeare [from Barrington] has written to a neighbouring vicar to get me the work of saving his church tower from falling which it will infallibly do this winter if it isn't taken in hand at once – (we had frosts this morning and last week). So I shall probably go to a place near here called Toft on Thursday... . Did I tell you I finished my stone gable cross and it has been up now nearly a fortnight and looks interesting and is I believe thought beautiful.[8]

The drawings referred to may well have been Powell's entry for the RIBA Owen Jones Travelling Studentship which he won in 1893, setting off for Italy in August with John Paul Cooper (22). They spent four months in Milan, Verona, Venice, Florence and Rome. Powell thought the RIBA might find the drawings he made on his travels inadequate but he wasn't too worried:

> I have done a few drawings and they are very dull with perhaps one or two exceptions and I rather doubt if the RIBA will think I have fulfilled my contract. This, I only mind as far as my pocket is concerned – not an inch further![9]

8 Unpublished letter from Alfred Powell to his father, dated 17 Sept 1892, in 'Autographed Letters, etc. ...', p. 130, amongst the Powell papers.

9 Unpublished letter from Alfred Powell to his father ('Carissimo Padre'), dated 10

Blow wanted to come out and join them in Venice early in 1894 but the plan came to nothing.[10]

When Powell returned he, like Blow, took advice from Philip Webb[11] and set about learning the carpentry trade in Abinger, near Dorking in Surrey. His stay in the area was a long one[12] although he originally planned to work at carpentry only until the end of 1894:

> The workman's life develops under modern conditions into a dull longing for Saturday from the first stroke on Monday morning. I am not quite so far developed yet myself but have very little doubt I should soon be if I went on. As it is I mean to stop at Christmas. I have had my wages "riz" this week from 14/9 to 19/8, thus from 3*d.* to 4*d.* an hour (58½ hours).[13]

This same letter makes reference to the construction of a school room, by the church at Bisham, for which Powell acted as architect. He extended the vicarage also. But letters from Powell to his family and to the SPAB show that his association with the Abinger area continued beyond this period. In October 1894 he wrote to his mother about a new project on which he hoped to work with Detmar Blow. It was for a house and garden, to be built in stages:

> A house with a history! This was my suggestion ... built slowly and well – according to means! What wisdom! It certainly seems wiser to do so than hurriedly complete it ... The garden is to have things growing in it by next spring so I must make up my mind as to its lines before long.

Blow visited Powell in March 1896 when the Chichester Market Cross campaign was at its height and may have worked at Long Copse (23), as the new house was called, then. He had asked Herbert North to supervise work on site

---

Nov 1893 from Pensione Caccianini, Firenze, in 'Powell Manuscripts', vol. 2, ed. Edgar Powell (1912), p. 159 in the possession of Mrs Thompson-Lewis, Petersfield, Hants.

10 'Autographed Letters, etc. ...', p. 101, amongst the Powell papers.

11 Letter from Philip Webb to Alfred Powell dated 17 March 1894, in W. R. Lethaby, *Philip Webb & His Work* (Oxford, 1935), pp. 123–4, quoted under the chapter heading.

12 In mid 1893 Powell disappears from the London scene and the pages of Cockerell's diary for more than eighteen months. When he re-appears it is only fleetingly due to a chance meeting early in 1895 when Powell and Lethaby visit the New Gallery where Cockerell worked as Secretary for nine months in 1893 between jobs with William Morris.

13 Unpublished letter from Alfred Powell to his father, dated 13 Oct 1894 from 'Smokejack', Ockley, Surrey, in 'Autographed Letters, etc.', p. 263, amongst the Powell papers.

23. Long Copse, Ewhurst, Surrey. The house seen from the garden, before 1922.

at Tintagel later that spring, not the sort of thing he would have done if he had not been busy elsewhere. Certainly Blow worked with Powell on a later stage of construction in 1899, delaying his services (and those of his 'colleagues') to Thackeray Turner at the SPAB as a result: 'at present we have some four to five months work building a small house for Mr Powell in Surrey.' The letter was written from Coneyhurst at Ewhurst, an earlier house by Philip Webb near Godalming, in whose grounds Long Copse had been built.[14]

Long Copse is stone-built with a long roof of thatch on the first build and stone tiles on the later work. Described by Pevsner as 'an extreme example of the primitive wing of the Arts and Crafts movement', it was built originally as a summer cottage with just two rooms, cranked about a winding stair that projects externally at the pivot point. However primitive, its picturesque qualities were much admired by G. F. Watts,[15] the portraitist whose mortuary chapel at Compton nearby exhibits similarly hand-crafted characteristics. At Long Copse Powell is recorded as having acted as 'Master of the Works' as well as designer, buying all the materials and according to a later description, 'all the craftsmen were university men save the plumbers, an entertaining exception.'[16]

[14] Unpublished letter from Detmar Blow to Thackeray Turner dated 16 October 1899. SPAB Archive: Clare Church file (Suffolk).

[15] Lawrence Weaver, *Small Country House of Today*, vol. 1 (London: Country Life, 1911), pp. 25–29.

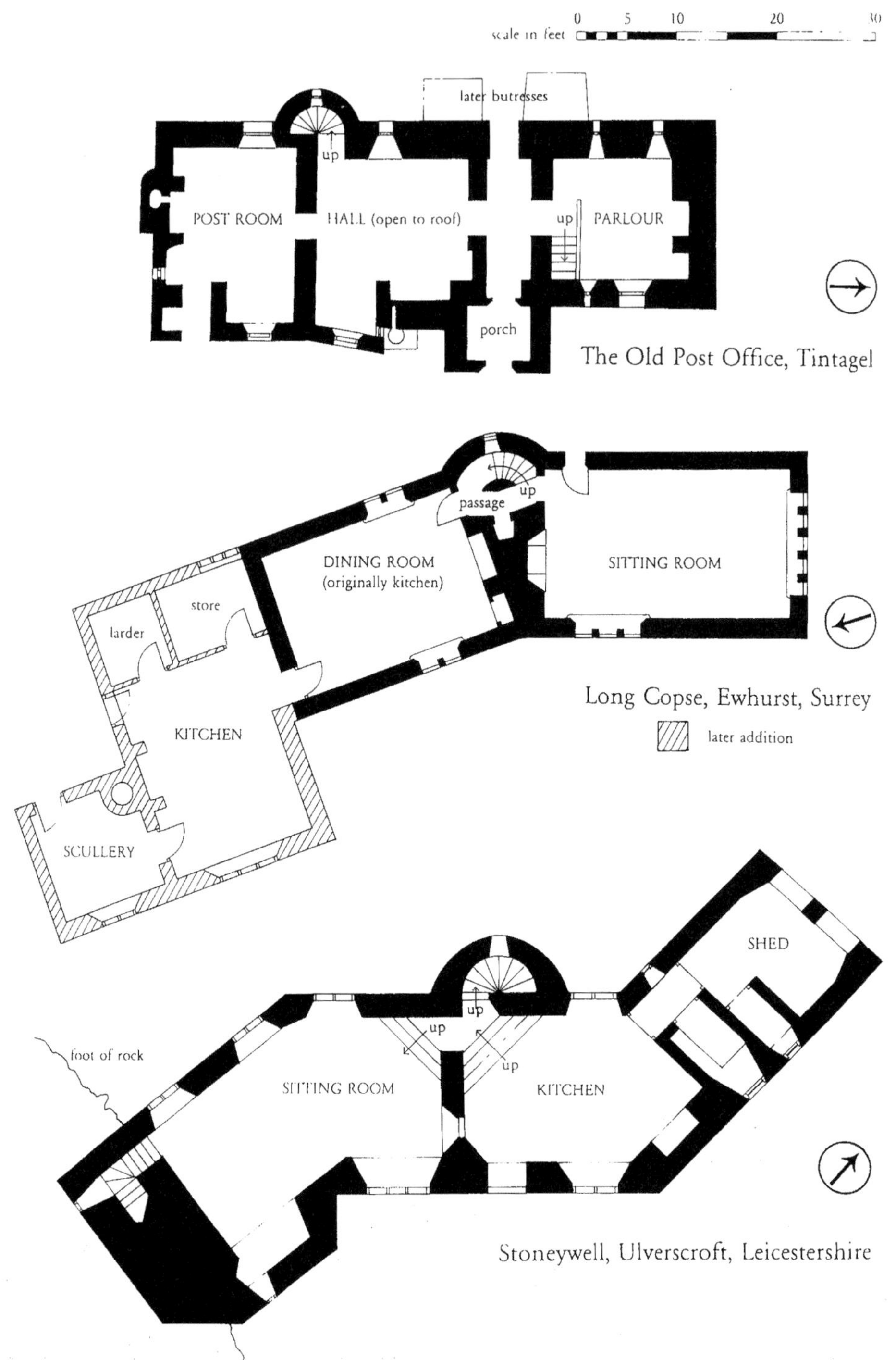

24. Comparative plans of The Old Post Office, Long Copse and Stoneywell (by A. F-K).

Some of the craftmanship however indicates a more experienced hand, 'the stonelaying being firm and neat' as Lawrence Weaver suggests in the same passage. Other features too suggest Blow's involvement, not least the newel stair, externally expressed. An uncommon feature locally, this does not derive from the Surrey vernacular. It is however common in the West Country where a late medieval example may be found at the Old Post Office, Tintagel. The plan at Long Copse also has similarities with Gimson's later double cranked plan for Stoneywell Cottage built by Blow and his masons in Leicestershire in 1899 and here the same stair arrangement appears again. The common threads within the three plans (24) suggest Blow's influence.

Whatever his activities in Surrey at the time, Powell was also working elsewhere in 1896. While Blow was involved at Tintagel on what was to become one of the earliest National Trust properties, Powell was, not entirely coincidentally, working on the repair of the first building the Trust owned. The common link between the SPAB and the fledgling National Trust was Cockerell who Powell had met at the Blows' in Chelsea as early as 1892.[17]

The Trust was founded in 1895 largely as a result of the efforts of Octavia Hill, a tireless campaigner for slum rehabilitation and the improvement of living conditions for city dwellers. During her work in deprived urban areas her attention had been drawn to the need for the protection of urban open space and she became fundamentally involved in several successful bids to save some of London's remaining tracts of common land from encroaching development. Her experience with the Commons Preservation Society formed an essential part of the foundation upon which the National Trust was built.

Octavia Hill's charitable ventures included work at the Red Cross Hall and here she was helped by Sydney Cockerell, who was involved from a young age, acting as its Secretary. Her work in the slums stemmed from the rehabilitation of 'Paradise Place', purchased with funds lent by Ruskin. She and Ruskin fell out but Cockerell, who knew them both, had succeeded in reconciling them. He was still not yet twenty. Shortly before departing for Northern France in 1888 with Detmar Blow both young men had attended 'Miss Hill's May Festival in her original houses purchased by Ruskin. May pole and Morris dancing' [Saturday 26 May 1888]. Another link between Cockerell, Blow and the Trust came through T. M. Rooke, the former pupil of Burne-Jones, neighbour of the Cockerell family in Bedford Park and Blow's mentor as an architectural draftsman. Rooke knew Octavia Hill too and joined the first Executive Committee of the National Trust in 1895.

16 Ibid, p. 25.

17 The Cockerell Diaries, 1 March 1892.

So, on 27 February 1896, the same day that Detmar Blow was making his initial inspection at Tintagel, the Cockerell connections resulted in a request from the committee of the SPAB that Alfred Powell should report on the condition of a medieval house in Alfriston, Sussex (25). It was the Old Clergy House, so named from its use by the clergy from the beginning of the seventeenth century. Built on a Wealden Plan with jettied bays either side of a central full height hall, its western jetty had since been removed and a floor constructed over part of the hall to provide additional accommodation. It became the vicarage and then, after about 1790, was converted into two cottages, remaining as such until 1885 when the vicar applied for authority to demolish it to avoid the expense of making good its dilapidated condition. The Ecclesiastical Commissioners consented but decreed that the old lady who let the house could live out her last years before it was taken down. This effectively saved the place for she lived until 1888 and soon after its future was secured when the Rev. Benyon was appointed to the living. His rescue appeal, eventually published in August 1892, describes the building:

> May I venture to draw your attention to the Old Clergy House at Alfriston which is in urgent need of repair. It is a building erected in the 14th century, apparently of contemporary date with the adjoining church of St Andrew, colloquially known as the 'Cathedral of the South Downs'. It is constructed of oak framing with the interstices filled in with wattle and daub. On plan it consists of a central hall ... with an open-timbered roof ... . On either side of this Hall are smaller rooms, two storeys in height (the one end now temporarily used as a Reading Room), which were probably the Dormitories and Offices, etc. The building is of a character rarely found in England, and is, therefore, of national interest, as it is an important piece of evidence showing the manner in which the Parochial Clergy, as distinguished from monastic establishments, lived in England in the middle ages.[18]

Benyon's first architect was Owen Fleming, later chief architect to the London County Council, Housing of the Working Classes Branch, and a close friend of C. R. Ashbee. His early assessment of the condition of the clergy house was supported by the Sussex Archaeological Society and the SPAB but the necessary funds were not forthcoming and it was the SPAB who suggested to Benyon that the answer to his problems might be to hand the building over to the National Trust.

The Trust was formally incorporated early in 1895. Immediately Octavia Hill wrote to Sydney Cockerell about the Old Clergy House:[19]

[18] From the SPAB Archive: Alfriston file (Sussex).

[19] Benyon having first written to the Rev. Canon H. Rawnsley, the Trust's first secretary, on the SPAB's advice only ten days after the decision to form the

25–6. Before and after: the Old Clergy House, Alfriston, Sussex, before repair (National Trust) and after (from *Old Cottages and Farmhouses in Kent and Sussex*, before 1900).

National Trust had been taken on the 16th of July 1894.

> ... as I understand, it is offered to the National Trust and the question of acceptance comes up at our Executive Committee on Tuesday. We should, very naturally, be asked to 'restore' it, and so far as that odious word means preserve from decay, of course we would wish to do so. Has your Ancient Monuments any information, which would give an approximate idea of the cost of doing what they would advise ... ?

Cockerell passed the letter on to the SPAB (his 'Ancient Monuments'?) who thought Fleming's initial estimate of £450 high. Owen Fleming, who had agreed to take on the project gratis, had pulled out due to pressure of other work, leaving the vicar with an unresolved builder's account assessed by the SPAB to be worth £150. Since then another architect had advised that a further £600 would be needed. The SPAB thought this preposterous and suggested Powell take control. Powell accepted[20] but things dragged on and the deeds were not signed until February 1896 when the building changed hands for a nominal ten pounds.

Powell's report was approved by the SPAB in March and was followed by his estimate[21] with a covering letter costing his own services at three guineas a week. For £350 he would overhaul the oak frame, repairing the joints where necessary, replace oak rafters and re-thatch. He included for laying a new stone floor, building a new chimney and fireplace in the hall, repairing or replacing oak window frames and leaded glazing, shoring, underpinning, strapping, bolting and 'rendering building in all respects secure and weatherproof with as little alteration of its present appearance as possible and compatible with modern occupation.'

Funds were needed and in June a letter from the National Trust appeared in *The Times*[22] concerning an appeal for £850 to fund two of their earliest acquisitions: the Old Clergy House and Barras Head at King Arthur's Cove, Tintagel. Money came in slowly and Octavia Hill, who herself gave £25 towards the Clergy House campaign, was obliged to ask Powell what he could achieve for £140.[23] Work started on 1 October and by December the framing to the front of the hall had been made permanently secure, working from the inside as with Webb and Blow's pioneering work at Knoyle:

20 Powell's acceptance was dated 7 October 1895 from Wrea Head, Scalby, Scarborough: 'as far as I can see it, it will suit me very well to take up the work. In the ordinary course of things I shall be at Mrs Edsom's, Abinger Hammer on Monday next.' Through the winter he kept the job in mind, writing again in November from Trinity College, Cambridge with reassurances.

21 From Abinger Hammer in May 1896.

22 *The Times* (15 June 1896), unpaginated press cutting to be found in the SPAB Alfriston file.

23 *The Standard* (16 October 1896), unpaginated press cutting to be found in the SPAB Alfriston file.

27. The Old Clergy House in 1992.

> All new oak timber used has been applied on the inside with the result that the appearance of the building from the outside has not been changed save for the heads of a few iron bolts ... the funds at present at the disposal of the National Trust are today virtually exhausted and the work will have to be stopped immediately.[24]

The infant Trust published another appeal in its annual report and with repairs eventually completed in 1898 (26), the hall was opened to the public. Access was by prior arrangement with the Trust's tenants, an early one being Lionel Curtis,[25] a friend of Owen Fleming and C. R. Ashbee. Ashbee, who may have heard of the building through the SPAB,[26] honeymooned at the Clergy House in 1898 with his wife Janet, ranging red apples along the beams and swimming in the Cuckmere river nearby. The Old Clergy House remains open to the public today (27).

Alfred Powell began to attend SPAB committee meetings regularly from March 1896, when Blow was staying with him at Abinger. Both he and Blow had served their time in the approved SPAB manner and the Society made the most of the skills they had acquired. While the National Trust was trying to

24 Ibid.

25 Private Secretary to the Chairman of London County Council.

26 Ashbee attended two meetings of the SPAB Committee as a visitor in the second half of 1895 at a time when the Clergy House would have been on the agenda.

raise funds for Alfriston, Powell was involved, through the SPAB, in preliminary work on another of the Trust's early acquisitions, a medieval craft guildhall known as the Joiners Hall in Salisbury. His report was passed on by the SPAB in July 1896 but it was nearly two years before they were able to tell Powell that the Trust had raised funds and were 'anxious to see their work carried out under your guidance'.[27] The fine frontage in St Ann's Street Salisbury remains as testimony to their efforts.

After Blow and Powell joined forces in 1897 their work for the SPAB was often undertaken together but never, it seems, as a partnership. One or the other was always the architect in charge. Powell was involved in Blow's work at Clare church in Suffolk and Blow and his men helped Powell at Navestock church, Essex.[28] At Navestock, Powell was to be found working on site again himself. Thackeray Turner had inspected the church for the SPAB, writing early in 1899 that Powell 'will be able to go and live at Navestock for a short time so as to start the job.'[29] The work, involving underpinning, damp proofing and the repair of external plaster, was spread over a period of two years or more and overlapped with another job of Powell's at Yatton in Somerset.[30]

27 Unpublished letter from Thackeray Turner to Alfred Powell dated 28 April 1898. SPAB Archive: Joiners Hall, Salisbury file. Powell's report recommended re-roofing, strapping loose joints in the timber frame and new lath and plaster in the framed panels. Another SPAB job was intended for Blow at about this time but came to nothing: Buscot Church near Lechlade, much loved by William Morris, was in need of attention and in November 1896, soon after Morris's death, Thackeray Turner of the SPAB had written to Sir Edward Burne-Jones who was mediating on the Society's behalf concerning repairs. Although nothing came of it, Turner had suggested Blow 'Whom we believe you know ... His skills and powers of dealing with an ancient building are quite exceptional' [unpublished letter from Thackeray Turner to Edward Burne-Jones, 13 Nov 1896. SPAB Archive: Buscot Church, Lechlade file].

28 Writing from Coneyhurst, a house designed by Webb adjacent to Long Copse, Blow told Thackeray Turner how he was placed. Blow was trying to plan his work in the long term, accounting for his team of craftsmen on various jobs: 'Two of the men, as you may know, will be busy ... for him [Powell] at Navestock' [unpublished letter from Detmar Blow to Thackeray Turner, 16 Oct 1899: SPAB Archive: Clare Church file, (Suffolk)]. On another occasion Blow and Powell visited Haddon Hall with Thackeray Turner on the SPAB's behalf but the trip was made in an advisory capacity and no work resulted.

29 Unpublished letter from Thackeray Turner to the incumbent dated 6 Jan 1899: SPAB Archive: Navestock Church file, (Essex).

30 Work at Navestock was finished by May 1900 but the plasterwork may have been left until later because Powell wrote to Turner on the subject in March 1901. In a postscript he added: 'Am getting on with Yatton. What a tale!' [unpublished letter

Yatton church was another SPAB case, this time inspected in the first instance by Blow who reported on the tower in June 1900. The vicar had previously been advised that the tower must be repaired and the spire taken down and rebuilt. Blow thought otherwise, as long as the work was 'executed and left in the care of dependable men under competent supervision.' His letter to the SPAB goes on to give an insight into the discomforts of life on the road: 'I regret my expenses being greater than I like, in these towns it is difficult to get a bed without (?) either in service or fleas. Enclosed my account, kindly reply to Clouds house by Salisbury where I am to go Friday to Monday next.'[31] Blow's report was accepted[32] but it was Powell who worked on site, the old spire being saved under his supervision.

Powell and Blow shared more than just their rooms, joining Cockerell at Kelmscott House for musical evenings on several occasions soon after Morris died.[33] Country songs were Powell's speciality. He often sang at social evenings, Cockerell recording one such event at Emery Walker's when Lethaby and Bernard Shaw were there.[34] But despite working in collaboration over several

---

from Alfred Powell to Thackeray Turner, 28 March 1901: SPAB Archive: Navestock Church file, (Essex)].

31 Unpublished letter from Detmar Blow to Thackeray Turner, 6 June 1900. SPAB Archive: Yatton Church file, (Somerset).

32 Blow's report was approved on 9 June 1900 at a vestry meeting in Yatton, Blow writing to Turner from Stockton House, Wiltshire (rented by Pamela Tennant, nee Wyndham) to say how pleased he is to hear his suggestions are to be adopted: SPAB Archive: Yatton Church file (Somerset).

33 Cockerell's diary records: 'Music in the evening at Kelmscott House. Miss De Morgan, Detmar and Alfred Powell' [Wednesday, 6 January 1897]; 'Miss Anderson, Detmar and Alfred Powell came to supper (at Kelmscott House) and there was music afterwards. D played two Tartini pieces better than I have ever heard him play' [Monday, 1 February 1897].

34 Cockerell's diary [Sunday, 7 February 1897]. Powell sang his country songs. Later that week Cockerell, Lethaby and Powell were together again, dining with Blow at Gatti's after the SPAB committee meeting. It was probably through Cockerell that Powell met Olive Garnett to whom he was briefly engaged later that year. Cockerell had shared Gimson and Barnsley's old rooms in Raymond Buildings with W. H. Cowlishaw, a young architect articled to Thackeray Turner who gave Lucy, Olive Garnett's sister, lessons in plasterwork [Cockerell Diary: Monday, 15 October 1894] and later married her. Cowlishaw built a house, The Cearne at Kent Hatch, for the Garnetts (A. Stuart Gray, *Edwardian Architecture* (London: Duckworth, 1985), pp. 152–3). Cockerell knew the Garnett family and when Powell stayed with him for a few days in Richmond, Cowlishaw and Lucy Garnett were amongst the visitors one evening [Tuesday, 2 March 1897]. Powell read to them all from 'Love is Enough' and The Rubaiyat of Omar Khayam. Powell's

years, Blow and Powell only shared premises for a short period, Powell moving back to Surrey and opening an office at 18 Quarry Street, Guildford in 1898.[35] Despite the move, Powell kept up with his old friends in London, Gatti's still being a frequent meeting place.[36] Wherever his office, Powell still worked on site. In 1900 he was resident at Mount Grace Priory near Northallerton in North Yorkshire where he was making a house from part of the old Carthusian Priory (28). Powell was engaged as master of the works by the new owner, Lowthian Bell, an old client of Philip Webb's:

> The building at this time was in a bad state of decay and was hardly more than a farmhouse, inhabited by a caretaker whose cows grazed in the inner courtyard of the priory.[37]

Bell had implored Webb himself to come and stay: 'You need do no sums, draw no plans, just tell me what you think.'[38] But Webb was not to be drawn from his approaching retirement despite the success of Rounton Grange, his previous commission for Bell.[39] Undoubtedly Webb was behind Powell's appointment but nonetheless it seems Webb did not advise on Mount Grace Priory himself. Powell re-opened the quarry at the back of the house and work commenced. While at Mount Grace, however, Powell became increasingly worried about his health. Blow visited him there in May[40] and soon after Powell described his situation in a letter to his mother:

> I am sitting in our farm kitchen after the week's work and everything at peace again after bustling about for six days. And we have had a

---

engagement to Olive Garnett was brief for on 7 August he told Cockerell it was over. Powell bounced back; at the end of September he visited Cockerell on two consecutive days with Cecilia Waern (on the second occasion for breakfast) [29 & 30 September 1897].

35 Cockerell visited him there on 22 October (Cockerell Diary).

36 The Gatti's occasions were almost invariably after SPAB committee meetings. Powell joined Cockerell, Webb, Lethaby and Emery Walker there several times in this period, according to Cockerell's diary. One evening, after the Guildford move, Cockerell found Powell at Lethaby's. Cockerell had been visiting Lethaby with Sara Anderson, a friend from Brantwood days: 'Sara read the first lecture in "The Two Paths" and Powell sang songs. We all went to supper at the Restaurant Margueritte in Oxford Street. Sara Anderson going to Brantwood on Saturday' [Wednesday, 16 November 1898].

37 *The Builder* (6 August 1904), p. 157.

38 Letter from Lowthian Bell to Philip Webb, 13 April 1900 from Rounton Grange, in W. R. Lethaby, *Philip Webb & His Work*, p. 203.

39 W. R. Lethaby, *Philip Webb & His Work*, p. 111.

40 Unpublished letter from Detmar Blow to Thackeray Turner, 10 May 1900 from Mount Grace Priory: SPAB Archive: Haddon Hall file.

28. 'West Elevation. The Manor House, Mount Grace Priory, Northallerton: Original State and Additions. Mr. Ambrose Poynter, Architect'. From *The Builder*, 6 August, 1904.

> really smashing afternoon for a great treat and I have been along the road on the bicycle to a place called Hutton Rudby, a most interesting looking place ... I went partly to see the doctor being convinced that at least three quarters of my right lung was absolutely lost and done for to say nothing more, but – like so many before him – he pronounced everything to be as sound as sound and 'if he'd 'a had a heart and lungs like that he'd a bin out fighting in South Africa.' So I came away naturally disappointed with strict injunctions to eat nothing and drink nothing except his pills and physic for which he demanded a half crown. So that incident is closed, and I think economically... . If it did not so incessantly pour with rain this place would be a Paradise just now. As it is all our boots over- or under-flow with cheesy clay of the heaviest. I have made a change in our working hours this next week, reducing them to ten instead of twelve which we have been doing hitherto. Now we shall begin at 6.30 instead of 6.00 and leave off at 6.30 having two hours off for our meals... . I hope you are all flourishing. I am not ill so don't distress yourself... . We are going to have some fine rooms here if I get my way – oak panelling and plaster-works. But there is a lot to do before that comes to be.[41]

Soon after Powell discovered he was suffering from pleurisy. He gave up work and Mount Grace Priory turned out to be his last building project for some time. T. W. Ridley & Sons of Middlesborough completed the scheme on day work under the superintendence of Sir Ambrose Poynter.[42]

41 Unpublished letter from Alfred Powell to his mother, dated 30 June 1900 from Mount Grace Priory, in 'Autographed Letters, etc.', pp. 294–7, amongst the Powell papers.

42 Poynter later decorated No. 34 Queen Anne's Gate, a town house designed by Blow in 1912 for Lord Glenconner.

Chapter 4
THE CALL OF THE COTSWOLDS
The Wandering Architects and the Cotswold Craft Communities

> How beautiful the little village with its grey stone houses had become; for we had now come into the stone-country, in which every house must be either built, walls and roof, of grey stone, or be a blot on the landscape.
>
> William Morris, *News From Nowhere*, 1892.

In September 1900 Alfred Powell cruised on the P & O ship *Peninsular* with his brother Malcolm in an attempt to regain his health,[1] but his recuperation was not complete. His friends were worried. Blow called on Cockerell 'in great anxiety about Powell who indeed looks very ill' [Thursday 18 October 1900]. Powell was worried himself and talked to Blow and Cockerell about moving to Colorado for his health.[2] He settled for the Cotswolds, staying first with Ernest Gimson and his wife at Pinbury early in 1901:

> Dearest Mother, [he wrote, describing his arrival] They are both more than kind and look after me with all the care and anxiety you could possibly wish! I got in about 4.30 or thereabouts and was just in time to catch the postgirl. Then we had tea and muffins which were very good. I bought a tin of cocoa in Cirencester to provide my beverage and any amount of boiled and boiling milk is always at my disposal. Mrs Gimson is a very nice little person with very brilliant blue eyes and does all she can think of to spoil me with comforts external and internal. I sit in a nice large porch and have my meals and write this etc. and in front of me is a great bank of yew trees beyond the lawn, with glimpses through to the wooded hill behind. The peace is perfectly exquisite and wherever you look are beautiful hilly woods

1 Cockerell supped at Gatti's with Webb and Lethaby on Thursday 27 Sept 1900: 'P.W. brought a nice letter of Alfred Powell's from amongst the Greek Islands.' This quotation as others in the text followed in brackets by a date that includes the day of the week, i.e. [Sunday 24 June 1888], are from Sydney Cockerell's diaries. These are to be found amongst the Cockerell Papers in the British Museum Manuscripts Collection.

2 Cockerell Diary [Wednesday 17 October 1900].

> and woody hills – red bracken in the first and red couch-grass in the second; and this morning, after a little snow in the night, we could see all the little crossing and recrossing rabbit runs, on the hill opposite, marked out in white, like cobwebs. After breakfast which took sometime, as usual, (Gimson says 'a nice protracted meal' and 'that's right, make the most of the incidents of the day!') we went for a walk up the road and made a round of about two miles, coming home through woods again.[3]

Gimson and the Barnsley brothers, Ernest and Sidney, had been at Pinbury since 1894. They were now well established, with cottages and a workshop where, from the start, Sidney Barnsley applied himself to designing and making furniture. His married brother Ernest lived in Pinbury House itself, devoting much of his time to alterations and improvements. By the summer of 1901 Powell was stronger and found himself accommodation nearby at Edgworth Farm. He set himself up, doubtless under Gimson's tuition, to make ladderback chairs using a pole lathe in the traditional Cotswold way that Gimson had learnt during a stay at the workshop of an old Cotswold chair bodger, Philip Clisset:

> I have been putting up my turning lathe – which is not quite done yet and then I hope to get three or four hours a day at turning – and more when I got used to it, meanwhile I have a letter from Abinger asking about some work they want me to do to the school there – but I think it is too far off – and I have had enough of trapesing over the country for 18 pences![4]

At this stage Ernest Gimson was less single minded than Sidney Barnsley about furniture making, his abilities in design being hampered by his more limited capabilities in its construction. Alfred Powell persuaded his old friend to face up to the problem[5] and soon after Powell's arrival another workshop was set up, employing several men, in the yard of the Fleece Hotel in Market Square, Cirencester. Sydney Cockerell and Emery Walker, by then in partnership, visited them all at about this time: 'Had supper followed by songs from Powell and Gimson in the yew walk, the whole place gloriously beautiful' [Saturday 3 August 1901]. They played croquet and 'went for a walk in the afternoon to see a beautiful old house called Daneway. Gimson very much

3 Unpublished letter from Alfred Powell to his mother, dated 19 Feb 1901 from Pinbury, Cirencester, in 'Autographed Letters, etc ... by Alfred Hoare Powell and Some Others. Written at Home and Abroad, AD MDCCCLXXIX to MDCCCCXII. Bound 1914' (by Edgar Powell), p. 298, among the Powell papers.

4 Unpublished letter from Alfred Powell to his mother, dated 26 June 1901 from Edgworth, Cirencester, in 'Autographed Letters, etc... pp. 309–10.

5 Mary Comino, *Gimson and the Barnsleys* (London: Evans, 1980), p. 97.

29 (right). 'The Cottage at Sapperton: South Side', from a drawing of Ernest Gimson's cottage by F. L. Griggs. The cottage, called Leaseowes, is now much altered.

30 (opposite). Sherwood Hill, Alfred Powell's house at Tunley, near Sapperton, Gloucestershire. The extension to the right hand side is recent. The wing to the left is one of the original pair of cottages that Powell joined together, the other being behind. Powell's dark boarded link section appears centrally.

married (his little cottage full of his wife's relations) but as nice as ever.' Powell, now living nearby, described Cockerell's visit:

> I am going over to Pinbury to stay till Tuesday for a little change... . Do you remember Mr Walker who came one day to see me in bed? He is come or coming for Sunday and Monday with Cockerell, another old friend – so we are going to have supper all together in the Nuns Walk – that's the great yew avenue, tonight and there will be sixteen of us I think. Ernest Barnsley very kindly suggested I should stay to Tuesday morning which I am very pleased to do.[6]

By the time Cockerell next visited in August 1902, Gimson and Ernest Barnsley had formed a furniture making partnership, and with Sidney Barnsley had leased Daneway, the house Cockerell had been shown the year before. They used it as show rooms for their furniture and plasterwork[7] and the outbuildings became workshops. Their landlord, Lord Bathurst, remained the same. He had wanted Pinbury back for his own use and agreed to a suggestion made by Ernest Barnsley whereby he would pay for the building of three new cottages in Sapperton, thus compensating his three tenants for the surrender of the Pinbury lease. Powell helped Gimson set out his aptly named cottage, Leasowes (29)

6 Unpublished letter from Alfred Powell to his mother, dated 3 Aug 1901 from Edgworth Farm, Cirencester, in 'Autographed Letters, Etc ...', p. 322.

7 Mary Comino, *Gimson & the Barnsleys*, p. 102.

telling later how he was 'astonished at the minute care and consideration given to the final placing, as if he had already lived in it and knew every requirement and every amenity of the house and its environment.'[8]

Powell decided to build too, first making use of existing accommodation at Gurners Farm, Oakridge Lynch to form a fairly *ad hoc* arrangement that suited his immediate needs. Later he found two tiny cottages just outside Sapperton at Tunley and undertook a similar exercise on a slightly larger scale. Overlooking a remote corner of pasture, surrounded by woodland on a steep site, the house he formed here, by joining the two cottages together, still stands (30). Known as Shepherds Hill, the linking section, hip roofed and weather-boarded, accommodates a winding stair, made with oak treads cut from the solid. The front door, sunk down between the two old cottages, appears only as the visitor descends the twisting front path.

Powell mastered various hand crafts in his early years in the Cotswolds but he had not given up architecture by any means. His brother Oswald had been the second master at Bedales School in Steep, Hampshire since its foundation in

[8] W. R. Lethaby, A. H. Powell & F. L. Griggs, *Ernest Gimson, His Life & Work* (Stratford on Avon, Shakespeare Head Press, 1924), p. 19. When Cockerell visited Powell in August 1902 he found him away but saw 'the rapidly rising new houses of the Barnsleys and Gimson and went on to Pinbury for tea' [Sunday 31 August 1902].

1893 and in 1901 Alfred designed a house for him that stands opposite the school gates:

> I am launched on Oswald's house at last, and have a good month's work ahead of me making the drawings and specifications etc. and have two or three other drawings to make sometime also and as everybody always wants things 'at once' if possible – somebody will have to wait![9]

The house was called Little Hawstead and like Long Copse it has a double pitched roof with a low eaves line (31). The big sheltering roofs are the principal element of both houses, offering a homely quality and a welcoming aspect. Row Cottage (32), next door to Little Hawstead is similarly constructed, its sloping roof coming nearly to the ground. Its builder was Geoffrey Lupton who worked with Powell nearby at the Red House [see (108) and ch. 8].

Although such commissions drew Powell back into architecture he was still far from enthusiastic about setting up an office: 'I am getting much more settled in now with my chair making which will I hope begin to get along soon. I have also another house to build, for my friend Cholmeley in Yorkshire – so I don't believe in offices any more than I ever did – which wasn't much, for bringing work.'[10] Powell's enlargement of Mill Hill for Fairfax-Cholmeley is sympathetic

9 Unpublished letter from Alfred Powell to his mother, dated 18 July 1901 from Edgworth, Cirencester, in 'Autographed Letters, etc.', p. 312, amongst the Powell papers.

10 Unpublished letter from Alfred Powell to his mother, dated 3 Nov 1901 from

31 (opposite). Little Hawstead, Steep, near Petersfield, Hampshire, designed by Alfred Powell in 1901 for his brother Oswald.

32 (left). Row Cottage, Steep, near Petersfield, Hampshire.

to Blow's earlier work. His new entrance elevation [see (13)] leaves Blow's original front [see (12)] to face the view over a new garden with a pergola on the terrace below. Powell's staircase, with its carved wheatsheaf newel tops [see (14)], is outstanding even in comparison with the Gimson plasterwork and Powell's own version of Delft tiles in the downstairs rooms he converted from Blow's former stables and coach house.

There was a group of patrons, including Hugh Fairfax-Cholmeley, for whom Alfred Powell worked over the years and with whom he often stayed, re-affirming the close association with both his clients and his work, whether architectural or craftwork, established earlier in his career. Amongst other such friends were the Biddulphs at Rodmarton, the Murrays at Painswick, St John Hornby who had a country home at Chantmarle in Dorset from 1919 and Bob Skinner at Bromham Hall in Bedfordshire. Whether he built with his own hands again for any of these clients may not be recorded but in 1903 Powell is known to have spent six months on site, repairing part of Queen's College, Cambridge. His workforce again consisted of 'University Men' and this may throw some light on his earlier building methods at Long Copse where the men on site were similarly described. Powell's position in the scheme of things at the university is left unexplained in his correspondence but it is clear from a letter to Cockerell that he tried to teach more than building work alone:

Sapperton, Cirencester, in 'Autographed Letters, etc ...', p. 327.

> I have been trying to sow rebellion in their hearts but they are far too happy to think of anything else ... You know our Dettie [Detmar Blow] has got the work at Kings Chapel to do? Just plain panelling work around the chancel or sanctuary I should have said.[11]

Powell described his own work to his mother:

> We are at present what is called underpinning a bay window... . We are so cramped for room to get at things that it makes it doubly long and difficult. They all seem quite satisfied so far in spite of the crumbs of architectural education I try and get them to swallow now and then. But they most always chokes'em up again. They've got their heads so full of book learning they hardly know a shovel from a barrow some of them! I believe I may get some more work here - woe's me! I don't want to live all my life in Cambridge! but as I have come out to seek my fortune I suppose I mustn't flout the hussy![12]

That Powell had lost some of his enthusiasm for such a way of life is made clear by his subsequent actions: by 1904 he had embarked upon a new career. It started in 1903 when he submitted designs for hand painted ceramics to Wedgwood, telling Cockerell about it one evening as the two men walked over Waterloo Bridge together after tea at Gatti's.[13] Later, in 1904, Powell wrote to Cockerell from Market Drayton:

> I am here presumably until the spring, having had a long talk with my employers, I am getting broken into the business view that popular taste is the only proper test of value... They want me to have a show in the spring in London and be showman, but I shall get out of that somehow... I had Mrs Blow at Oakridge for a week last month. I never

11 Unpublished letter from Alfred Powell to Sydney Cockerell dated 13 Dec 1903 from Queens College, Cambridge, amongst the Cockerell Papers in the British Museum Manuscripts Department. Blow's work at King's College Chapel was not executed until 1907 and consisted of a reredos and panelling both sides of the chancel linking the stalls from one side to the other. His work was removed when the Rubens Holy Family was installed. Blow portrayed his proposals in a large picture dated 1906, retrieved by his family who found it at King's College in a cellar. It seems likely that Blow was already considering the design in 1903 when Powell was in Cambridge as Powell met a pupil of Blow's called Twining there and took him sketching on the backs (unpublished letter from Alfred Powell to his mother, dated 16 Sept 1903 from Queens College, Cambridge, in 'Autographed Letters, etc.', pp. 346–7, amongst the Powell papers).

12 Unpublished letter from Alfred Powell to his mother, dated 27 Sept 1903 from Queens College, Cambridge, in 'Autographed Letters, etc. ...', pp. 348–9, amongst the Powell papers.

13 Sydney Cockerell Diaries [Thursday 12 May 1904], British Museum Manuscripts Collection.

> saw her look so young and strong and healthy! truely she be a wonderful lady ... I hope to carry on my ceramics there after this next six months is over.[14]

In 1906 he married Ada Louise Lessore whose own connections with Wedgwood went back to her grandfather, Emile Lessore, himself a celebrated decorator of Wedgwood pottery. The Powells worked together thereafter, their joint association with the firm continuing for forty years. They returned to the Cotswolds, as Alfred hoped, although much of their work was undertaken in London, Wedgwood setting up a studio for the Powells in Red Lion Square in 1907. Alfred taught the craft of ceramic decoration to Sidney Barnsley's daughter Grace and reintroduced the hand painted tradition to Wedgwood by teaching some of the girls then working there at transfer printing. The Powells encouraged others, like Lethaby and Thackeray Turner, the SPAB's Secretary, to produce designs for Wedgwood too.[15] Alfred taught china painting at the Central School of Art when Lethaby was co-principal with George Frampton and continued his association with Lethaby and Turner at the SPAB over a long period too.[16] He was still campaigning on the Society's behalf after the Great War to prove that old cottages could be economically made good, on sound SPAB principles, to provide homes fit for those who survived the trenches. The selection of a pair of suitable cottages for such treatment at Drinkstone in Suffolk made a considerable impact at the time and proved the economic viability of the hypothesis.

Although the Powells moved back to London in the 1920s, they later returned to the Cirencester area, living at Tarlton near Rodmarton where they built themselves another curious little house in 1933.[17] Known as The Studio (33), for that was its primary function, it followed the familiar Powell pattern,

14 Unpublished letter from Alfred Powell to Sydney Cockerell dated 1 Oct 1904 from Tyrley Castle, Market Drayton, amongst the Cockerell Papers in the British Museum Manuscripts Department.

15 Maureen Batkin, *Wedgwood Ceramics 1846–1959* (London: Richard Dennis, 1982), p. 144.

16 Powell's SPAB cases included work in 1902 in collaboration with Randall Wells concerning proposed alterations to the church at Abbey Dore (see Chapter 7). He underpinned the Roman pavement in the park at Cirencester in 1908 and repaired the west window of the town church there soon after (unpublished letter from Alfred Powell to Sydney Cockerell dated 22 Dec 1909 from Oakridge Lynch, Stroud, amongst the Cockerell Papers in the British Museum Manuscripts Collection).

17 Powell told Cockerell it was newly built in a letter of that year (unpublished letter from Alfred Powell to Sydney Cockerell dated 5 Dec 1933, amongst the Cockerell Papers in the British Museum Manuscripts Collection).

being timber framed, on the medieval cruck principle, from local larchwood. It was roofed in oak shingles.

Some of the finest examples of the Powells' hand-painted ceramics reveal their connections with the area (34). At Rodmarton Manor, near Tarlton, Alfred's huge heraldic platters decorate the walls. Built over a period of seventeen years from 1909, Rodmarton was Ernest Barnsley's major work and represents one of the great achievements of the direct labour method of building favoured by the group (35). Barnsley visited frequently at all stages of its construction, sometimes cycling over from Sapperton with a book on the handlebars.[18] Alternatively, he would walk over Tarlton Down although the direct route was often foresaken in favour of another on which mushrooms might more frequently be found.[19] Ashbee visited Rodmarton on 24 October 1914 and wrote in his journal:

> I see no modern work to equal it, nothing I know of Lutyens or Baker comes up to it, and when I ask why, I find the answer in the system, the method rather than the man. It is a house built on the basis not of

18 Norman Jewson, *By Chance I did Rove* (privately published, 1951; reprinted by the Roundwood Press, Barnsley, Nr Cirencester, 1973), p. 340.

19 Norman Jewson, *By Chance I did Rove,* p. 99.

33 (opposite). The Powells' studio and summer cottage at Tarlton, Gloucestershire.

34 (left). Punch bowl decorated by Alfred Powell with views of Gloucestershire (Cheltenham Art Gallery & Museums).

35 (below). Rodmarton Manor, Gloucestershire: the garden front.

> contract but of confidence and Barnsley has been allowed a free hand to put all his personal knowledge and technique into the work. The English Arts and Crafts Movement at its best is here, so are the vanishing traditions of the Cotswolds.

The art of freehand decoration that the Powells applied to ceramics was equally applicable to furniture and their work can be found on products from Gimson's Sapperton workshop. It was Powell who had initially encouraged

Gimson to involve himself seriously with furniture design[20] but neither Gimson nor Powell divorced themselves entirely from architecture. In 1911 Powell executed the fine drawings for Gimson's unsuccessful competition designs for the city of Canberra and later it was Powell who secured the commission for the library at Bedales for Gimson [see Ch. 8 and (109)], that was to mark the architectural culmination of his career.

Powell outlived most of his contemporaries, working to the end. A month after his eightieth birthday he wrote to Cockerell to say that he only felt about sixty and that the end of the fighting in Europe would push it back another ten.[21] He was still working and living at Tarlton and had just finished a thirty-six piece tea service. He died in 1960 at the age of ninety five, his obituary in *The Times* suggesting that: 'Powell was connected with an interesting event, amounting to a minor revolution in the history of British Architecture.'[22]

That Powell's way of working should be seen as revolutionary was an astute observation in 1960 for he had long outlived the movement of which he had been a part. With the benefit of further hindsight the assessment becomes increasingly valid. The minor revolution in question was at its height in the Cotswolds for the Sapperton group were only one of several within the area following revolutionary principles. The best known was that of C. R. Ashbee and his Guild of Handicraft who, in 1902, picked the old wool town of Chipping Campden as a centre in which to relocate their craft enterprises from the East End of London. Another was observed by Norman Jewson, an assistant of Ernest Gimson's. This, the Whiteway community at Miserden near Stroud, appeared to Jewson to offer a bleak contrast to his own pleasant life. Ashbee described Whiteway in his journal:

> We found here people who seemed to be 'back to the land' in grim earnest. I had long talks with some of them. They hold the other end of the stick we are ourselves shaping at Campden, but their problem, could they work it out, is a much more important one. How to live by its produce on a given piece of English land. Treating their agriculture not as exchange but for the purpose of produce only and paying their rates, for the 90 acres of land they farm, out of a common pasturage and grass crop. They have little home-built cabins of wood and brick

20 *Architect-Designers: Pugin to Mackintosh*, catalogue of exhibition held at the Fine Art Society 5–29 May 1981 (London: Fine Art Society with Haslam & Whiteway Ltd, 1981).

21 Letter from Alfred Powell to Sydney Cockerell dated 7 May 1945 from Tarlton, Cirencester, in Viola Meynell (ed.), *Best of Friends* (London: Jonathan Cape, 1956), p. 155.

22 Obituary, Alfred Powell, unpaginated press cutting from *The Times* (1 June 1960), in the RIBA biographical file.

> dotted about among their allotment patches. 'Tis all very uncouth and experimental.[23]

Gimson himself obtained the land he needed for the 'craft village' he too had always envisaged but his untimely death in 1919 meant that it all came to nothing. Others followed the early settlers. Although Detmar Blow did not start building his own house, Hilles, near Painswick until 1913, the sense of becoming part of an existing community of old friends contributed to his choice of location, as it did for Philip Webb who had earlier tried to find accommodation in the area for his retirement in 1900.[24] Blow, Cockerell, Gimson and the Barnsleys had searched high and low to find the cottage Webb needed:

> My dear Sidney Barnsley, [Webb had written from No. 1 Raymond Buildings] Just as I was closing my outer door this evening on my way to the post, and for a constitutional, Detmar Blow mounted the stairs. He told me he had just come from Pinbury, and that a cottage near Cirencester Park gates was to let... . This news ... has set me all agog not to miss a chance of finding a decent home on high ground, if only for a year's trial to see how it goes with me... . Should I be thought to trespass too rudely on your known good nature by asking you on your next visit to Cirencester to have a look at said cottage? ... Perhaps when I have found my country legs once more I might be able to walk as far as Pinbury and back in the day, and you could cheer me up when you came marketing, and take your bread and cheese with me; ... the Cotswolds I would rather like as well as the Barnsleys and the Gimsons.[25]

23 Ashbee Journal, quoted in Fiona MacCarthy, *The Simple Life* (London, Lund Humphries, 1981), p. 100. Another who witnessed the Colony at Whiteway was Malcolm Muggeridge whose sight of two young nudists from Whiteway (Elfie and Doddles) apparently gave him his first intimation of sex: Malcolm Muggeridge, *The Green Stick* (London: Collins, 1972.)

24 It all started with a visit made to Pinbury, via Wells with Lethaby, by Cockerell and Emery Walker who saw a cottage which they thought might do [Sunday 2 April 1899]. Webb was informed and wrote to Gimson: 'That dragoman of friends; the interpreter of all wants; Sydney Cockerell, has told me of his visit to Pinbury and of the kindly entertainment he and Emery Walker had from you and the rest of the little colony. He may have told you of my failing in South Wales to find a place of retirement in my old age, and that may have suggested the possibility of finding a sufficient hut or Diogenes tub near Cirencester. With regard to Cockerell, I need hardly say I am as clay in his hands, so that when he produced a simple sketch of a possible and vacant cottage, with an exclamation amounting to "there you are" – what was I to say? The limestone of the Cotswolds would I think, be good seating for my worn bones ...' (letter from Philip Webb to Ernest Gimson dated 10 April 1899, in W. R. Lethaby, *Philip Webb & His Work* (Oxford, 1935), pp. 198–9).

The cottage did not work out but the search went on, as Lethaby later described: 'In June 1900 Webb visited the Cotswolds again, lodging a week at the house of Richard Harrison,[26] a fine man and wheelwright of the old sort. Webb had a little knowledge of the crafts. I can picture him now sitting in Dick's yard watching the making of a wagon, telling how it should be done and why.'[27] It all came to a head in August. Webb, writing to Powell about his work at Mount Grace, advised him about choice of builders ('Good builders, my good Alfred Powell, do not hang plentiously on the prickly gooseberry bushes of architectural practice') and continues:

> It may interest you to know that the convulsions of second childhood are on me, ... there are still just hopes of the Gimson and Barnsley folk finding that the smallest of steddings, Tunley Farm, may be had for me; and failing that coveted situation I may get housed in Sussex.[28]

For Webb the Cotswolds were not to be and coincidentally, it was Powell that ended up at Tunley and not Webb. Later that week, at Gatti's, Webb told Lethaby and Cockerell that he would probably go to Sussex after all [Thursday, 9 August 1900]. His Pinbury friends were disappointed, after all their efforts, to lose the company of their old guide and mentor. They tried to persuade him to wait but to no avail. Webb wrote, told them of Powell's sea cruise and continued:

> None ... of you could have been so disappointed as I am that I did not get to the good district of Pinbury, for I was so at large with all of you there ... and there will be no childish sheepdog and undignified deerhound to welcome me ... alas and alas! ... Cockerell, the faithful Dragoman to friends in difficulty, with his boundless energy, ... does the thing, and I smile as if the sun had broken through a cloud.[29]

Notwithstanding all Cockerell's efforts, Webb was still reluctant to go, writing to Powell in October:

> My delight was great in getting your cheerful letter from on board ship off the Greek coast and on your way to Smyrna. It cannot be said when I have had so entertaining a note of travel. You made the famous

25 Letter from Philip Webb to Sidney Barnsley dated 9 March 1900, in *Philip Webb & His Work*, pp. 201–2.

26 Harrison's work with Gimson and Blow is described in Chapter 6.

27 Letter from Philip Webb to Sidney Barnsley dated 5 May 1900, in *Philip Webb & His Work*, p. 204.

28 Letter from Philip Webb to Alfred Powell dated 7 Aug 1900, in *Philip Webb & His Work*, p. 206.

29 Letter from Philip Webb to Sidney Barnsley dated 31 Aug 1900, in *Philip Webb & His Work*, p. 207

> land I have never seen fairly dance before my mind's eye. Personally I am in the throes of decided indecision ... . Having limpet-like stuck so tightly here for so many years it takes a strong oyster-knife to unfasten me.[30]

Webb moved, in the end, early in 1901 by which time Caxtons, his Sussex cottage, had been re-roofed and overhauled. Had he found his place in the Cotswolds his presence would have reinforced its claim as a centre for Arts and Crafts excellence, but it should not be supposed that there were no others. A Guild of Handicraft flourished in Birmingham and the Bromsgrove Guild of Applied Art, where George Bankart was in charge of plasterwork, did likewise. Craft communities were not the isolated and self-contained organizations they sometimes appear and the Birmingham enterprises were cross-connected with those in the Cotswolds. Bankart's work shows this clearly. Teaching plasterwork at the Art School in Leicester where he and Gimson had both studied in the 1880s, he undertook plasterwork for Gimson, carrying out exuberant pargetting work at the White House, Clarendon Park, Leicester, designed by Ernest Gimson in 1897.[31] They remained friends and, each developing his technique independently, became the two leading exponents of hand-modelled plasterwork in the country. They had a great deal in common. Both had been articled to the same Leicester architect, Isaac Barradale; Gimson from 1881 and Bankart from 1883. Both met William Morris when he came to Leicester in 1884 and both men's careers were shaped accordingly, Gimson joining Sedding as a result of Morris' introduction.

Bankart worked in the Cotswolds. At Hartpury House in Ashleworth he first undertook decorative plasterwork in 1901 for Guy Dawber (1861–1938), undertaking most of Dawber's plasterwork thereafter. Dawber had come to the Cotswolds in 1887, sent from London to Batsford Park as clerk of works by the fashionable office of George and Peto. Batsford Park was near Bourton-on-the-Water and Dawber spent his weekends walking, cycling and sketching, being joined on occasions by Herbert Baker, then Chief Assistant at George and Peto. In 1890 he set up in practice in Bourton on his own account, renting a room at the Village Institute for 9*d.* a week.[32]

30 Letter from Philip Webb to Alfred Powell dated 23 Oct 1900, in *Philip Webb & His Work*, p. 209.

31 Gimson's client was his half brother Arthur (Mary Comino, *Gimson & the Barnsleys*, p. 90). The panels were modelled in Keene's cement with a design based on the oak tree. Illustrations of these panels appear in *Plastering, Plain and Decorative* by W Millar, edited by G. Bankart, 1926, and crediting the design to Gimson and the execution to Bankart.

32 Dawber's early Cotswold work includes alterations at St David, Moreton-in-the-Marsh and the rescue of the Manor House, Bourton-on-the-Water in 1890.

Although craft communities were to a greater or lesser degree transplanted into Sapperton and Campden, the craft revival in the Cotswolds was in the end fairly widespread and generally evolved more slowly. A typical example was the village of Broadway whose inherent quality had been appreciated by William Morris himself as early as 1876. Once prosperous from wool, it had, by the mid-nineteenth century, atrophied by degrees. Its fine stone houses were sub-divided and patched; the railway passed it by. Nonetheless Morris extolled the virtues of a farmhouse there in one of his lectures:

> 'tis an ideal house I am thinking of, ... everything about it is solid and well wrought; ... there is a little sharp and delicate carving about its arched doorway and every part of it is well cared for; 'tis in fact beautiful, a work of art and a piece of nature no less.[33]

When Morris preached, many followed. John Singer Sargent was amongst the earliest to arrive in Broaway in 1885.[34] Next year Henry James joined the little group who thought they had 'discovered' the village.[35] He wanted to keep Broadway quiet and advised the actress, Mary Anderson, against buying Bell Farm, possibly the subject of Morris' lecture. She ignored him and by 1899 her house guests were able to field a cricket team, her visitors including Elgar and J. M. Barrie. The eventual arrival of the railway in 1904 was due in part to the increasing demand generated by these early settlers. The Lygon Arms changed from a run down inn to become one of the best hotels in the country. Its proprietor S. B. Russell bought and sold a few antiques and his son Gordon built up the trade. After the war Gordon Russell Ltd started producing new furniture in Broadway and became an international success.

Although he immediately set up a London office in 1891, commissions in and around the Cotswolds continued and it is for these stonebuilt smaller country houses that he is best remembered. They include Nether Swell Manor (1903–13); Bibsworth Manor, Broadway (1904); Conkwell Grange, Bradford upon Avon (1907) and Eyford Park, Upper Slaughter (1910). Dawber's houses show his identification with the countryside in which they rest and this is borne out by his work as a founder of the Council for the Preservation of Rural England (now the Council for the Protection of Rural England). Although his work is often on a larger scale than that of the Sapperton architects, it continues the quiet traditions of the region in the same way as their furniture and their cottages. Dawber's published works include *Old Cottages, Farmhouses and Other Stone Buildings in the Cotswolds* (London: Batsford, 1905).

33 William Morris quoted by Alan Crawford, in 'New Life for an Artist's Village', *Country Life* (24 Jan 1980), pp. 252–254, p. 252.

34 Alan Crawford, 'New Life for an Artist's Village', p. 252

35 In 1889 Henry James wrote about the village and its artistic colony in *Harpers Magazine* (see Crawford, 'New Life for an Artist's Village', p. 253).

Broadway attracted other crafts and was always likely to appeal to those who sympathised with the Morris viewpoint. One such was Katie Adams who set up her book bindery here in about 1905. Another old friend of Sydney Cockerell, they came close to marriage: 'I would have married her' Cockerell reflected later but 'she was five years older than I and by the time I could afford to marry we could not have had a family.'[36] Instead he ended up with a fine collection of her bindings, each volume 'Katied' (as he put it) to perfection. Opposite her Eadburgha Bindery, Ernest Barnsley repaired and adjusted a stone cottage, then known as York House, for her in 1907.[37]

Then, as now, changes in the rest of the Cotswolds were similar to those experienced in Broadway but to a lesser degree. It was in 1907 that Norman Jewson first came to the Cotswolds and he thought it still 'a part of the country little known at that time except to a few architects and artists.'[38] Jewson became Gimson's assistant after approaching him one day in his garden at Sapperton, leaving with an offer of a month's work on trial. He stayed for forty years, from the outset supervising much of Gimson's architectural work on site and learning the arts of decorative plasterwork and lead casting. Jewson continued an architectural practice in Sapperton after Gimson's death and assisted Peter Waals, who had been Gimson's workshop foreman, with furniture design.[39] It was Jewson too who finally brought Rodmarton to completion after the deaths of first Ernest and then Sidney Barnsley.

Before coming to Sapperton, Norman Jewson spent three years at Cambridge and a further three in London, articled to Herbert Ibberson who had worked with Gimson under Sedding.[40] Jewson never had any intention of staying in London after his articles, although he was aware that: 'it was generally considered impossible to become a successful architect without living in a town, spending much of one's time making social contacts while most of the actual work was done by one's office staff, but for me it was architecture I was interested in, not making a large income as an architect. My own buildings I wanted to have the basic qualities of the best old houses of their locality, built in the local traditional way in the local materials, but not copying the details which properly belong to the period in which they were built. By working on these lines I hoped that my buildings would at least have good manners and be able to take their natural place in their surroundings without offence.'[41]

36 Quoted in Fiona MacCarthy, *The Simple Life* (London, Lund Humphries, 1981), p. 104.

37 Mary Comino, *Gimson & the Barnsleys*, p. 131.

38 Norman Jewson, *By Chance I did Rove*, p. 1.

39 Mary Comino, *Gimson & the Barnsleys*, p. 197.

40 Norman Jewson, *By Chance I did Rove*, p. 15.

Before he approached Gimson, Jewson spent a month in the Cotswolds, anxious to fill his sketchbook and learn something of the local building tradition to impress his prospective employer. He arrived by train at Cirencester, bought provisions, hired a donkey and trap, threw in his luggage, which included a small tent and set off:

> The donkey trotted at a fair pace down Gloucester Street, and then branching off along the Cheltenham Road, proceeded so far as the inn at Perrott's Brook where he stopped, no doubt assuming that my habits coincided with those of his former master. Here I asserted my preference for a by-road instead of a main highway; we took a lane to the right, slowly climbing a long hill. From the top there was such a charming view of the beautiful little saddle-backed tower of North Cerney church, rising among magnificent trees on the opposite hillside, that I filled the first page of my sketchbook while the donkey nibbled the grass at the roadside.[42]

Jewson, who was a Norfolk man, was astonished to find oxen still in occasional use for ploughing in Gloucestershire in 1907. He picked his way around the lanes and villages, visiting Campden but basing himself near Bourton-on-the-Water. He saw stone tiles quarried at Eyford and, befriending the foreman in charge, watched the construction of the almshouses designed by Lutyens at Upper Slaughter.

Working for Gimson, Jewson lived, like Powell before him, at Oakridge Lynch. One of his first jobs involved site supervision of Gimson's alterations to a house at Water Lane nearby which he would visit on his way to work at Daneway. By the time the Water Lane project was complete, a pair of tiny cottages had fallen vacant in Sapperton and Jewson moved in. He was joined there in 1910 by another of Gimson's assistants, Walter Gissing, son of the novelist George Gissing, but only for a year. Gissing went on to work with William Weir to learn the methods of the SPAB, for whom Weir was now the principal architect (see chapter 10). Gissing returned to Gimson later, supervising the construction of a pair of cottages for May Morris at Kelmscott. He was killed in the First World War.

Another of Gimson's assistants, Basil Young, also arrived in 1910. He too only stayed for a short time but commissioned Gimson to design a house (36) which he built for himself at Budleigh Salterton in Devon in 1912. Long Orchard (37), as it was known in its final form, was built of cob, a material chosen by Gimson in a conscious attempt to continue the revival of a dying craft started by Detmar Blow at the turn of the century in Wiltshire (see ch. 6).

41 Norman Jewson, *By Chance I did Rove*, pp. 13–14.

42 Norman Jewson, *By Chance I did Rove*, p. 2.

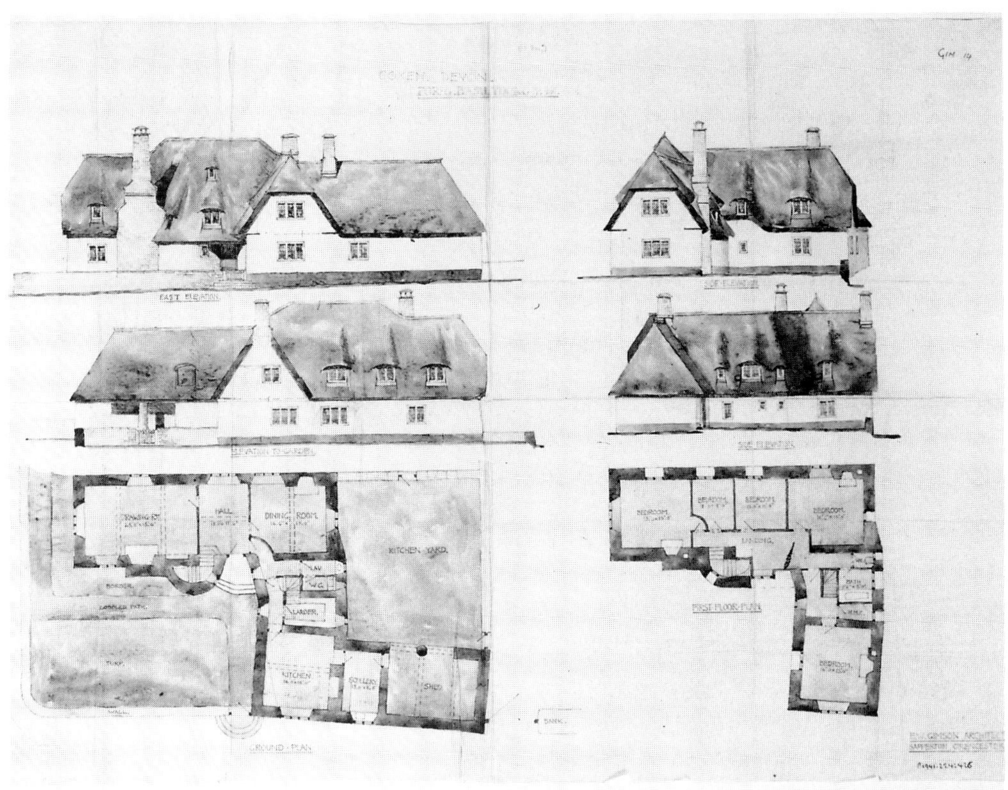

36 (top). 'Coxen, Devon. For G Basil Young Esq. E. W. Gimson Architect, Sapperton, Cirencester', an early scheme, unbuilt.

37 (below). Long Orchard, Budleigh Salterton, Devon, from *Ernest Gimson, His Life and Work*, 1924. The house was built traditionally in Devon cob.

> The cob was made of stiff sand found on the site; this was mixed with water and a great quantity of long wheat straw trodden into it. The walls were built 3 foot thick pared down to 2' 6" and were placed on a plinth standing 18" above the ground floor, and built of cobble stones found amongst the sand. The walls were given a coat of plaster and a coat of roughcast, which was gently trowelled over to smooth the surface slightly. I believe 8 men were engaged in the cob work, some preparing the material, and others treading it into the top of the walls. It took them about 3 months to reach the wallplate... . Building with the cob is soon learned - of the 8 men only one of them had any previous experience, and I believe he had not built with it for 30 years.[43]

Jewson often spent considerable lengths of time superintending work on site for Gimson. But he came to know the Barnsleys well too, spending much time at Upper Dorvel (38), the house Ernest Barnsley had made in Sapperton by building onto either end of an earlier part. The little formal garden in front of the house shows the thinking that later led to Barnsley's compartmented garden design at Rodmarton (39). Jewson helped Ernest Barnsley at Rodmarton (40) and became engaged to Mary, his daughter. His engagement was a long one because of enforced absences whilst working for Gimson at Muchelney in Somerset, and Salle in Norfolk - both SPAB projects, the first involving repairs to a medieval priest's house now belonging to the National Trust (41). At Salle he worked, like Gissing, as site architect for William Weir. They repaired the magnificent hammer-beam roof to the church and fitted new seating made by Gimson. Jewson worked there for three months, married and then returned with his wife, thus making him a rarity even amongst his itinerant friends: an architect who spent his honeymoon on site.

As a married man he started work on his own account whilst helping his father-in-law at Rodmarton. He still had time to assist Gimson too and the young couple spent six months in Oxford whilst Jewson supervised Gimson's repairs to the Great Tower at Magdalen College. He found the dons most hospitable, lodging out beyond Magdalen Bridge and dining at the high table not only at Magdalen but at Balliol too, where he did a little work in the chapel. While there he superintended alterations and redecoration of the rooms that the Prince of Wales, later King Edward VIII, was to occupy whilst at Oxford. Mary's youngest sister, Elisabeth Barnsley, came to visit and made a dramatic impact:

43 *Ernest Gimson*, catalogue of an exhibition held at Leicester Museum (Leicestershire Museums Service, 1969), p. 5, quoted in Mary Comino, *Gimson & the Barnsleys*, pp. 140-1.

38 (top). Upper Dorvel, Sapperton, Gloucestershire; Ernest Barnsley's house, formed from an existing core, extended at both ends.

39 (left). The summer house by Ernest Barnsley at the end of the Long Walk, Rodmarton.

40 (right). Cast lead hopper decoration at Rodmarton, probably by Norman Jewson.

> One day when I was on the tower, a message came that I was wanted at once. When I reached the gateway I found my wife and her youngest sister, who was staying with us, wet through to the skin. They had been out punting on the Cher and had both fallen in – one in a vain attempt to help the other – luckily they had been able to get to the bank and climb out. So I had to find a cab and bribe the cabman to take them home and fortunately they were none the worse for the adventure. We spent many pleasant summer evenings on the Cher, punting or canoeing and there were no more accidents. We also went to Henley Regatta and explored the country round on bicycles, a pleasant enough way of doing so in those days. Oxford was then a much smaller and quieter city, with no traffic problems.[44]

Oxford was still the city that Morris had known and loved although another Mr Morris was by now making his first cars in a small workshop in the town. As yet there were no huge factories or housing estates for those who worked in them. Jewson remembered a song of the period that, he said, showed the attitude of ordinary country folk to motoring. It began: 'The rich folk go by in their madcap machinery; They kick up the dust and they spoils all the greenery,' but, Jewson continues: 'cars were still so comparatively rare that one could cycle for miles along country roads without meeting one, though the roads, being still untarred, when one did meet a car one got smothered in dust in dry weather.'[45]

During the last years of his life, Gimson went into partnership with F. L. Griggs who lived in Chipping Campden. Jewson stayed with Griggs often and mixed with those who remained from Ashbee's Guild of Handicraft. In 1927 Griggs began building Dover's House in Campden for himself, using local craftsmen, local materials and traditional methods. Griggs is said to have supplied his workmen with a rough sketch rather than detailed plans and was later to boast that there was not a right angle or straight line in the whole house.[46] Frederick Griggs is best known for his etchings and book illustrations but he also had a passion for bellringing and would entertain the Campden bellringers at an annual feast at the Lygon Arms. He did much for Campden, his lasting memorial being Dover's Hill which he bought for the National Trust.

Jewson's practice continued in the tradition of Gimson and the Barnsleys. Much of his work involved alterations and repairs to old buildings although he did build cottages and houses, mainly in the Sapperton area. His house at Coates

44 Norman Jewson, *By Chance I did Rove*, pp. 100–1.

45 Norman Jewson, *By Chance I did Rove*, p. 101.

46 Thomas A. Clark, *Silences of Noons – The Work of F. L. Griggs (1876–1938)*, exhibition catalogue for Cheltenham Art Gallery and Museum's Exhibition, 5 Nov–31 Dec 1988.

41 (top). The Old Priests House, Muchelney, Somerset.

42 (below). 'House at Coates: Cirencester, for A. G. McKillop Esquire. Norman Jewson M.A. Architect'.

for A. McKillop in 1924 (42) typifies his new work whilst his rescue of Owlpen, a Tudor manor house in a wooded valley beneath the Cotswold Edge, shows how completely he understood the local building traditions. Jewson bought Owlpen at auction in 1925, repaired it as a labour of love and sold it again in the following year. He engaged tradesmen who had trained, like him, under Gimson (43), describing the work they did as 'the nearest I got ... to satisfying myself or my own standards.'[47] Frederick Griggs made an etching of Owlpen as a tribute to Jewson's work (44) but the house itself is perhaps his best testimonial.

[47] Nicholas Mander, 'Norman Jewson at Owlpen Manor', in *Norman Jewson – Architect – 1884–1975*, exhibition brochure at Arlington Mill Museum, 1987.

43 (top). The tradesmen and craftsmen at Owlpen Manor, 1926. *Back row:* Fred White, Tom Coles, Jack Fern, Reg. Kilby, Reg. Gardiner. *Middle row:* Harry Drinkwater, Charlie White, Ted Hunt, Ray Parsloe, Frank Hogan, Herbert Howley, Bill Chappell. *Front row:* Leslie Brown, Bill Woodward (foreman), and Wilf Hunt (motorcycle).

44 (below). Owlpen Manor, from an etching by F. L. Griggs.

Chapter 5
A WANDERING ARCHITECT
Detmar Blow and His Itinerant Masons, 1897–1900

> The real architect of a building ... must be his own clerk of works, his own carver, his own director, he must be the familiar spirit of the structure as it rises from the ground ... to make the most of the site and the building as applied to it.
>
> J. D. Sedding, 'Architecture – Old and New', 1881

One of Norman Jewson's first projects away from Sapperton on Ernest Gimson's behalf was in Leicestershire where Margaret, one of Gimson's sisters, wanted a summer cottage. Jewson described his visit:

> The Charnwood Forest is a grand tract of primitive woodland country, in which are several disused slate quarries which have become picturesque lakes, with steep rocky sides formed of the beautiful many coloured slates of that district... . The builder took me to one of them to select some slabs of slate for lintels over the doors and windows of the cottage ... While on this excursion I stayed in a cottage in the forest with an old retired farm labourer and his wife, a real Darby and Joan couple.[1]

Rockyfield Cottage (45), built in 1908 for £600, was the result of Jewson's efforts and it is here in the Charnwood Forest, in fact in the very slate quarries that Jewson describes, that we pick up the tracks that Detmar Blow had left ten years before during what was the most intensive phase of his career as a journeyman architect and mason. Rockyfield was the last of four cottages in the forest designed by Gimson and Detmar Blow was the builder of the first three. It was he who selected their massive slate lintels in the disused quarries nearby and his use of them emulated those over the medieval fireplace at the Old Post Office in Tintagel. Lawrence Weaver noticed these lintels at Stoneywell, the second of the cottages, built for Gimson's older brother Sydney and completed in 1899: 'The lintel over the fireplace is an amazing bit of construction, a single gigantic slab weighing a ton and a half, a rough shard of slate that had lain neglected in an old quarry until Mr Detmar Blow spied it.'[2]

1. Jewson, *By Chance I did Rove* (as ref 18, ch. 4), p. 42.
2. Lawrence Weaver, *Small Country Houses of Today*, Second Series (London: Country

45 (top). Rockyfield Cottage, Ulverscroft, Leicestershire, from a photograph taken before 1913 in *The Country Life Book of Cottages*, by Lawrence Weaver.

46 (below). Pair of cottages at Ulverscroft, Leicestershire, designed by Ernest Gimson and built by Blow for Mr. Billson (Cheltenham Art Gallery & Museums).

Opposite page: 47 (top) Stonywell Cottage, Ulverscroft: stone slates replace the earlier thatch; and 48 (below), drawing of the cottage by F. L. Griggs from *Ernest Grimson, His Life and Work*, 1924.

Blow built the three cottages as a continuous sequence.[3] The first was in fact a pair (46), built in 1897 for James Billson from whom land for the other three came. After Billson's cottages came Stoneywell, a double cranked plan [see (23)] with a spiralling stair externally expressed, as at Tintagel. Built into the hillside, the floor levels rise with the ground and despite the fact that the original thatch has been replaced with stone slates, the ridge line still twists and climbs like the sheep path that winds from the lane to the front door (47). The sitting room at the upper end of the cottage is cut into a granite outcrop into which another steep narrow stair has been fashioned and out of which the masonry rises in such a way that it is hard to tell where the outcrop ends and the massive chimney begins (48).

Life, 1919), p. 18.

3 S. A. Gimson, Random Memories of the Building of Stoneywell, unpublished, private collection, 1938.

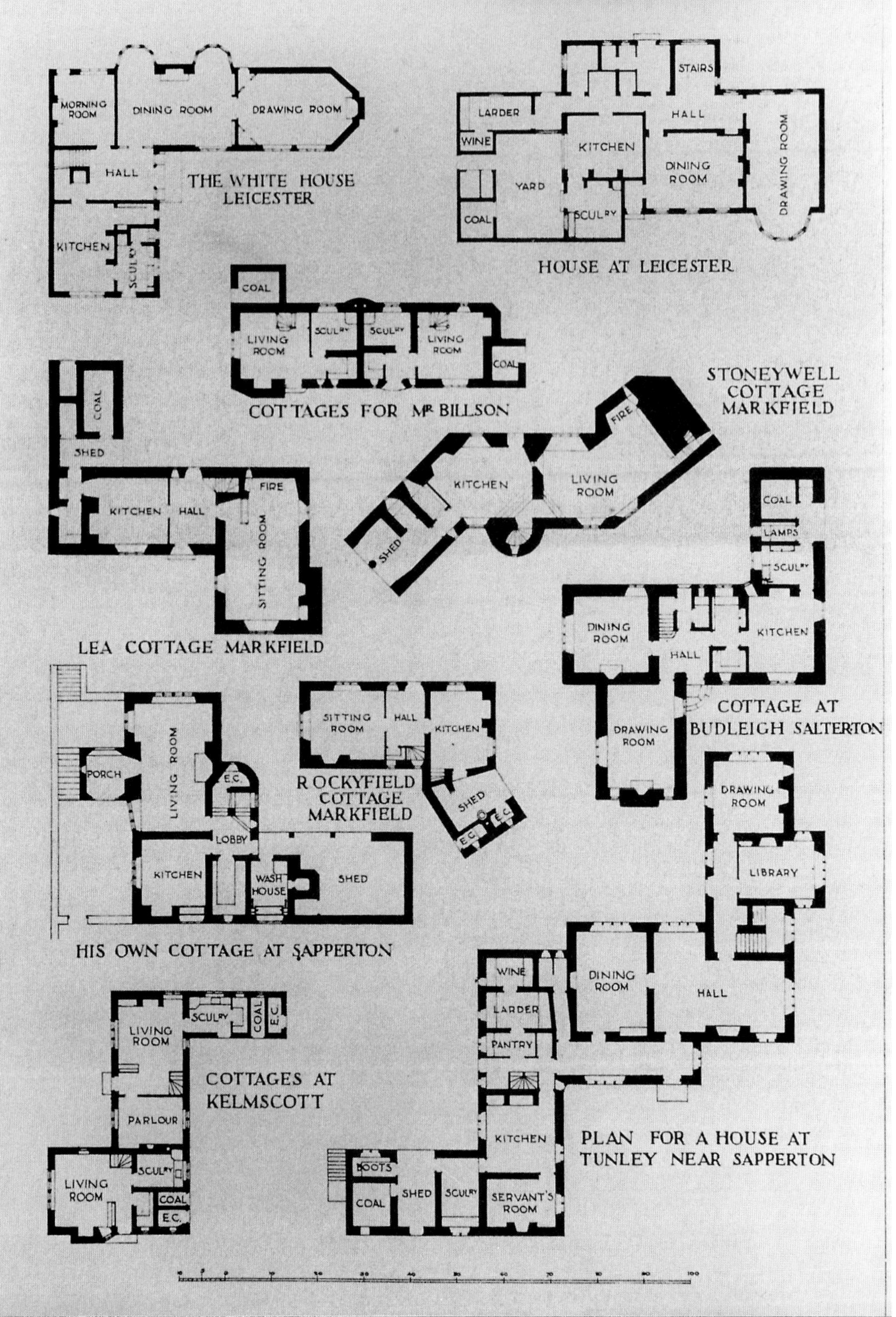
THE WHITE HOUSE LEICESTER
MORNING ROOM
DINING ROOM
DRAWING ROOM
HALL
KITCHEN
SCULRY
HOUSE AT LEICESTER
STAIRS
LARDER
HALL
WINE
KITCHEN
DINING ROOM
DRAWING ROOM
YARD
COAL
SCULRY
COTTAGES FOR MR BILLSON
COAL
LIVING ROOM
SCULRY
SCULRY
LIVING ROOM
COAL
STONEYWELL COTTAGE MARKFIELD
FIRE
KITCHEN
LIVING ROOM
SHED
LEA COTTAGE MARKFIELD
COAL
SHED
FIRE
KITCHEN
HALL
SITTING ROOM
COTTAGE AT BUDLEIGH SALTERTON
COAL
LAMPS
SCULRY
DINING ROOM
KITCHEN
HALL
DRAWING ROOM
ROCKYFIELD COTTAGE MARKFIELD
SITTING ROOM
HALL
KITCHEN
SHED
E.C.
E.C.
HIS OWN COTTAGE AT SAPPERTON
PORCH
LIVING ROOM
E.C.
LOBBY
KITCHEN
WASH HOUSE
SHED
COTTAGES AT KELMSCOTT
SCULRY
COAL
E.C.
LIVING ROOM
PARLOUR
LIVING ROOM
SCULRY
COAL
E.C.
PLAN FOR A HOUSE AT TUNLEY NEAR SAPPERTON
DRAWING ROOM
LIBRARY
WINE
DINING ROOM
HALL
LARDER
PANTRY
KITCHEN
BOOTS
COAL
SHED
SCULRY
SERVANT'S ROOM
0 5 10 20 30 40 50 60 70 80 90 100

49 (opposite). Ground plans of houses and cottages designed by Ernest Gimson; and 50 (above). Lea Cottage, Ulverscroft, Leicester (both from *Ernest Gimson, His Life and Work*).

At Stoneywell the plan form is sinuous and follows the contours. At Lea Cottage, the third and the last built by Blow, the land lies less steep and the cranked wings are at right angles one to another (49), giving an enclosing form of a less rugged and more sheltering character (50). Its roofs step up from the road, wing by wing and only the highest section has anything like a full upper floor. The lowest, that containing the stores, is built off the roadside, its eaves projecting over the boundary wall. The stone walls were whitewashed inside and out, in contrast to Stoneywell where Blow left the masonry simple and strong, as Lawrence Weaver describes it:

> Roughly, even rudely, built ... no tool has been lifted to mark a false impression of age. If it has the air of being old, it is only because old ways have been followed not because the least effort has been made to impart a false air of antiquity, and herein lies an important distinction and a very real difference. The walls have a notable texture. This, however, is not the result of working the stones in any special way, but of choosing them carefully for their varied colours and laying them with thick mortar joints in an 'admired confusion' of size and plane that gives the surface a changeful life in sunshine and in softer

> lights. Thatch, too, gives a cottage an age-long air if it is laid in the old way, not unduly smoothed down. The practical question as to whether it is wise to build a cottage, of a sort which it would be idle to deny is very draughty, which one suspects is in cold weather very cold, and is certainly inconvenient if measured by ordinary standards of convenience, is one clearly for the owner and the owner alone to decide. He has got a house in which it must be entertaining to live, and if there are some drawbacks it is clear that he has weighed them, and that to him and his they are not, in fact, drawbacks but amusing incidents. Moreover, there are people hardy enough – shall we say sensible enough? – not to think about draughts, or to recognize them when they blow. And if there is a draught that is felt, well – il faut souffrir pour etre belle.[4]

Stoneywell cost £920 to build. Sydney Gimson had wanted to spend less and suspected the original estimate to have been unrealistic:

> Ernest said to Detmar 'If we say £500 Sydney will have it, if we say more I don't think he will. Can we do it for that?' 'Oh yes' said Detmar, 'I should think we can.'[5]

Ernest designed stables and outbuildings for Stoneywell later and one of the working drawings bears the following note:

> Dear Sid, I should like your comments on this plan – I have been into the cost of the carpentry with Harrison [Richard Harrison of Sapperton] carefully and inclusive of railway carriage and hauling from Bardon it comes to about £165 – in larch – in addition to this of course there is the mason's work in the foundations and chimney and the cost of the slating, glazing and small painting – and also the yard. If you are really inclined to have it done this year, it would be a great help to Harrison if it could be quickly decided as the trees could then be cut before the sap begins to rise. I should like this time to get estimates from Harrison and Chapman so that you don't have to rely on my "probable cost" (as if you ever would again).[6]

Sydney Gimson was under no illusions and took Blow's opportune optimism in good part: 'Detmar Blow was a very handsome and attractive young man, he had a charming irresponsibility and an elastic conscience which ... sometimes acted to my advantage.'[7] When Blow saw a particularly good boulder by the wayside he would surreptitiously borrow a pair of large and heavy wheels from

4 Lawrence Weaver, *Small Country Houses of Today*, Second Series, pp. 20–1.

5 S. A. Gimson, op. cit., not paginated.

6 Ernest Gimson, working drawing: 1941. 224. 13: Cheltenham Art Gallery and Museum, quoted in Comino, 'Gimson & The Barnsleys'.

7 S. A. Gimson, op. cit.

Billson and the stone would appear in the wall of the cottage. Billson, perhaps less tolerant, grew a little weary of Blow's cavalier attitude towards material possessions but his sarcasm was water off a duck's back, as Sydney Gimson's continuing account reveals:

> Detmar stayed with Billson while his cottages were in hand and Billson told of his casual way of using stationery and even stamps from his host's store. One day as he was annexing a stamp in Billson's presence, James [Billson] remarked sarcastically 'Why do you trouble to take them one at a time? Why not take a dozen?' 'Oh, thank you.' said Detmar and took them!

Although Blow was sometimes unable to see a clear differentiation between what was his and what was not, he no doubt perceived such requisitions as being for the good of the common cause and his charm was such that forgiveness seemed a matter of course. Philip Webb called him a 'honeysuckle villain'[8] but acted towards him like a godfather.[9] Sydney Gimson tolerated his easy going ways too and extolled his virtues:

> Most of the time he was building my cottage he lodged with old Mr Crooks in the cottage at the bottom of Lea Lane ... and would often go up to work in a pair of trousers of the old man's. Jean and I gave a dance that winter in Leicester, Detmar was one of the guests and was the unquestioned most attractive and sought after man there. He had that charming easy natural behaviour which made him a welcome and valued guest in any company, either of working people or aristocrats.[10]

Although this glowing description of his social graces does much to explain his later success as a society architect, he could also be frustrating. As Sydney Gimson complained: 'Detmar was often not at Stoneywell when I hoped to find him there. The walls at one end were some feet high before he appeared at all.'[11] Blow's letters and drawings often have no date and appointments were given no great priority. He preferred doing things to organizing them and seems to have been more concerned about the eternal qualities of his work than the temporal. But it was not just his character that militated against his continued presence at Stoneywell, his frequent absence being due also to the fact that the cottages he built in the Charnwood Forest were not the only work he had on hand at this time. Another major project was the repair of Lake House, an Elizabethan

8 Unpublished letter from Philip Webb to Sydney Cockerell dated 30 November. 1892, V & A Manuscripts Collection, Ref MSEPWM.

9 Recalled by Mrs Rosamund Caffrey, Hugh Fairfax-Cholmeley's daughter, in a telephone conversation with the author, 17 Sept 1988.

10 S. A. Gimson, op. cit.

11 Ibid.

house near Salisbury. When in 1897 its new owner, Joseph Lovibond, had asked the SPAB for advice, Thackeray Turner carried out a survey and recommended Blow: 'I hear he is busy, nonetheless I hope the committee will arrange with him to give his services for I feel sure there is no man more competent to do the work which you need.'[12]

The problems at Lake were twofold: defective foundations and the separation of the inner and outer faces of the walls. Philip Webb again added his inspiration and counsel, as at East Knoyle, and there are similarities between the two jobs in terms of approach and working methods: 'the core of the wall was removed piece by piece from the bottom upward, and re-built in strong materials, bonded to the outer facework, which remained untouched but for the filling in of the open joints with new work from the inside.'[13] Much ingenuity was shown in the repair. In unpanelled rooms, where oak lintels had decayed, original plasterwork was retained by leaving the old timber in place and relieving them with a cambered tile lintel above. The old transoms and mullions were repaired in a painstaking fashion too, being secured by copper cramps or dowels, bedded in sulphur, run in hot.

Such painstaking efforts to ensure the retention of ancient material may not seem unusual today but the work must be seen in the context of its time.[14]

12 The archives of the Society for the Protection of Ancient Buildings provided considerable source material for this chapter. To avoid repetitive references it may be assumed that such information, if not referred to elsewhere, is to be found in the topographical SPAB archive file relating to the repair project concerned.

13 G. Ll. Morris, 'Lake House, Near Aymesbury: An Account of its Sustentation and Repair by Mr Detmar Blow, with the Counsel of Mr Philip Webb', *Architectural Review*, vol. 5 (March 1899), 171–80, p. 173.

14 Blow's work at Lake was upheld by the SPAB when their criticism of the proposed 'restoration' of Peterborough Cathedral was questioned in 1896. Sometimes accused at that time as being a 'do nothing' organization, they put forward Lake as an instance where they had had 'an opportunity to justify their position, and to carry out with a free hand a critical, and at the same time, very careful piece of preservative work.' (G. Ll. Morris, loc. cit.) The campaign at Peterborough culminated in the preparation of a specification suggesting conservative repair rather than the re-building favoured by the Dean and Chapter. It was signed by Turner, Lethaby, Blow, Webb and J. T. Micklethwaite (then Surveyor to the Fabric at Westminster Cathedral). A further group appended their names as being 'of the opinion that the methods proposed in the above specification are eminently practical, and they are such as we would recommend for repairing work of this nature.' The list included Robert Weir Schultz, F. W. Troup, Edward Prior, Halsey Ricardo, Mervyn MacCartney, Henry Wilson, Ernest Newton, Guy Dawber and Charles Ashbee. The SPAB went on to claim many signatures to a petition to support their cause – all to no avail.

Restoration, a process associated by Morris and his colleagues at the SPAB with the pulling down of old work in order to renew it, was still the norm. Such a course of action would have seemed almost inevitable ten years earlier and Lake was fortunate to avoid such a fate, Blow's efforts receiving critical acclaim as a result: 'Keeping unchanged the ancient stones that shared the sunrise of Shakespearian England, Lake House will retain its place in the chronological chain of architecture.'[15] Blow brought credit to the SPAB too: 'the architectural world at least should be unanimous in its agreement concerning the repair of ancient buildings and the Institute of Architects and the Society for the Protection of Ancient Buildings ought to have an almost identical membership.'[16]

51. The fire at Lake House, Wilsford-cum-Lake, Wiltshire, Good Friday, 1912.

Not much of Blow's early work at Lake remains. In 1912 the house was gutted by fire (51) and Lovibond wrote to the SPAB:

> Knowing the interest your society has taken in the past preservation of the building it will be a source of satisfaction that the rebuilding has been placed in the hands of Mr Detmar Blow ... If the walls can be preserved as they stand at present there will be but little alteration in the outside, although a strong west wind may do mischief. The interior is utterly destroyed and little can be said about it until the rubbish is cleared.

15 G. Ll. Morris, 'Lake House', pp. 176–7.
16 G. Ll. Morris, 'Lake House', p. 178.

The house as it stands today bears witness to Blow's second careful reinstatement, despite an addition which, when proposed in 1930, had caused him great concern. Then in his sixties, he urged the SPAB to protest. In the corner of his letter to them is a little sketch plan and, written within a heart, a note: 'This is Lake I had twice to repair with my own hands.'

James Billson's pair of cottages in the Charnwood Forest[17] must have been well under way when Blow was still completing the first repair at Lake. These jobs probably represent the first undertaken after he set up his shared rooms in Lincoln's Inn with Powell. By the time Blow moved on to Clare in Suffolk to repair another church tower, starting work in July 1898, accounts indicate that work on Stoneywell cottage had also commenced. But Blow was committed to work in London as well that year and began to find himself overstretched. The Clare commission had come through the SPAB twelve months earlier and although the intervening period gave the parish time to raise funds, Blow could delay commencement no longer, despite family problems. Thackeray Turner wrote to him at Lake in April, asking about start dates at Clare, having to explain to the incumbent: 'Mr Detmar Blow has recently lost his father. This I presume has put him behind in his correspondence.'[18]

As at East Knoyle, the church tower at Clare (52) had been pronounced dangerous and beyond repair. In fact its condition was worse than Knoyle and stretched the techniques learned there and refined at Lake. Clare was the first project Blow worked on for the SPAB without Webb's help. Nonetheless he reported back to the committee as work proceeded and this correspondence indicates that things did not go easily. They thought Blow was spending too much time in Leicestershire, Turner warning him: 'I considered the case a serious one, it required the utmost caution and constant observation on your part till the structural repairs gradually reduced the risks, which I think are considerable.' James Vatcher, the incumbent, had agreed that a representative from the society would visit from time to time to approve the work and Charles Canning Winmill, a young LCC architect who joined the committee that year, visited on their behalf in August. He reported in such a way that Webb was obliged to write to Blow direct:

> The committee asked me to communicate the result of our consideration to you. We were unanimous in thinking that a serious effort should be made by you to be much more continuously on the ground; watching, scheming to meet difficulties as they occur, and

[17] Now known collectively as Chitterman House and much altered.

[18] Jellings Blow had died suddenly on May 23. Cockerell heard the news from Detmar's brother Sydney two days later and went down to Petworth to see the family next day. (Cockerell Diaries)

52. 'The Preservation of Our Old Churches: Restoring the Tower of Clare Church, Suffolk', from *The Daily Graphic*, 15 December 1889 (SPAB).

personally directing the work of your men. With the waste of time now occuring from constant railway travelling by you, this very necessary attention is not possible on your part ... could you not see Mr Gimson, and put the case plainly for him and see if he could arrange for some weeks at least to look after the Leicester cottages? It might be more difficult with the unfortunate London work, but if you gave Saturday, Sunday and Monday to that, it would give you 4 consecutive days in each week for Clare, and the loss of time in mere travelling would be reduced ? ... You know enough of me I am sure to understand, that I have not undertaken to speak, and write in this way, willingly ? It has gone much against the grain – but the responsibility both to the society and you are too great to allow of my shirking the disagreeable.[19]

19 Unpublished letter from Philip Webb to Detmar Blow dated 9 September 1898, in SPAB Archive: Clare Church file (Suffolk). 'The unfortunate London work' probably referred to proposals Blow was putting together at the time for a site in Chelsea, on the corner of Cheyne Walk and Danvers Street. C. R. Ashbee had put forward a scheme for the same site in the previous year. Neither was built. Blow's client was Johnstone Douglas of Ruthwell, for whom he had worked in 1896 (Andrew Saint, 'Ashbee, Geddes, Lethaby and the Rebuilding of Crosby Hall', *Architectural History – Journal of the Society of Architectural Historians of Great Britain*, 34 (1991), 205–23, p. 206).

Blow replied, reassuring Webb about some specific aspects arising from Winmill's observations: 'I am sure you will understand that the purpose of this reply isn't to blame your reporter (a very young man) but to re-establish myself in your holinesses mind ... Believe me, yours cheerfully yet ever anxious in these works.'

As costs rose the SPAB appealed for funds on behalf of the parish and sufficient money was raised to complete the work, eventually involving the complete re-building of all the inner faces of the tower – a considerably larger undertaking than that at East Knoyle. But, as Blow's reports indicate, supervision was still a problem:

> one of the men ... who had been temperate for 18 months, got into bad company at Clare and for a second offence of getting drunk, got himself dismissed from the work by the foreman. The vicar told me the man had wasted a day or so, which I said should not be charged for; but of course this is not the reason for the vicar's distress, the work will cost more than expected, which I told the committee at their last meeting – and we cannot do more as to speed than has been done all through ...[20]

Vatcher remained dissatisfied with progress and by June 1899 he had had enough: 'I really think if this work is to be carried through, you must come down here and spend your time amongst the men. It is a well known thing that the master's eye makes the men go and as I consider you have so grossly misled us, as an honourable man you should do your utmost to pull us through! I am convinced it will be your presence alone that will finish this work – if you pay no attention to my wishes, I will write to the society you represent. And if they take no notice I will publish all the correspondence in the daily papers. Believe me, yours truly.'[21]

He must have written to the SPAB simultaneously for Blow was obliged to justify his actions to Turner in a letter dated two days later and written from Stoneywell, where he was presumably staying while working on Lea Cottage, the next in the Leicestershire series: 'I left Clare a week ago after 4 or 5 days stay. I have been there very constantly about every fortnight on a visit. I wrote three days ago that I would be there again this week and have taken no payment ... (save expenses) ... since end of last year.' Blow himself was clearly worried about the situation for he took on a young architect, Basil Stallybrass, to help out soon after but he was never concerned about the eventual outcome, writing

20 Unpublished letter from Detmar Blow to Thackeray Turner, 11 February 1899. SPAB Archive: Clare Church file, (Suffolk).

21 Unpublished letter from James Vatcher, the incumbent, to Detmar Blow, 2 June 1899. SPAB Archive: Clare Church file, (Suffolk).

to Turner from Stoneywell to assure him that the work, when completed, would defend itself. And so it did. *The Builders' Journal* told the story on 4 October:

> The work of restoration involved the scooping out of the old core and the insertion of concrete blocks of Portland cement and tiles [see 53, overleaf], which were solidly united to the outer shell by the pouring of grout in the interstices. The strength of the structure has been further increased by bonds of the best blue Staffordshire bricks, which line it in places, and also secure the turret to the tower, and the latter again to the church. Altogether, it is estimated that 43,000 bricks have been used, besides all the old flints which have been put back.[22]

The *Daily Graphic* went further on December 15:

> The work has been so successful that one would hardly believe, looking at the outside, that a restoration had been effected at all, except for the disappearance of the cracks. This beautiful tower ... has been preserved, indeed, in all its ancient beauty, stronger and better than ever, and will now be handed down to posterity from generation to generation and a priceless heirloom.[23]

In the end James Vatcher shared the enthusiasm with which Blow's work was received. This is born out by further correspondence with the SPAB in 1903 concerning the repair of his choir stalls. The society suggested Ernest Gimson for the work but although Vatcher was happy for Gimson to do the joinery, he insisted on Blow in a supervisory capacity: 'The people here would not consent to anything else.'[24]

22 A party from the Athenaeum Club visited during the summer on a perambulation through Suffolk. Their magazine tells how the work was placed in the hands of Mr Detmar Blois [sic] and how, when they visited, the church was described to them by Mr Blois and Mr Micklethwaite (the Surveyor to the Fabric of Westminster Abbey, who had acted with Blow at Peterborough): 'Suffolk Visit', *The Athenaeum Magazine*, no. 3745 (5 August 1899), p. 200.

23 An inscribed stone at Clare recorded the repair: 'This tower, built in the thirteenth century, added to and partly re-built in the fifteenth century, which last work gave way under the strain of the bells, was mended with a new inside from ten feet off the bottom under the advice of the Society for the Protection of Ancient Buildings at a cost of £1,160. A.D. 1899.'

24 Unpublished letter from James Vatcher to the SPAB, in the SPAB archive. Later James Vatcher became Rural Dean and had Blow re-build a neighbouring church at Hundon after a fire in February 1914. Blow worked at Clare Priory also and in 1920 a new owner contacted the SPAB on Vatcher's recommendation, William Weir visiting to make a report. Vatcher's correspondence with the Society continued as late as 1928 when he wrote about an old pargetted house for sale

old rubble walling
plucked out and
replaced as concrete
between bonds of
concrete
tile lintel
concrete of old material
concrete
single course
tile
concrete
sill bonding of sole tiles
Bonding of Staffordshire brick
Detmar Blow
View of interior of Belfry Clare Church Tower Suffolk.
Built in the 13th Century added and enlarged in the 15th cent
which later work gave way under the strain of bells.
was made good with a new inside

53 (opposite). Clare Church Tower: internal repairs, from a sketch by Detmar Blow inscribed 'View of interior of Belfry, Clare Church Tower, Suffolk. Built in the 13th Century, added and enlarged in the 15th Century which later work gave way under the strain of bells was made good with a new inside 10 foot off the bottom'.

As the Clare saga indicates, the success of Blow's work, here and elsewhere, was dependent not on him alone but also upon those who worked with him. His repair methods developed progressively from one job to the next and such a process was facilitated through continuity in his workforce. At Lake, Clare and in the Charnwood Forest he worked alongside a group of itinerant masons, some of whom remained with him over a considerable period of time. Indeed Blow's foreman at Clare was James Neale who first worked with him even earlier at East Knoyle in 1892 as part of the workforce employed by Albert Estcourt of Gloucester, the builder Webb had used at Clouds.[25] Blow worked with James Neale again at Lake[26] before putting him in charge of the work at Clare and in 1904 when Blow returned to West Wiltshire to build a house near Tisbury he found 'the descendants of former craftsmen' ready and able to carry out the work required:

> Each a giant at his trade and often in stature, they hate to leave their old homes and so they farm a few acres when building is not plentiful. When a very noble church tower was repaired close by, the mason was not addressed by his name, Jim or Neale but as Farmer Jim and once I heard this friendly warning coming down the tower, 'Jim, thee must tap the rick, there be snowstorm coming.'[27]

For men that hated to leave their old homes, these Wiltshire masons did a lot of travelling. Blow's other mainstay was Frank Green, his foreman in the Charnwood Forest. Green was as itinerant as James Neale over a similarly lengthy period. He too would have known of Blow's work at Knoyle and may well have worked there too as he came from the area. Blow's mason at Mill Hill is said to have been John Ward but Green could have helped out there as well, for Lawrence Weaver describes how Blow

---

adjoining Clare churchyard. It was rumoured that it had been sold for dismantling and re-erection in the United States. Vatcher told the SPAB: 'When we were repairing the tower, Detmar Blow lodged at this house. He did many things exposing its beauty and if you could get in touch with him he would be able to tell you of its great value.'

25 Unpublished letter from Blow to Webb, 14 January 1893, in the SPAB archive.

26 His name is spelt Neil in the accounts that survive in part at Hilles. Another mason named Benjamin Gale also features in these accounts.

27 Lawrence Weaver (attributed), 'Little Ridge, Wiltshire, a Seat of Mr Hugh Morrison', *Country Life* (26 October 1912), pp. 570–1.

> had built several farm steadings and cottages in Yorkshire when Ernest Gimson asked him to undertake the building of Stoneywell Cottage, of Lea Cottage, and of a house which stands near them. Mr Blow took with him to Leicestershire his foreman mason and a small band of men, who had worked with him before ... The foreman mason was Mr Frank Green, who came from East Knoyle, Wilts, a birthplace of happy augury, for it was there that Sir Christopher Wren first saw the light. With him worked Henry Shepheard and Jimmy Snook (delightful name!). Three Leicestershire men joined the band. The other two were known simply as 'Harry' and 'William' and Mr Detmar Blow writes of them: "Both dear giants in stature, and totally unlike their comrades, being (I grieve to record it) too fond of beer. The trowels that they brought matched their stature, for they were nearly two feet long." All the early part of the work was superintended by Mr Blow himself ...[28]

This description of the workforce in Leicestershire related specifically to Lea Cottage but Sydney Gimson confirms that Frank Green worked on Stoneywell too: 'The foreman of the little gang of masons was Frank Green and one or two of them stayed at Crooks Cottage. Jean brought them a pork pie and was surprised to hear that they 'hotted it up' ... to us this was a new way to treat pork pies.'[29] Frank Green's nephew John would not have found a pork pie so strange, for one of the largest manufacturers is today located in Wiltshire, where the family remained. John Green quarried, as did his father before him, at Newtown, Tisbury, less than five miles from Knoyle. He died in 1980 at the age of ninety-two and is remembered locally as a tall man who 'worked too hard to ever get fat'.[30] He is said to have untopped a new piece of quarry when he was over eighty and to have had a crowbar, with which he worked, three inches square at the butt and tapering over its seven foot length: 'It must have weighed 1½ hundredweight and he used to laugh when others could hardly lift it.'[31] John Green's quarry was the last in the Chilmark/Tisbury area of South Wiltshire to close and although two have since re-opened, much of the experience of that stone, passed down by word of mouth from father to son, died with him.

In 1900 Frank Green travelled with Blow from Leicestershire to Norfolk to build Happisburgh Manor (54). Gimson was going to be involved too, continuing the successful association built up in the Charnwood Forest, indeed Blow gives him the credit for the 'double butterfly' plan: 'He [Blow] does not

28 Lawrence Weaver, *Small Country Houses of Today*, vol. 1 (London: Country Life, first published 1910, third edition revised 1922), pp. 34–6.

29 S. A. Gimson, op. cit.

30 Unpublished letter from Ben J. Lloyd to the author, 2 March 1985.

31 Ibid.

54. Happisburgh Manor, Norfolk, seen from the north-west, soon after completion (BAL).

himself lay claim to the idea but says that it "originated with my friend Mr Ernest Gimson who sent the little butterfly device on a postcard." As in the Leicestershire cottage illustrated ... these two men, who combine the faculties of the artist craftsman with the training of the architect, had wished to join forces at Happisburgh. Circumstances, however, prevented this, and the whole of the planning, drawing and execution is to be put down to Mr Blow.'[32] There is, however, an early drawing by Gimson (55) suggesting that he was responsible for a little more than just the initial concept.

Happisburgh is the first of Blow's major works and is situated on the north east coast of Norfolk, on high sandy ground close to the sea: 'in a small village of flint-built houses with reed-thatched roofs and a church with a very lofty tower. The house is built entirely of beech shingle and flints bonded with bricks; the roof covered with reeds grown on the estate; with the exception of some wood and glass, nothing was imported. It was built by the men of the district, assisted by a foreman and other leading men who worked with the architect on buildings in various counties.'[33] Elevationally the treatment at Happisburgh

32 'The Work of Mr Detmar Blow and Mr Fernand Billerey', Architectural Supplement to *Country Life* (26 October 1912), v–xxxvi, p. xvi.

33 Anon., 'A House at Happisburgh, Norfolk', *Architectural Review*, XV (1904), 214–19 (p. 214).

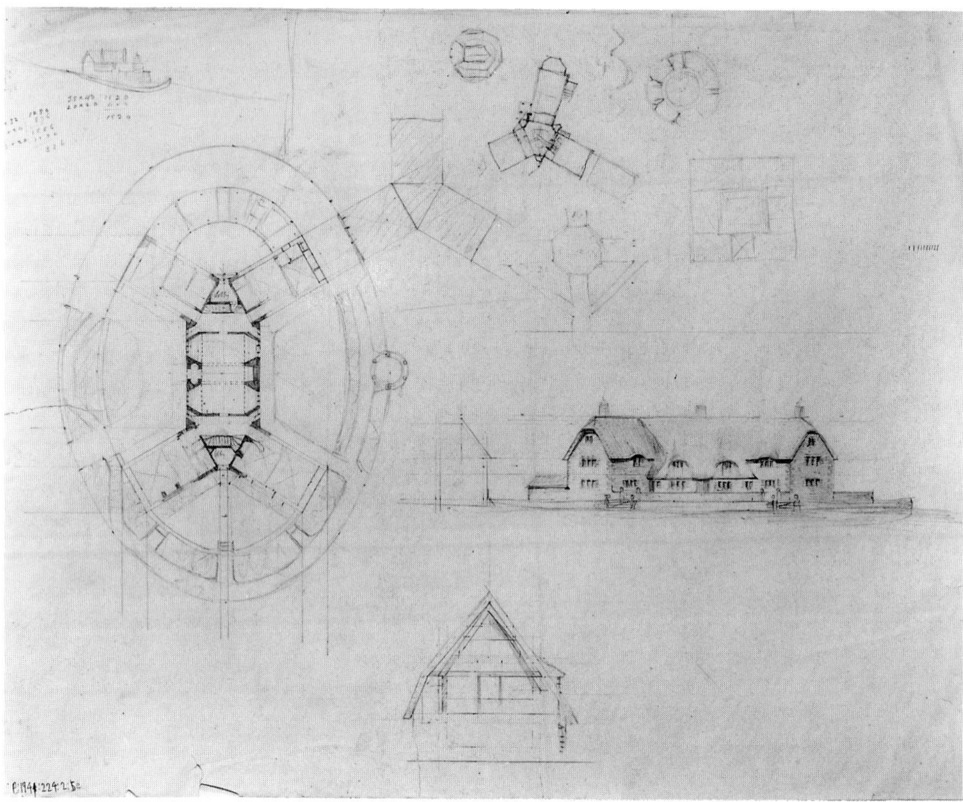

has none of the quietly unpretentious repose of the Leicestershire cottages or indeed of that suggested in the Gimson drawing. In its place there is a restless, changing quality which is reinforced by the plan form. Although the parapeted gables with their tumbled brick details follow local precedent, their disposition one to another is rearranged with every slight shift in viewpoint. These gables are the dominant element in the composition from whatever angle one approaches and a single word appears in each, picked out in brick amongst the shingle. Walking round they read: AVE MARIA STELLA MARIS. The fifth gable, over the central entrance porch, carries the date 1900.

Blow's materials were indigenous but not all the labour on site at Happisburgh was local: 'It uses methods and materials which make it perfectly right where it is and perfectly wrong if we were in another locality. But it uses them with individuality and intelligence, an intelligence which does the highest credit to Mr Blow, and which he will be the first to wish in some measure to share with the man he wisely chose for his foreman, Mr Frank Green. He, in the manner of the medieval craftsman, had an instinct as well as a practical knowledge of local needs and local possibilities. He acted under Mr Blow as master-builder and lived largely on the spot in order to watch every little detail of the work.'[34]

55 (opposite). Undated design for a butterfly plan house by Ernest Gimson. The plan closely resembles Happisburgh Manor, although the elevational treatment shows little similarity (Cheltenham Art Gallery and Museums).

56 (left). 'The Wyndham Sisters', painted by John Singer Sargent in 1900. Left to right: Lady Mary Elcho, Mrs Pamela Tennant, Mrs Madeline Adeane. The portrait of their mother, Mrs Percy Wyndham, painted by G. F. Watts in 1877, can be seen in the background (Metropolitan Museum of Art).

Happisburgh Manor was built for Mrs Albermarle Cator, a friend of the Tennants for whom Blow later built Wilsford Manor. His reputation spread through a network of clients who were all socially interconnected and after the turn of the century his workload shifted away from historic building repair towards country house work. His clientele stemmed from contacts originally made much earlier at Clouds, Pamela Tennant being the daughter of Percy Wyndham. Her marriage to Edward Tennant linked two families at the centre of a social circle known as 'The Souls'. A somewhat incestuous clique of affluent, highly intelligent socialites, they lived their lives at a high pitch both emotionally and intellectually. It was the magnetism of Edward Tennant's sisters that was the force that initially bound the Souls together as an identifiable group but the three Wyndham sisters - painted by John Singer Sargent in 1900 (56) - were an essential component also. Blow worked for all three, and for many of their friends too. Mary, the eldest, became Lady Elcho and later Lady Wemyss, and for her he altered and extended Stanway in Gloucestershire. He worked for Madeline, the youngest, at Babraham near Cambridge from 1899, and built Wilsford (described later) for Pamela between 1904 and 1906. Other

[34] 'The Work of Mr Detmar Blow and Mr Fernand Billerey', p. xx.

Souls included their brother George, then a promising young politician, and more senior political figures such as Arthur Balfour, George (later Lord) Curzon and Herbert Asquith.

Blow's connection with the Souls lasted throughout his career. When, in 1902, Sydney Cockerell was a house guest at Hewell Grange in Worcestershire, the Cators and Pamela Tennant were amongst the party. Gay Windsor, later Lady Plymouth, was their hostess and another mainstay of the Souls. Later Blow worked on the chapel at Hewell Grange for her, in turn buying furniture for Hilles, his own house near Painswick in Gloucestershire, from the craft workshops she ran. After her husband, the Earl of Plymouth, died in 1913 she left Hewell to live near Hilles. Her house, called Holcombe, was leased from Blow and he extended it for her in 1925.

Happisburgh proved a turning point in Blow's wandering lifestyle. Webb had tailored his long 'apprenticeship' specifically to the needs of the SPAB and the historic buildings for which that society cared. But Blow's career had always maintained a second strand, typified by new building projects like Mill Hill and the Leicestershire Cottages. Although the SPAB continued to put cases his way after the turn of the century, Blow balanced these with other commissions and Happisburgh gave him an opportunity to show how his way of working could produce domestic architecture of the highest quality. Pulled in two directions, he wrote to Thackeray Turner at the SPAB early in 1901 suggesting that since Clare his time on other jobs had prevented him getting round to casework for the SPAB: 'The last six months I have been so very hard at new work so pray forgive. I could have done any number [of SPAB cases] after Clare, instead of journeyman masoning.'[35]

As opportunities presented themselves more rapidly in the late 1890s Blow had found that concentrating his time on one project alone was too restrictive. Nonetheless he did not give up his way of building. He continued to use directly employed craftsmen, thus avoiding the contracting system that he and his friends held responsible for many of the problems they perceived in the architecture of the day. He felt confident to depend on others within his team to maintain the essential presence on site and his continuing association with his leading masons can best be followed through his connections with the Green family. He worked with them again at Amesbury Abbey,[36] at Wilsford (see next

[35] Unpublished letter from Detmar Blow to Thackeray Turner dated 16 Jan 1901: SPAB Archive: Stonehenge file.

[36] When Blow was working in Norfolk in 1900 he sent a telegram to William Green at Tisbury: 'Can you or son build 4 weeks work Amesbury Abbey – building gate piers and meet me there Monday morning. Mr Blow, Happisburgh.' Blow's draft for the telegram appears in the corner of a drawing now at Norfolk Records Office.

chapter), and at Heale House (see Chap. 11). He continued to use Tisbury stone from the Greens' quarry in his later houses. Wallingford Court [see (139)], an unbuilt mansion in Berkshire, the design for which he exhibited at the Royal Academy in 1913,[37] was to have been in rubble walling with Chilmark dressings, Chilmark being the generic name for stone quarried in the Tisbury area.

57. Richard Harrison, the Sapperton carpenter, by Alfred Powell.

Blow and his associates knew that it was not just masons who had to be carefully selected. The men who built the Charnwood Forest cottages were all hand picked whatever their trade, Gimson's brother Sydney recalling: 'Ernest wished Detmar to do the mason's work, Harrisons of Sapperton to do the timberwork and Durham to do the thatching.'[38] In addition 'Chapman of Markfield [a local builder] was also employed by Detmar Blow to help in the building'[39] The thatcher, John Durham, came from Fifield, Oxfordshire and thatched Ernest Gimson's own house in 1902. Richard Harrison (57) was the Sapperton carpenter and wheelwright that Philip Webb lodged with when house-hunting in the Cotswolds. Harrison was responsible for all the constructional timbers and internal woodwork at Stoneywell. Kelly's *Directory* for Gloucestershire in 1894 describes him as a carpenter, provision dealer and beer retailer and his building and undertaking business was still thriving in Sapperton in Norman Jewson's time. According to Jewson:

Later Blow carried out further extensive alterations to Amesbury Abbey. His drawings, dated 1904, are uncatalogued in the RIBA drawings collection. See John Bold, *Wilton House and English Palladianism – Some Wiltshire Houses* (London: HMSO, 1988). See also note 6. 6 for the extent of Blow's work at Amesbury Abbey.

37 'Wallingford Court, Berkshire', anon, *The Building News* (11 July 1913), p. 46.

38 S. A. Gimson, 'Random Memories of the Building of Stoneywell', unpublished, private collection, 1938 (unpaginated).

39 S. A. Gimson, op. cit.

> after the rector and the farmer, not including Gimson and the Barnsleys, who were comparative newcomers, the most important man in the village was Richard Harrison, the wheelwright, whose workshops and yards backed onto Ernest Barnsley's garden. He was a short little man, with a face reddened by exposure, small, humourous blue eyes and a tight mouth holding entirely toothless jaws ... if ever a man loved his work, old Richard did. He seemed to live for nothing else, starting work at six in the morning and often working as long as it was light in the evening, or at any rate pottering about the shop, seeing all was in order for the next day ... To anyone who really appreciated his craft he enjoyed explaining the reason for using oak for the spokes, elm for the hub and felloes of a wheel, why ash was better for shafts and that the stop-chamfering that added so much to the appearance of a wagon was only, or at any rate mostly, to reduce the weight while that could be done without reducing the strength.[40]

Harrison's work, or the tradition that it continued, was the inspiration for the furniture produced by Gimson and the Barnsleys. The chamfering and chip-carving that constituted much of their decoration derived from the local techniques, tested by time, that Harrison used. The wagons inspired their wagon-backed furniture and even the hay rakes he made reappeared in another form, as stretchers bracing some of their tables.

Blow's masons other than Neale and Green are more difficult to trace. There is no further record of Henry Shepheard and Jimmy Snook but the search for them revealed another Wiltshire mason who used to talk of his work with Blow. This man was Charles Gauler. He was born, the story goes, within the sound of Bow Bells in 1885 (making him three years older than John Green).[41] When he was six his father had come to Tisbury as foreman of the Chilmark stone masonry works at Tisbury Station. Charles was the oldest of six but was too young to have travelled with Blow in the 1890s. Nonetheless, before he died in 1956 he told of how he worked on the new wing of a house at Temple Guiting in Gloucestershire, about a mile north of the quarry there. The house in question must have been Stanway where Detmar Blow built a new wing in 1913, demolished in 1948. Blow's client, Lady Elcho, was one of the Wyndham sisters and a neighbour and frequent visitor to the Ashbees in Campden.

Charles Gauler also used to talk of his connections with Lake House and with a house at Fonthill that must have been Little Ridge[42] (see chapter six).

40 Jewson, 'By Chance I did Rove', p. 79.

41 One of Charles Gauler's brothers died young and is buried in Tisbury; another became a postman in Salisbury in the 1930s and another worked for John Green in his quarry at Newtown near Tisbury.

Blow was working at both in 1912/13. Gauler left school when he was twelve in 1897, but it is said that he did not undertake journeyman work until after 1902 after which time he worked a seventy-two hour week, starting at 6 a.m. He had beer for breakfast at 8 a.m. and again at noon and again in the afternoon and 'if slightly merry with beer, it was economical as it made the mallet swing up and down faster.'[43]

Gauler is interesting because he continues the association between Blow and the South Wiltshire masons that runs from James Neale at East Knoyle in 1892 via the connections with the Green family and on over a period of more than twenty years to some of Blow's later commissions, before the Great War. It was an association that was important to Blow not just for his work but socially and this is epitomised by the presence of his mason friends in pride of place in the front pews at his society wedding in St Paul's Cathedral in 1910.[44] Afterwards, when the family moved into Hilles, the house Blow built near Painswick (58), he tried to combine the running of his household with hospitality to the masons still working there. They were to be part of the family. For Blow this was no idle social experiment, it was the natural result of a life that had been led in close conjunction with his fellow craftsmen. He was, as Sydney Gimson had observed at Stoneywell, equally at home with the masons and with the aristocracy.

The masons were not the only ones who shared Blow's itinerant life. Among others who travelled with him was Oliver W. F. Lodge, the son of the eminent Victorian physicist and psychic researcher Sir Oliver Lodge, who rented Lake House from 1919. Sir Oliver was a regular visitor to Clouds in the 1890s and it was Madeline Wyndham who recomended his son to Blow, young Oliver writing to her to express his appreciation while working with Blow at Clare: 'I have begun to learn stone carving this week, I have levelled some surfaces and am now copying a 13th century dripstone moulding with a row of dogs teeth in it ... I have struck Architecture here, at last, and it is my calling ... I meet lots of real people here and Detmar Blow is very nearly an ideal person.'[45]

42 Charles Gauler told too how as a young man, turning balusters on piece work, he innocently turned one in eleven minutes when his boss was watching and consequently had his piecework rate reduced. The tale is attributed to a house at Newton Tony (unpublished letter from Ben J. Lloyd to the author, 8 Feb 1985). The big house at Newton Tony is Wilbury, an altered but very early Palladian house of 1710 by William Benson. Although it was rented by the Wyndhams while Webb was building Clouds for them, there is no record of Blow having worked there. Gauler's brother was however employed by John Green at Newtown (not impossible to confuse with Newton Tony?) where Blow worked at Hatch House in 1908; Charles, 23 at the time, might perhaps have worked with them.

43 Unpublished letter from Ben J Lloyd to the author, 2 March 1985.

44 Simon Blow, telephone conversation with the author, 26 Feb 1985.

58. Hilles House, Painswick, Gloucestershire. Stone slates now replace the original thatch, lost in a fire which nearly destroyed the whole house in 1951.

Eleven years younger than Blow, Sir Oliver's son later became an acclaimed playwright and a published poet. A trial period of work on site was clearly not an uncommon way of gaining some insight into the building world, Detmar's brother Sydney spending a similar interlude with the bricklayers for Lutyens in 1895. Like Sydney Blow, Oliver Lodge was after a taste of the building industry before deciding on a career, perhaps as an architect but (again like Sydney) the experience was not sufficiently seductive to sway him from the stage. A lasting friendship was made nonetheless, Lodge later becoming a close neighbour of the Blows, settling at Upton St Leonards, near Hilles. He lived until 1955 and the family remembers him reminiscing about the old wandering days. He told how, in the evenings at Clare, he used to tramp the country lanes with Blow, visiting other churches nearby or swimming in the river Stour. They sounded like happy times for Lodge, and they must have been for Blow too as twelve years later he named his first child Clare. When asked what they talked about on such walks, Lodge replied, 'Why, the revolution of course.'[46]

[45] From a letter in a private collection quoted by Caroline Dakers, *Clouds. The Biography of a Country House* (London & New Haven: Yale University Press, 1993), p. 166.

[46] Philip Warre-Cornish, Detmar Blow's son-in-law, recalled this in conversation with the author, 10 Jan 1985.

Chapter 6
THE WAY CONTINUES IN WILTSHIRE
Basil Stallybrass, and Detmar Blow's Continuing Career, 1901–1906

> No-one knows better than Mr Blow the difficulty of wedding the airy spirit of three centuries ago to the sturdy needs of today, and no-one has learnt how to overcome it more successfully.
>
> Lawrence Weaver, *Country Life*, Oct 1912.

Basil Stallybrass was Detmar Blow's first architectural assistant. He joined Blow in 1899 at Clare[1] and from there moved on to Babraham Hall, near Cambridge,[2] which Blow altered for Mrs Madeline Adeane, the youngest of the three Wyndham sisters from Clouds.[3] Not long after, in 1901, Detmar Blow talked to Sydney Cockerell about taking on a partner,[4] but nothing came of it and when a partnership was eventually formed in 1906 (see Chapter 11), Stallybrass was not

1 That April he made drawings of the nearby church tower at Belchamp St Paul, which Blow had been asked to look at by the SPAB.

2 Both Blow and Stallybrass used headed writing paper from Babraham for correspondence relating to Clare. A letter to the SPAB, requesting copies of a fund-raising pamphlet for a prospective donor who wanted to help save the tower, was initialled 'B.S. for and on behalf of Detmar Blow', and came from Babraham. Soon after, Blow borrowed the Adeane's stationary too, crossing through the heading and marking it 'Clare, Suffolk'. This letter to the SPAB thanks Thackeray Turner for donations and proposes both Stallybrass and Oliver Lodge as members of the society (unpublished letter, Detmar Blow to Thackeray Turner, 23 July 1899, SPAB Archive: Clare Church file, Suffolk).

3 Blow must have become a family friend as he accompanied Charles Adeane on an early motor tour in 1902 ('Detmar called. He is going on a motor car tour with Mr Adeane in France to Chartres.' Cockerell Diary, Tuesday 15 July 1902). They drove from Windsor to Southampton, crossing the Channel and on to Chartres and Orleans. Blow was an enthusiastic passenger and kept detailed notes, typically: 'No sounds but the powerful thud of the regulator and we run freely down the long hill into the boulevards of Southampton.' Each arrival and departure time was logged, on the move if the handwriting in his sketchbook is anything to go by (Blow sketchbook No. 12, no date, Ref 1987. 55, pp. 2–32, RIBA Drawings Collection).

4 Sydney Cockerell's diary [Wednesday 1 May 1901].

the man. Nonetheless Stallybrass worked with Blow for at least eight years and his responsibilities indicate that he held a position of trust in Blow's organization from an early date. Blow needed such a man for in 1901 he found himself entrusted with the repair of one of the oldest and most important structures in the country. On 31 December 1900 two stones of a trilithon in the outer ring at Stonehenge fell during a storm (59). The SPAB had been worried

about the future of the stones for ten years or more and had already collaborated with the renowned Victorian archaeologist General Augustus Pitt-Rivers. The Society of Antiquaries, the Hon. Percy Wyndham from Clouds and Sir Edmund Antrobus, the owner of the monument, had all become involved in the debate thereafter. Public access and the army's increasing use of Salisbury Plain were the main concerns and a correspondent advised the society, only shortly before the fall: 'I was told at the close of the manoeuvres at Salisbury Plain last autumn that the grand march past was held close to the circle and the earth shook as the cavalry and artillery galloped past.'[5]

A debate concerning re-erection followed the fall, Webb writing from Caxton's to put forward the rejected suggestion that all the stones be

[5] Here and elsewhere in this chapter, source material is from the SPAB archive.

underpinned to prevent further collapse. Blow, already working nearby at Amesbury Abbey for Sir Edmund Antrobus,[6] was well placed to implement the chosen course of action whatever it might be. The committee told Blow that although they opposed a general restoration of all stones, they approved the re-erection of the recently collapsed trilithon including the repair of the lintel, broken in the fall, which Blow suggested be pinned together by the insertion of

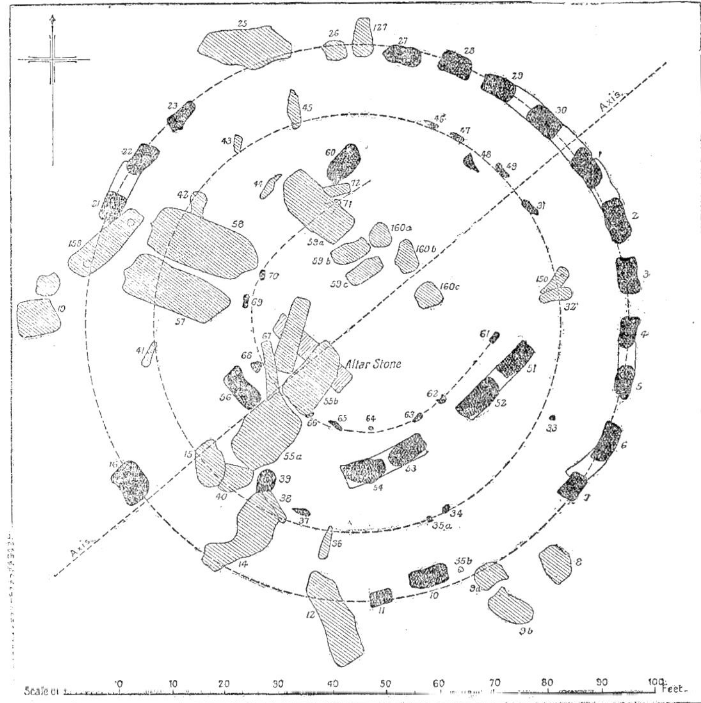

59 (opposite). Stonehenge in Sept. 1899, by Hedley Fitton, published in *The Daily Chronicle*. The trilithon on the left is the one that fell on 31 Dec., 1900. To its right lie the stones of the trilithon that fell on 3 Jan., 1797. The leaning stone centrally is the remaining upright of a trilithon that fell in the early part of the 17th century and was straightened under Detmar Blow's supervision in 1901.

60 (left). Plan of stones standing on 30 Dec. 1900 (recumbent stones shown hatched), from *The Times*, 9 April, 1901. The trilithon that fell is no. 21–2.

granite dowels. He informed the SPAB that 'Sir Edmund Antrobus requests the work should be carried out under my supervision, the honour of which I must

6 Blow's work at Amesbury dates from 1900 (See note 34 in the previous chapter) but it seems likely that his major alterations are later. His drawings, dated 1904, are uncatalogued in the RIBA drawings collection. This work included the paving of the entrance hall, a revised stair arrangement in the galleried stairwell, the remaking of the octagonal lantern and the refitting of the long saloon, later known as the ballroom or music room. The room has since been sub-divided. Blow took pains to ensure his work copied previous details where possible for a note appearing on one of his drawings reads: 'All details marked like this are existing and must be used again – the remaining should be cast in plaster from them.' See John Bold, *Wilton House and English Palladianism – Some Wiltshire Houses* (London: HMSO, 1988), p. 115.

ask the society to regard and acknowledge as theirs, whilst it remains my duty and pleasure to further its views.'

Blow attributed the fall of the two stones (an upright and the lintel over) to the condition of the ground: 'which being well trodden down immediately around the stones with the tread of millions of feet, retains the rain water running down the stones instead of distributing it as it might otherwise do.' His concern about the trampling effect of visitors gave rise to a controversy about fencing off the monument, indeed Blow was among the first to see that the increasing popularity of the stones must in the end result in the control of public access. He felt that the collapse of the stones:

> must be connected with the general control of the visiting public. Their number grows annually and already on some days nearly one thousand people visit the place. His Majesty's camp begun a year or so ago will be ready for the housing of troops speedily and railway communications will shortly be established.

This point was taken up by *The Times* which suggested that 'colonies of rats, attracted by the remains of luncheons, have burrowed about the foundations ... We must be prepared to face some limitations of access and some restrictions of use ... there is only one alternative – an unclimbable wire fence carried around a really large portion of the ground.'[7]

The fence went up and the uproar started. Blow defended the decision: 'The fence has been erected to meet an urgent temporary need caused by the sudden transformation of a once quiet rural neighbourhood into a popular district.' Others thought differently. The local parish council in Amesbury complained of the stoppage of alleged public rights of way through the stones and Percy Wyndham tried to sort this out with a letter to the Times: 'The public who visit Stonehenge do so as licensees, in the same way as many places of interest or beauty are visited on land in private ownership, without it ever being intended or supposed that public right has been established by their so doing.'[8]

The question of the re-erection of the fallen stones still remained unanswered. In his report Blow contended that the trilithon should be made good for the well-being of the remaining standing stones: 'The gap that has been made is a danger to the rest in the same manner as a gap in an avenue or a clump of trees ... the rest must in their turn follow unless the gap be planted up or other precaution taken ...' He pointed out that the weights of the stones were not unusual by the standards of his day and that every precaution could be

7 From an unpaginated press cutting from *The Times* (9 April 1901), in the SPAB Stonehenge file.

8 From an unpaginated press cutting from *The Times* (28 April 1902), in the SPAB Stonehenge file.

taken to avoid marking the stones during re-erection. Both Blow and Webb had been adamant about the need for experienced craftsmen and well-qualified supervision for such work: 'so very much would depend on the intelligence as well as the experience of the foreman or clerk of the works, and of his being there.'[9] 'The Society has already done two important buildings in the neighbourhood with local men who would again be at liberty.'[10]

Antrobus decided to entrust the preservation of the monument to a joint committee composed of the SPAB, the Society of Antiquaries and the Wiltshire Archaeological Society. As a preliminary exercise, Blow, in conjunction with Dr William Gowland, an archaeologist, was instructed to straighten a leaning stone, all that remained standing of the central and largest of the five trilithons forming the inner ring or horseshoe. In the end this was the only work carried out under Blow's direction (60). Its fellow stones had fallen in the early part of the seventeenth century followed by the neighbouring trilithon to the north (61) on 3 January 1797. This neighbouring group was eventually re-erected, together with the 1900 fall, but not until 1958.

Stallybrass was in charge of Blow's operations on site. He had become a SPAB member himself a little earlier, Blow thanking the committee for electing Stallybrass (and Wells, see Ch. 7) in his first letter to the SPAB concerning the fallen stones. Stallybrass attended committee meetings with Blow in April 1901, meeting Cockerell amongst others.[11] In September when work had commenced, Cockerell and his friends found Blow's accounts, given over the supper table at Gatti's, fascinating:

> Detmar very interesting about the discoveries of Roman coins and lower down of flint implements at Stonehenge, showing conclusively that the monument is of the Stone Age, as Lord Amesbury told me he thought it was. The Roman coins were found a foot below the surface and the implements two foot six inches to three foot six inches down. The surface of the part of the leaning stone that was below the ground still shows very marked signs of the tooling. Must go and see it.'[12]

Cockerell went down to visit on the following Monday, walking the six miles from Porton station:

9 Unpublished letter from Philip Webb to Thackeray Turner dated 16 January 1900. This is presumably a case of new year forgetfulness and must have been written on 16 Jan 1901.

10 Report from Detmar Blow to the SPAB, undated, SPAB Archive: Stonehenge file.

11 Stallybrass came to know Sydney Cockerell well, visiting him in Richmond and joining him, Blow and others at Gatti's on many occasions (Cockerell Diaries 1901: 23 & 25 April, 20 June, 24 Oct., 7 & 14 Nov., 12 Dec. Also 1902: 9 & 23 Jan.).

12 Cockerell Diaries, Thursday 26 September 1901. Lethaby, Cockerell and Emery Walker were amongst those present.

61 (above). 'Starting for Straightening with Ropes Strained'. Detmar Blow (in white panama) and Prof. Gowland, straightening the leaning stone, 1901 (Wiltshire Archaeological and Natural History Society).

62 (below). 'Sifting Soil Through Four Different Meshes down to ⅛ inch size'. Basil Stallybrass is second from the right (WANHS).

> I found Dr Gowland and Stallybrass with two or three workmen busy sifting the earth taken from the base of the great stone behind the altar which they have recently set upright. (62)[13]

Stallybrass helped Gowland in an experiment to ascertain the method by which Stonehenge's builders formed the tooling exhibited on the finished surfaces of the stones: 'This tooling was apparently executed with the small quartzite hammers. In order to demonstrate this a small piece of sarsen was tooled in a similar manner by Mr Stallybrass with a quartzite pebble. On comparing it with the blocks tooled by the builders of Stonehenge they were seen to be almost perfectly identical. I may say in this connection that Mr Stallybrass failed to produce anything at all like it with any of his mason's tools.'[14]

Like Blow, Stallybrass was, it seems, no stranger to stonemasonry himself. He was back in London by the end of October and early in 1902 Blow read a paper at the RIBA on their findings. Cockerell was not impressed: 'A poor paper (D hadn't taken enough pains) but the excellent slides partly made up for it.'[15] Perhaps Blow had other things on his mind. His widowed mother was tiring of her country life in Sussex and although he still had an address at Lincoln's Inn,[16] ten years of wandering had left him without a proper home to which he could invite her. His new rooms at 9 Kings Bench Walk, in the Temple, were chosen with her in mind.

One might be forgiven for taking this move to mark the establishment of Blow's first proper London office. With a practice already too large to allow him to continue journeyman masoning himself, he was talking to Cockerell in May 1901 about 'starting an "office" with a clerk and perhaps a partner',[17] but if 9 King's Bench Walk was Blow's idea of an office, it was certainly no conventional one. Sydney Blow, having given up bricklaying, shared the new premises and, still set on a career in the theatre, was trying to persuade his brother to sponsor the production of a play he had co-written. They read the play, called 'Where Children Rule', to Lady Pamela Tennant[18] who advised

13 Ibid., Monday 30 September 1901.

14 William Gowland, 'Recent Excavations at Stonehenge', *Wiltshire Archaeological Magazine*, XXXIII (June, 1903), 1–62, p. 35.

15 Cockerel Diaries: Monday 20 January 1902. Blow's paper, 'The Architectural Discoveries of 1901 at Stonehenge', may be found in the *Journal of the RIBA*, Vol. IX, 3rd series (25 Jan 1902), 121–42.

16 Blow had moved from Old Square, where he shared with Powell in 1897, to No. 3 New Square in 1898.

17 Sydney Cockerell's diary for Wednesday 1 May 1901: British Museum Manuscripts Collection.

18 In her house at 34 Queen Anne's Gate, later extended by Blow in 1912.

Detmar to back Sydney and form a syndicate. Detmar designed the costumes and scenery and their mother, then aged seventy, acted as accountant. Mrs Blow was a remarkable woman. German by birth, she was taught piano by Clara Schumann and learned to swim when she was seventy-two. She lived with them at King's Bench Walk as Sydney describes:

> My mother, when she realised there was no chance of my throwing up the theatre and going back to grow flowers with her in West Sussex, had come to live with us there... We provided her with the one bedroom that the chambers boasted, and Detmar and I re-organised the large living room. Two deep recessed bookcases that stood each side of the fireplace were dismantled, and in their place two patent beds were erected that shut up in the daytime flat against the wall and hidden by beautiful William Morris curtains. Not even the nosiest of parkers would have guessed that beds were produced from behind those curtains every night.[19]

Where Detmar got any architectural work done is not clear but Lethaby would have had no hesitation in confirming that these were not the type of 'respectable offices with the framed perspectives on the walls and clerks slaving in the background'[20] that he and his friends found so unconducive to their kind of architecture. Sydney engaged his cast from King's Bench Walk, interviewing numerous children for the play. He was amused by a twelve year old who solemnly presented his card:

> Solomon Marks
> Hind legs of crocodile,
> Peter Pan, Duke of Yorks Theatre
> Mile End Road, E.[21]

According to Sydney the play got wonderful notices and did equally wonderful business.[22] Perhaps it was fortunate for Detmar's architectural career that his brother married soon after and moved to Regents Park.

Working on site at Stonehenge, Stallybrass avoided such distractions but early in 1902 he disappears from Cockerell's diaries and thereafter his movements go unrecorded until 1904 when he reappears in a supervisory capacity at Little Ridge, a Wiltshire house for Hugh Morrison, the inheritor of a haberdashery fortune.[23] Little Ridge and Pamela Tennant's Wilsford Manor

19 Sydney Blow, *The Ghost Walks on Friday* (London, Heath Cranton, 1935), p. 106.

20 W. R. Lethaby, A. H. Powell & F. L. Griggs, *Ernest Gimson, His Life and Work* (Stratford on Avon: Shakespeare Head Press, 1924), p. 8.

21 Sydney Blow, *The Ghost Walks on Friday*, p. 107.

22 Sydney Blow, *The Ghost Walks on Friday*, p. 105.

23 Hugh Morrison's mother inaugurated the South Kensington School of Art

63 (above). Sandell's Farmhouse, West Amesbury, Wiltshire, designed by Detmar Blow in 1902

64 (right). 28 South St, Mayfair, by Detmar Blow.

were built at about the same time and these two houses represent Blow's most significant work in south Wiltshire, a part of the country that provided him with many commissions. Pamela Tennant, the Wyndham sister to whom Sydney had read his play, had Blow build Wilsford Manor virtually next door to Lake House, in the Avon Valley north of Salisbury, an area in which his work is particularly concentrated. Neither Stonehenge nor Amesbury Abbey are much more than a couple of miles away. In addition, Blow worked on the church tower in Amesbury in 1901 and in West Amesbury, on the road to Wilsford, he built a farmhouse for the Antrobus estate. It was called Sandell's, after its tenant farmer and the drawings for it are dated 1902. It is in a plain and provincial mid-eighteenth-century style (63) and it is interesting to compare this house with its urban equivalent, 28 South St, Mayfair designed by Blow at about the same date (64).

Pamela and Edward Tennant stayed elsewhere at West Amesbury[24] while Blow was building them Wilsford Manor. There had been an earlier house on the site, which they had bought early in 1902, living there for a while before

---

Needlework with Mrs Percy Wyndham [Edith Olivier, *Four Victorian Ladies of Wiltshire* (London, Faber & Faber, 1945), p. 62].

24 As indicated by an unpublished letter from Pamela Tennant to Sydney Cockerell, 16 March 1905 from West Amesbury House. Amongst the Cockerell Papers, Ref. 52769, British Museum Manuscripts Collection. West Amesbury is another but smaller gabled stone house seemingly of the same era as Lake House but in which Blow found what he thought to be a twelfth-century roof, similar to one he knew at Amesbury Church [*Country Life* (1 March 1902), p. 277].

embarking on re-building. Sydney Cockerell knew the Tennants through Blow and Pamela wrote, inviting him to stay in this earlier house while they were

> settling in ... whitewashing over bad wallpaper ... I wish we could change the house even more but we cannot do that just now. The garden is altogether delightful – a rambling farmhouse garden that has never been spoiled and some yew hedges of a noble size ... there is a most beautiful house close by called Lake House ... would you care to come down to us next Sat. to Mon?[25]

Wilsford Manor is close to Lake House in more ways than location. The early drawings that Blow sent Gimson show stone gables, mullioned and transomed windows and massive chimneys rising above stone slate roofs with a thatched service wing and a mature walled garden. He signed them: 'To EWG, Wilsford House; built with parts of old material, DB 1904.' (65) This inscription implies that the house was up by 1904 but in fact completion was not until 1906 when Detmar and his mother stayed for Christmas.[26] Thus the 1904 drawings probably mark the inception of the scheme and it is of interest that Blow shared his early thoughts with Gimson, his old collaborator.

Pamela Tennant loved her house for it suited her ideals. It is a house that seemed never to have been new and it relates to its surroundings in much the same way that she felt she should relate to hers. Like many of her friends, Pamela Tennant idealised the countryside and its traditions, for the Souls set themselves apart from the smart society that associated itself only with palatial grandeur. They were amongst the first to seek 'a house in the country' as opposed to a country house, loving the land not because they had owned it for generations but because it sustained the way of life with which they identified – that of the countryman, not just the Lord of the Manor. Pamela Tennant sat on her Morris chairs in the open Stone Parlour at Wilsford and published her 'Village Notes'. In this outdoor sitting room, a loggia beneath deep thatched eaves, she felt perhaps that she shared something of the accommodation enjoyed by her dairyman in the cottage she had Blow build near the entrance to her house (66). Her Morris chairs were part of the same ethos and if her dairyman could not afford such things, it was no more her fault than it was Morris's, who wished it were otherwise and made them to ensure that traditional ways of

[25] Unpublished letter from Pamela Tennant to Sydney Cockerell, 22 April 1902 from Wilsford House, amongst the Cockerell Papers, British Museum Manuscripts Collection. Cockerell went down in July, visiting Stonehenge and Lake House whilst there (Cockerell Diaries, 26 & 27 July 1902).

[26] Unpublished letter from Pamela Tennant to Sydney Cockerell, 29 December 1906 from Wilsford Manor: 'We have just had Detmar and his mother spending Xmas with us'; amongst the Cockerell Papers, British Museum Manuscripts Collection.

65 (top). Wilsford House, Wilsford-cum-Lake, Wiltshire, from the walled garden. Sketch sent by Detmar Blow to Ernest Gimson during or just before construction. The drawing is inscribed 'To EWG, Wilsford House; built with parts of old material, DB 1904' (Cheltenham Museum and Art Gallery). Wilsford House was known as Wilsford Manor from 1906.

66 (below). Dairyman's Cottage, Wilsford-cum-Lake, Wiltshire.

67 (right). Wilsford Manor. Carpenters, perhaps from Sapperton, in front of the recently-raised trusses over the thatched wing. Roof carpentry and panelling were undertaken by Ernest Gimson.

68 (opposite). Wilsford Manor, virtually complete. The stone parlour is the open loggia on the extreme right beneath the thatched wing. Note the creepers already well established after transplanting (Cheltenham Museum and Art Gallery).

doing things continued at a time when factory production was threatening to make them history. For the same reasons, Pamela Tennant had Gimson make her panelling and design hand-modelled plasterwork for her ceilings.[27] As at Stoneywell he was responsible for the roof carpentry too, the exposed truss blades in her room above the stone parlour showing the marks of the adze, although they were produced in the days of machine milling (67).

As at Hilles later, Blow built no steps up to the front door at Wilsford. Deliberately unpretentious, this is typical of Arts and Crafts houses. The low door is in the same vein but the window introduced above it suggests that more grandiose proposals for an entrance in the Early English Renaissance style, as shown in another of the early sketches Blow sent to Gimson, might only have been abandoned at the last minute. Instead, a simple cartouche appears over the

[27] Nearly all of the panelling has gone and only the designs survive for the plasterwork.

door with crossed fishing rods, the initials of Pamela and Edward and the date, 1906; trout from the Avon that bounds the garden stand on either side as supporters.

Pamela was deliberately unworldly according to Margot, her sister-in-law, who married Herbert Henry Asquith. Although Margot confirms that Wilsford was built 'stone by stone with their own hands',[28] she intended this as no compliment, being of the opinion that Pamela was not 'a citizen of the world'. She implied the same criticism often levelled at the Arts and Crafts architects – that their approach to traditional craftsmanship and the building materials of the local countryside represented an unrealistic attitude not only to craftsmanship and the countryside but to life in a post-industrial society generally.

That Wilsford was indeed built with their own hands was nonetheless much appreciated by those in sympathy with its ideals:

> It is difficult to express the great interest of house-building where almost each stone is chosen and discussed ... There are two kinds of flint when you have knapped them ... The right kind is a flint of a grey agate colouring, and not the dark glossy flints that are like bottle-ends. These last, unless repeatedly cautioned, were invariably the ones preferred by the workmen for use. And many a course was picked out and altered if not perfectly convenienced to the eye. This was possible

[28] Simon Blow, *Broken Blood* (London: Faber & Faber, 1987), p. 131.

> owing to an estimation of time that was Oriental. The winged chariot hurrying near of contract work was absent, for there was no contractor, and with the exception of woodwork in the interior skillfully carried out by Mr Ernest Gimson and his men, the house was built by local labour. Sand was found in a paddock two fields distant, and all the stone of the smaller building that stood on the spot previously was incorporated in the present house.

It was not only the old building material that was saved:

> One beauty the previous house could boast – it had luxuriant masses of creeping plants upon its walls. These, it was resolved, should be saved if thought could do it. They were taken down most carefully, and a temporary wall – a wooden rack – prepared for them at the bottom of the garden ... And so it came about that, long before the house was completed and habitable they were all 'blowing and growing' on the walls ... Even two vines that had dwelled in a conservatory, crouching to man's cultivation, and bearing enormous grapes, allowed themselves to be transplanted outside.[29] (68)

Frank Green was on the spot from the start, a drawing marked for his attention and showing the foundation[30] being dated 2 March 1904. It clearly indicates that before the smaller house that Wilsford Manor replaced, a larger house had stood on the site:

> The foundations of this were in fact discovered when the digging and displacing of the earth began. A low wall was found built in the chequer pattern of stone and flint, characteristic of many Elizabethan buildings in South Wiltshire. Fragments of old mullions were also found. Some of these were saved, and after years of interment set up once more to face the weather in the windows of the present house.[31]

Although Wilsford's triple gables and chequer pattern of stone and flint may seem to spring directly from Lake, Wilsford is no copy, deriving its inspiration from a whole genre of local houses. The chequer walling pattern found in the earlier excavated foundations can be seen again at West Amesbury House, where the Tennants lodged during the building process. Previously they had rented Stockton House, another Elizabethan manor house half way between Wilsford and Clouds and here too the plan is four square with triple gables on each face. Then there was Clouds itself – an inspiration to a whole generation of architects, not just Blow. However Webb's interpretation of Wiltshire

29 'Wilsford Manor, Wiltshire', *Country Life* (29 September 1906), 450–7, p. 454.

30 The drawing that remained in Blow's office was annotated: 'this is only a rough tracing, sent Green which dr.g had to be sent away by evening post.' (RIBA Drawings Collection.)

31 'Wilsford Manor, Wiltshire', p. 450.

Elizabethan at Clouds is freer than Blow's at Wilsford which owes its inspiration ultimately and perhaps most of all to Kelmscott. The stone slated roof may even be a direct reference, tempting Blow for once into a vernacular solecism in an area where stone slates are foreign.

If Pamela Tennant loved her house, she was also very fond of her architect. Her husband Edward, later Lord Glenconner, was not her first love nor her last[32] and Neville Lytton confirms that Blow 'was a man of singularly good looks and there is no doubt that many of his commissions were due to the favour he found with the fair sex'.[33] Indeed the Wyndham sisters were all old friends by the time Wilsford was built and as his grandson later wrote in his account of the Tennant family Detmar 'had a strong Byronic face and he dressed in a slightly wayward manner which would have appealed to her idea of "the artist"... he liked to travel in a gipsy caravan sketching buildings as he went. Detmar's bohemian leanings provided flights of excitement that Pamela's more constricted society world denied her. Detmar fulfilled her concept of the romantic artist, but the physical affair did not last. Finally he was to find Pamela too emotionally demanding, and he had to snuff out his candle when he heard her coming down the passage.'[34]

To Pamela Tennant and Detmar Blow the gipsy caravan was a symbol of an alternative society. One in which Pamela brought up her children, in the hope that they might one day people an idyllic vision of a future in which she saw gipsy caravans wandering down endless Wiltshire lanes. Her children would accompany her on caravanning trips and in poetic fantasy she would be accompanied by one or other of her romantic companions:

> February followed with glittring days,
> Primrose air, and amethyst skies,
> And we two drove through the country ways,
> Of beech-wooded Wiltshire, with deep-seeing eyes.
>
> We shall remember how clear the days were;

32 Amongst her admirers were Harry Cust and Ivor Guest, two of the most brilliant of the Souls, although neither perhaps fulfilled their early promise. Pamela seems to have had a fascination for such men and Osbert Sitwell, a close friend of her eldest son, remembered her sitting room with 'a collection of photographs of the most astonishing rakes and rips in whom she still believed, and whose conduct she would unflaggingly, and with the greatest display of ingenuity defend, or, where defence was plainly outside the capacity of any human being, ignore. All her black sheep, as it were, became swans' (quoted by Simon Blow, *Broken Blood*, p. 135).

33 Neville Lytton, *The English Country Gentleman* (London, Hurst and Blackett, 1925), p. 25.

34 Simon Blow, *Broken Blood*, p. 133.

How far we could see on the downs wide curves
We heard the rooks cawing, high in the still air
By the broad-timbered mill, where the Avon's bed swerves.

The sickle-shaped roads led us on and away,
Over high-shouldered Downs, where the land and sky meet,
By school-grounds where children were shrill in their play,
And pollarded lime trees bordered the street ...

White-roaded Wiltshire, your water-fed ways,
Your cloud-shadowed Down where the green plover cries –
We two shall remember those February days,
When we drove through your by-ways, with deep-seeing eyes.[35]

Caravans were no passing fancy for Blow. He owned his own and used it at Wilsford, perhaps at times as on-site accommodation. Indeed it was in his caravan, on a sketching trip in Suffolk, that he drove into the grounds of Helmingham Hall and met his future wife Winifred, the second daughter of the Hon. Hamilton Tollemache.[36] Blow was forty-three when he married, in 1910, and by then his practice vied with that of Lutyens for supremacy in the country house market.[37] But to be still on sketching trips in gipsy caravans at this stage of his career suggests a man who did not readily let go of youthful ideals. In 1913 Augustus John, another gipsy aficionado, drew two portraits of Blow (69). John's own identification with a gipsy lifestyle outlasted Blow's, but although at differing stages their careers both took on an itinerant aspect, in many ways Blow's early way of working was closer to the nomadic ideal.

According to John Betjeman 'Arts and Crafts cottages were the last rumble of a farm cart in an uneven country lane'[38] and certainly the cottages that Blow built at the turn of the century have a sense of belonging, to whatever place the uneven country lane may have led him. Two examples, on site at the same time in about 1900 but in very different parts of the country, demonstrate this sensitivity to the location. South of Wilsford and over the river in Netton, behind clipped yew hedges, stands a thatched cottage built in 'sun dried mud'[39]

35 Pamela Tennant, 'The Avon Valley', *Country Life* (18 Feb. 1911).

36 Clive Aslet, *The Last Country Houses* (New Haven and London: Yale University Press, 1982), p. 247.

37 On Oct 26 1912, *Country Life* published a 30-page *Architectural Supplement* to its magazine entitled 'The Work of Mr Detmar Blow and Mr Fernand Billerey'. Even Lutyens never achieved this.

38 John Betjeman's introduction to *English Cottages* by Tony Evans and Candida Lycett-Green (London: Weidenfield & Nicholson, 1982), p. 154.

39 As Blow himself described it on an uncatalogued drawing in the RIBA Drawings Collection. It was known as Miss Bramwell's cottage and completed by 1902 (a

69. Detmar Blow, one of a pair of portraits by Augustus John, 1913.

(see plate 70, overleaf), perhaps the earliest of the Arts and Crafts attempts to revive cob construction. Meanwhile in Norfolk, close to the stables at Happisburgh Manor, another cottage called St Annes was under construction (71). The contrast between the two is that of regional variation, and both are truly raised from the soil on which they stood – 'of the soil racey' as the Arts and Crafts architects themselves termed it.[40] The differences between them are the very

---

photograph of that date survives amongst the Blow family papers at Hilles). It was built under Blow's direction by estate labour for Mr Greville at Heale House, itself extensively altered and enlarged by Blow in about 1910.

40 Gavin Stamp, 'Of the Soil Racey – Arts and Crafts Rogues in North Norfolk', *Victorian Society Notes* (24 April 1971), quoted in Roderick Gradidge, *Dream Houses* (London, Constable, 1980), p. xviii.

70 (above). Heale Cottage, Netton, Wiltshire. Designed and built by Detmar Blow in chalk cob, about 1900.

71 (below). St Anne's, Happisburgh, Norfolk. A cottage at the gates to Happisburgh Manor, built in local stone from the beach and thought to date from 1900. Another cottage by Blow, built in 1902 in similar construction nearby at Bacton, was washed into the sea.

differences between south Wiltshire itself and the coast of north-east Norfolk.

On a larger scale there is a comparison to be drawn too between Wilsford Manor and Little Ridge (72), the other Wiltshire house Blow built between 1904 and 1906. Basil Stallybrass was in charge on site, working with James Neale probably as his foreman mason. Little Ridge was rooted in the same tradition and locality as Wilsford and so, according to the rule that made the Netton and Happisburgh cottages so different, Little Ridge and Fonthill are similar. The archaeological approach, adopted at Wilsford to identify the foundations of an earlier house and its flint and stone chequer construction, was carried a stage further at Little Ridge. For Little Ridge was not to be a new house at all: 'It was decided to re-erect what remained of the old manor house at Berwick St Leonard, distant about three miles, and Mr Detmar Blow's professional advice was sought to bring to the old ruin a new life and yet retain the spirit of the old.'[41] Like Wilsford and its antecedents, the manor house at Berwick St Leonard stood four square with triple gables (73):

> In 1905 it stood gaunt, roofless and derelict - merely an outside shell, and even of that, part was fallen and all decayed. The material, however, was the fine stone of the district, in good preservation and beautifully weathered by time. It was therefore decided that the remnant should form part of the new building, and be the model for the rest. The most accurate measured drawings were first taken of the irregularity of the old mason's work in order that this might be retained. Then each stone was taken down, labelled, penned in hurdles, removed to the new site and set up again in complete harmony with its former position and appearance ... [42]

Unfortunately Little Ridge no longer stands, making this contemporary account doubly valuable:

> Mr Blow [felt] secure that the fragmentary skeleton of the Berwick St Leonard manor house could be re-vivified and re-clothed as a modern house on a modern site and yet not lose its ancient savour. What it should be like his well-practised mind's eye could see. But that is not all that is necessary. How often a client, thoroughly pleased with his architect's inviting plans and charming drawings, is yet much disappointed in the ultimate result! Somehow all the charm seems gone; there is something harsh, awkward and repellent that has been introduced, although, seemingly, the plan has been carried out. And

41 'Little Ridge, Wiltshire, A Seat of Mr Hugh Morrison' [no author credited but attributed to Lawrence Weaver by Simon Blow in 'Blow by Blow' the story of the house's destruction in *The Guardian* 24 Feb 1979], *Country Life* (26 October 1912), 566–74, p. 566.

42 Ibid., p. 568.

72. Little Ridge, Fonthill, Wiltshire. The south-west front (*Country Life*).

73. The Manor House, Berwick St Leonard, Wiltshire, from a watercolour by John Buckler, 1804. The house was dismantled in 1903 for re-errection to form the basis of Little Ridge in the neighbouring parish of Fonthill (WANHS).

this may not be the architect's fault beyond his falling in with the client's demand that the 'job' should be 'contracted' for and the lowest tender accepted without due inquiry made or even a passing thought given as to whether the builder and his men either have or are capable of acquiring any understanding of what the architect has in mind. Thus tone and texture are missed; form is very slightly but quite disastrously warped; there will be something in the laying of the stones and in the working of the timber that falsifies the whole original conception ... Assuredly an architect must realise that his work will be a failure if there is not some measure of mutual understanding and some sympathy of aim between him and those who execute his designs. No-one knows better than Mr Blow the difficulty of wedding the airy spirit of three centuries ago to the sturdy need of today, and no-one has learnt how to overcome it more successfully.

At Little Ridge he realised what he wanted was at hand. He had only to seek and find. Masons, carpenters,[43] plasterers, some already knowledgeable, all quite receptive, were collected, and the old-new house took shape excellently well ... No form of decoration was more popular in Wiltshire three hundred years ago than plasterwork, and therefore this was largely resorted to at Little Ridge. Not, however, in the form of exact reproduction of old examples, but in new designs founded on precedent. Mr Stallybrass, who also acted as clerk of the works to Mr Blow, was the chief craftsman and modeller[44] ... The birds and animals seen in several [of the schemes] recall the delightful manner of mediaeval beasts. Ceilings of varied and original design are to be found in most of the principal rooms ... Plaster, too, was used for some of the over-mantels, recalling many an example dating from Elizabethan days.[45] (74)

43 'The dining room is lined with oak panelling, with lightly-carved stiles, that recalls the days of the old manor house. A recessed cupboard, still standing in its ruinous walls, had formed a cache where a remnant of old panelling was discovered surviving. This was faithfully reproduced - Stephens, the joiner, with his men, carrying out the work to perfection by treating in traditional manner oak from trees felled long before in the park and seasoned in the estate yard.' *Country Life* (26 October 1912), p. 573.

44 Stallybrass 'was assisted by most capable local men - by Charles Lamb and his son, of an old race of plasterers who could model and cast anything, and who, though seemingly spoilt by modern influences, were only too ready to be brought back to the right traditional lines; and so enthusiastic did they become over this effective but inexpensive form of decoration, that they perhaps outstrode the imagination of their forbears in the craft', *Country Life* (26 October 1912) p. 573.

45 Ibid., p. 573.

The garden at Little Ridge was laid out on a formal Elizabethan plan contrived by constructing a stupendous rampart on the downhill side of the house to give the flat terrace needed. Later Blow built such a rampart again at Hilles and here he repeated the pattern of the Berwick St Leonard porch too. In fact the original staircase from Little Ridge was salvaged by Blow for Hilles when the Morrisons extended their house for the second time. It survived the fire that so nearly destroyed Hilles and although a little charred in places still gives something of the flavour of the now vanished Wiltshire house from which it came. It was these extensions, in 1908[46] and again after 1912,[47] that were responsible in the end for the destruction of the whole. They turned what had been a house the size of Wilsford, still serving its purpose today as a family home, into the sort of Edwardian dinosaur whose future was uncertain as soon as the 'House in the Country' superseded the 'Country House' in the public imagination (75).

The enlarged Little Ridge was re-named Fonthill House and inherited the curse that has turned the Fonthill estate into a graveyard for houses that bear its name. James Wyatt's Fonthill Abbey, built for William Beckford, is the best

46 Ibid., p. 572.

47 Simon Blow, 'Blow by Blow', *The Guardian* (24 February 1979).

74 (opposite). The dining room at Little Ridge. The plasterwork is attributed to Basil Stallybrass (CL); and 75 (above): Fonthill House, Wiltshire, from a painting by C. Geoffrey Dechaume, 1925. This view shows the enlarged Little Ridge extended to either side of the original centre section formed from the rebuilt Berwick St Leonard Manor House.

known but not the first or the last to go before Little Ridge. In 1830 Hugh Morrison's grandfather had bought all that remained standing of the abandoned Fonthill Splendens, a nearby ruin that had preceded Beckford's Abbey, repairing and rebuilding part of it for himself. The tower of Wyatt's extravaganza had itself collapsed by then and Fonthill Abbey was never rebuilt, Beckford having sold it before the disaster and moved to Bath. One afternoon in about 1843 Hugh Morrison's father walked over to look at the ruin to find another visitor there before him:

> An old gentleman, mounted on a sturdy little cob had halted some way off, and he was gazing at the wood and at the ruins in so absorbed a fashion that he never observed the young man who had come upon him. It was William Beckford. He had ridden over from Bath to look for the last time on all that remained of the most stupendous of all the follies that he and his contemporaries had set upon a hundred hill tops.[48]

[48] Edith Olivier, *Four Victorian Ladies of Wiltshire*, p. 47. The estate had been split soon after the abbey collapsed, its ruins going to the Marquis of Westminster whilst the majority of the estate had gone to the Morrisons. Westminster built himself a Scottish baronial mansion with William Burn as architect, the house eventually coming down in 1955 after being requisitioned by the army in 1940. The re-born

76. The present Fonthill House by Trenwith Wills, standing above Blow's bastioned garden.

Blow's Little Ridge ignored the gothic romance of Wyatt's work and the classical collonades of Fonthill Splendens. It harked back instead to an even earlier Fonthill, a dignified Elizabethan house of gables and mullioned windows. Despite this stylistic disassociation with its immediate predecessors, his house fared no better, becoming in fact the sixth great house called Fonthill and the sixth to fall. That it should have survived until 1972 makes its loss all the sadder.[49] A fire that had destroyed the remains of Fonthill Splendens became confused with a supposed fire in the Blow house; the Department of the Environment, apparently thinking it already gutted, failed to spot-list and allowed it to be demolished. A few months later, Sir Nikolaus Pevsner received a letter from the Ministry clarifying the confusion but too late; Blow's

Fonthill Splendens, rescued and extended with Papworth as architect, was abandoned after a fire at the turn of the century. Along with his haberdashery fortune, Morrison had inherited a collections of paintings which had outgrown Fonthill Splendens. These survived the fire and Little Ridge was commissioned to re-house it (Simon Blow, 'Blow by Blow').

49 As John Harris pointed out in the book that accompanied an exhibition at the V & A: *The Destruction of the Country House*, Roy Strong, John Harris and Marcus Binney (London: Thomas & Hudson, 1974), p. 100.

77. Breccles Hall, Norfolk, the west front showing the rebuilt porch (CL).

bastioned garden was all that remained and now a smaller neo-Georgian house by Trenwith Wills, ironically a pupil of Blow's, stands on the site (76).

If Little Ridge and Wilsford share a Wiltshire genealogy, Breccles Hall is back in a Norfolk idiom (77), albeit different from the one exemplified by Blow's work at Happisburgh. Blow and Stallybrass worked here in 1907 for Charles Bateman-Hanbury. Of similar date to Berwick St Leonard, Breccles Hall had fallen to the status of a tenant farmhouse and much was ruinous, but Mr Hanbury wanted to live there himself and Blow considered re-instating the hall to its full height, taking out an upper floor inserted at a later date. Work had already started by the time Blow wrote to the SPAB about the proposal and Thackeray Turner visited him there 'with Mr Stallybrass, who is in charge of the work.'[50] The SPAB advised against the reinstatement of the hall and it remained at its reduced height as a result.

Nonetheless the north wing was rebuilt, the entrance front re-fenestrated and a simple brick gabled service wing added. They excavated the position of the old porch too, finding below-ground evidence of octagonal corner piers and reconstructing a replacement, simple and unadorned:

50 Unpublished letter from Detmar Blow to Thackeray Turner, 9 February (? unclear) 1907, SPAB Archive: Breccles Hall file (Norfolk).

> There has been no renewal of anything that was not ruinous; no imitative or conjectural replacing of decayed details not important to the structure; no unnecessary removal of features added to the original building at a later time and in a different manner. The house is not a sheet of paper scrawled over by the self-laudatory comments of an ignorant modern architect, as are so many 'completely restored' fabrics. It is a closely-written historical manuscript, and anyone with an eye at all practised in these matters can walk round the house and easily read, in general terms, its architectural past.[51]

The work by Blow and Stallybrass indicates their shared belief in the importance of a building's archaeology, both above ground and below. It was ahead of its time, such an informed approach to conservation being less common than it should be, even today. As at Fonthill, further alterations and additions were made later but the fate of the house was happier. Although demolition was rumoured when Breccles was sold in 1954, it fell into sympathetic hands.[52] The later work was this time by Lutyens, who described it to Lady Emily: 'An old tumbledown house restored by Blow! in a tumbledown fashion. I am glad I did not do it – as he did it! It made me feel lonely.'[53] Nikolaus Pevsner disagreed: 'The house was extremely well repaired by Detmar Blow shortly after 1900 and added to and (less well) altered by Lutyens after 1918.'[54]

Stallybrass left Blow soon after completing his work at Breccles Hall. A craftsman as well as a capable conservation architect, it is a shame that more of his craftwork does not survive. His plasterwork at Fonthill appears, from photographs, to have been of a quality that would have placed him with Norman Jewson as a worthy follower in the tradition of Gimson and Bankart. Fortunately, one interior remains to show his capabilities: The Old Bell House at Ludford, Shropshire. Formerly an inn serving travellers locked out when the city gates of Ludlow, over the river, were closed at nightfall, Stallybrass worked here for Henry Mahler in 1909 and 1910. Stripping away nineteenth-century work, he modified the plan, repaired the old structure, laid out a new garden (78) and fitted out the interior:

> The plasterwork is almost all new. The hall ceiling is in a style characteristic of Ludlow... . The drawing room ceiling is an echo of the famous old example at the Feathers Inn, and each compartment is

51 *Country Life* (20 Nov 1909), p. 710

52 The new owner, who bought it for £3,000, told the *Eastern Daily Press*: 'I just could not see the old place demolished' (undated press cutting in the SPAB archive).

53 Letter from Edwin Lutyens to his wife Emily, 14 October 1917, in Clayre Percy and Jane Ridley (eds), *The Letters of Edwin Lutyens* (London: Collins, 1985), p. 356.

54 Nikolaus Pevsner, *Norfolk: North-West and South*, Buildings of England (Harmondsworth: Penguin Books, 1962), p. 96.

78 (above). The Old Bell House and the mill beyond, at Ludford, Herefordshire, from the north-west; from a photograph taken before 1914, in *Small Country Houses, Their Repair and Enlargement*, by Lawrence Weaver.

79 (left). The drawing room at the Old Bell House with plasterwork by Basil Stallybrass (same source).

devoted to a different tree, which shelters the bird or beast that lives amid its branches. There is the oak with the squirrel, and the willow with its kingfisher (79). The new panel over the dining room fireplace shows a bell and the initials of Mr & Mrs Mahler contrived in bell ropes. All this work was designed and modelled by Mr Stallybrass himself, who closely superintended everything that was done, with the aid of his foreman and jack-of-all-trades, Mr H. Gibbon, who cast the plaster, laid the bricks and tiled the roof.[55]

55 Lawrence Weaver, *Small Country Houses – Their Repair and Enlargement* (London:

The garden Stallybrass laid out on the bank high above the Teme is small in scale with changes in level, terraced walks, walls and hedges. Its compartments echo the divisions in the drawing room ceiling and both plasterwork and garden in turn reflect the framework and character of the house itself.

Other work by Stallybrass at this time includes garden suburb cottages at Fallings Park in Wolverhampton,[56] designed within an estate plan laid out by Blow for Sir Richard Paget before 1908. Fallings Park was the first garden suburb to be initiated by a private landowner, rather than a local authority or a society of public utility, but only about seventy-five of the 1000 houses planned were built. The lay-out was innovative and anticipates more recent thinking, with footpath access to amenities such as laundry, playground and gardens carefully separated from traffic circulation.[57] The Stallybrass cottages have the low eaves and sweeping roofs characteristic of much of the work of Parker and Unwin at Letchworth or Hampstead. Blow too maintained an interest in such work, designing thatched cottages for Letchworth in partnership with Gimson[58] and taking part in *Country Life*'s 1912 holiday cottage competition[59] for which Herbert North, his assistant at Tintagel, also entered (see Ch.8). North's entry has Gothic touches (80), Blow's being simpler and thatched (81).

A final example of the care and thoroughness that Basil Stallybrass put into his work is to be found at Quennell House, Plaistow in Sussex (82). This small timber-framed farmhouse, built around a massive brick chimney stack, was typical of many in the home counties, sold in increasing numbers to those who sought traditional village houses within easy reach of London before the First World War. Its faithful repair was carried out by Stallybrass in accordance with the precepts laid down by the SPAB.[60] He would not rebuild the subsiding frame but raised the sunken structure using screw jacks, having inserted damp proof coursing and laid concrete below all the floors,

> the stone paving flags being numbered and relaid in their old positions. It is practically impossible to detect that the stone roof slabs have ever been disturbed, because not only were they numbered in like manner before being taken down, but exact note was made of the

Country Life, 1914), pp. 67–9.

56 Lawrence Weaver, *The Country Life Book of Cottages* (London: Country Life, 1913), p. 221.

57 J. S. Nettlefold, *Practical Housing* (Letchworth: Garden City Press, 1908), pp. 96–7.

58 RIBA drawings collection: 'Cottages at Letchworth' amongst Detmar Blow drawings, as yet uncatalogued, marked 'Detmar Blow and Ernest Gimson, 9 Kings Bench Walk, Temple and Daneway House, Sapperton, Cirencester.' Inserted in a different hand are the words 'and Fernand Billerey'. Dated [unclear] August 1914.

59 Lawrence Weaver, *The Country Life Book of Cottages*, pp. 124, 128, 130–1.

60 Lawrence Weaver, *Small Country Houses – Their Repair and Enlargement*, p. 12.

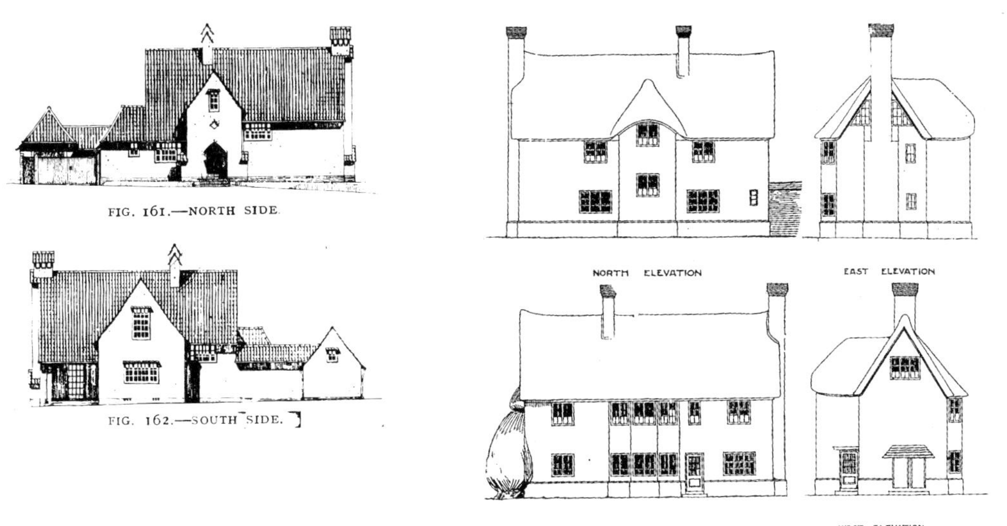

80 (left) Design for a holiday cottage by Herbert North, for the Country Life Holiday Cottage Competition (*Country Life Book of Country Cottages*, 1913); and 81 (right) Design for a country cottage by Detmar Blow and Fernand Billerey (same source).

82 (below). Quennell House, Plaistow, Sussex, view from the east (*Small Country Houses, their Repair and Enlargement*, 1914).

conformation of the old surface ... It must not be supposed, however, that this is a kind of work which can be done by contract with a written specification as the sole lamp to the feet of the local builder, and the architect visiting the site every week or so, as is usual where new works are in progress. Mr Stallybrass was on the spot the whole time and personally supervised every scrap of the work; and this is the ideal arrangement to ensure that close attention to detail is the essence of dealing successfully with an old building.[61]

In 1914 Stallybrass went into partnership in Plymouth. His move completed a historical circle for his partner was Edmund Sedding, nephew of Blow's mentor J. D. Sedding. Having won a competition for a new church in Newton Abbot, Edmund Sedding had been invited to design a cathedral for Dunedin in New Zealand in 1906. Stallybrass joined the practice as the cathedral started on site but although an involvement in its construction might have appealed to him, the scheme was built under the local direction of a New Zealand architect, Basil Hooper.

The majority of Edmund Sedding's practice was church work in the West Country and the introduction of Basil Stallybrass into the practice reinforced the connections with the SPAB that J. D. Sedding had forged many years earlier.[62] Immediately after he moved to Plymouth Stallybrass corresponded with the Society concerning the re-roofing of Tregony Church in Cornwall and later SPAB casework included a church tower at High Bickington and work at Gidleigh Castle on the edge of Dartmoor near Lutyens' Castle Drogo. Then seven years into a building programme that was to last twenty, here Lutyens too had abandoned conventional contract procedure for the way of working that Stallybrass had learned through Blow. Building work had begun under contract, with a clerk of works from London, but at an early stage his place was taken by J. C. Walker, a Yorkshireman who combined the offices of clerk of works and master mason, making full size templates from Lutyens' instructions.[63] After the first year every stone was laid by two men alone, Devon masons named Cleeve and Dewdney.

Only five miles from Castle Drogo a house attributed to Blow exhibits far fewer craft-generated qualities. But the provenance of North Bovey Manor (83), completed in 1907 for the Second Viscount Hambleden, millionaire proprietor of W. H. Smith the newsagent, is clouded.[64] A later visit by Stallybrass to North

61 L. Weaver, *Small Country Houses – Their Repair and Enlargement*, pp. 14 and 17.

62 When Thackeray Turner, concerned about a recommendation to straighten a leaning arcade at Broadhempston church, wrote to Edmund Sedding, he recalled the family connections: 'I remember very well the pleasure of meeting you at your uncle's house' (unpublished letter from Thackeray Turner to Edmund Sedding, 22 June 1896, SPAB Archive: Broadhempston Church file, Devon). Presumably the uncle referred to was J. D. Sedding [the work at Broadhempston church was mentioned in *The Builder* (6 June 1896) according to a clipping in the SPAB archive].

63 Christopher Hussey, *The Life of Sir Edwin Lutyens* (London: Country Life, 1950), p. 225.

64 The Blow attribution appears to derive from the architectural department of W. H. Smith & Sons and from a letter in *Country Life* from Warren Davis, headed 'Manor

Bovey, in 1919, was in no way associated with the Manor. He was in fact reporting to the SPAB on work to the church, coincidentally by Charles Nicholson, himself a pupil of J. D. Sedding. Living at Horrabridge, on the Plymouth side of the moor, Stallybrass had time on his hands after a serious illness. He kept his hand in with a little church work,[65] but in 1921 the SPAB were told that Stallybrass was still convalescing, now in Sicily.[66] He never recovered. The SPAB heard of his death from Humphrey Gimson, nephew of Ernest and son of Sydney Gimson of Stoneywell, who had been tidying up the loose ends of the practice because Edmund Sedding had died too, earlier the same year.[67] The office was closed down and a letter from the SPAB to Humphrey Gimson concerning future arrangements was answered, fittingly enough, from Stoneywell, the cottage Blow had been building when Stallybrass first joined him at Clare twenty two years before.

House Mystery', published on 15 January 1981, p. 127. There is, however, no mention of this house in any of Blow's obituaries or in the list of works undertaken by the Blow/Billerey partnership at the RIBA. This list was prepared by Billerey himself. More to the point, North Bovey does not appear in Blow's own list of works, submitted with his Fellowship nomination papers to the RIBA in September 1906. The foundation stone at North Bovey is dated a year earlier ('Laid WHS Oct 1905') and a new house of such proportion from such an important client would have been a prestigious commission - not the sort of thing to leave out when applying for Fellowship of the Institute. Another commemorative stone, set low down but in a different part of the house, reads 'Walter E. Mills Arch.t Oxford'. The house was extended later and its Great Hall floored through at first floor level but the original build has a restrained and dignified neo-Elizabethan central section which appears on both the entrance and garden fronts. There are good interiors too, despite the alterations. The rear lodges or gate houses, square on plan but set on the diagonal either side of the gateway are, like the garden building to the west of the house, picturesque. The garden layout is a grand one, with terraces looking over a magnificent Dartmoor valley, its stream landscaped to form a sheet of water, visible from the house. If Blow was involved it seems likely that he was not involved from the start, that his work did not pre-date September 1906 and that his contribution was not substantial. If he was involved after 1906 it is curious that the meticulous Billerey did not record it in his list of partnership works at the RIBA.

65 For example, at High Bickington where his involvement came about as a result of an earlier visit for the SPAB. Stallybrass had suggested re-bonding the tower buttresses and his correspondence with the SPAB continued for some time (SPAB Archive, High Bickington file).

66 Albert R Powys (1881–1936) had succeeded Thackeray Turner as Secretary to the SPAB in 1911.

67 A. Stuart Gray, *Edwardian Architects* (London: Duckworth, 1985), p. 324.

83. North Bovey Manor, Devon. The entrance elevation.

84. Kelling Place, Holt, Norfolk. The garden front (CL).

Chapter 7
ANOTHER ARCHITECT ERRANT
A. Randall Wells

Digging fresh earth with the scent of new cut wood in the air
W. R. Lethaby, 'Education in Building', *RIBA Journal*, 1901

Between 1901 and 1907 Randall Wells (1877–1942) built three of the finest free style churches the Arts and Crafts movement produced: one designed by W. R. Lethaby, one by E. S. Prior and one by himself. Wells worked for Lethaby first and it may have been Detmar Blow who made the introduction, for early in 1901 Blow wrote to the SPAB thanking them for electing Wells and Stallybrass to their membership, among whom Lethaby was a key figure.[1] Stallybrass was already working with Blow but although Randall Wells's father Arthur was an architect in Hastings, little more is known of his early architectural background and if Wells had no previous experience, he would certainly have needed a recommendation from someone Lethaby trusted.

Blow had just completed Happisburgh Manor and there is a dynamic, unrestrained quality in the interpretration of the Norfolk tradition here that links Happisburgh with another house, Kelling Place, also known as Home Place and Voewood (84), built near the Norfolk coast at Kelling between 1904 and 1905. Its architect, Edward Prior, was known to Blow and his circle. Prior's collaborator and site architect, Randall Wells was even more closely associated with the group and Wells would have known Happisburgh before working at Kelling.

Wells's work with Edward Prior, at Kelling Place and afterwards at Roker church in Sunderland, kept him busy for three years and the nature of the partnership, as with Gimson and Blow at Stoneywell, was peculiar to the working methods of this group of Arts and Crafts architects. Wells is named as co-architect to Prior on drawings for Roker Church but although no drawings survive for Kelling Place, on the back of a photograph there too is the pencilled inscription 'architects E S Prior and A Randall Wells'.[2] There is even an

1 Unpublished letter from Detmar Blow to Thackeray Turner, 16 Jan 1901, SPAB Archive: Stonehenge file.

2 Nikolaus Pevsner and Enid Radcliffe, 'Randall Wells', *Architectural Review*, 136

85. The Barn at Exmouth, as seen in an early photograph (BAL).

indication that a third man, William Comley Roles, contributed, although his involvement as clerk of works appears to have been largely with the landscaping and not with the house.[3]

The houses at Happisburgh and Kelling both use a fully developed butterfly plan but there are similarities that go further. Shared Arts and Crafts roots in the Norfolk soil account for the local materials chosen for both houses, but it is the restless way the materials are used in both that mark them out and suggest that the collaboration between the free style Arts and Crafts exponents may

(1964), 336–8.

3 William Comley Roles came from Romsey in Hampshire and practiced there in a long and varied career. He was employed as clerk of works by Lutyens at Great Maytham in about 1908 and by Prior both at Voewood and at St Oswalds, Parkstone in Dorset (Frank Green, 'William Comley Roles of Romsey', *Hampshire Field Club and Archaeological Society Newsletter*, New Series, 14 (Autumn 1990), p. 26).

have been more complex. For in fact the affinities between the two are in many ways as close as those between Kelling Place and Prior's earlier butterfly plan house, The Barn, in Exmouth (85).

The collective design process typifies much of the output of the Wandering Architects. To a greater or lesser degree there was a shared responsibility for the designs for Mill Hill, Long Copse, Stoneywell and Happisburgh also. This co-operative way of working reflects the shared aspirations and lack of concern for personal recognition amongst the young architects at the SPAB and the Art Workers Guild. Together they formed a design school, by a collective achievement if not by a collective name. Indeed there is a developmental thread that runs through their projects from Mill Hill, via the Old Post Office at Tintagel, Long Copse and Stoneywell (see 23), through cranked plans and butterflies, and on to Happisburgh and Kelling Place. This thread ties together a shared evolution that is built up, like the best team efforts, in such a way that it becomes hard to establish individual contributions.

Another common aspect was their stance over the way architecture was defined and perceived. Randall Wells never joined the RIBA. Like others he thought the Institute was sacrificing the art of architecture to the god of professionalism. Norman Shaw, his pupil Lethaby and many of their circle felt strongly enough about the issue to resign membership or, in the case of younger men in the 1890s, not to apply in the first place. Detmar Blow was among these but like most of the others he eventually came to terms with the situation, joining as a fellow in 1906. Wells did not, becoming the first representative on the Admission Committee under the Architects Registration Act on behalf of 'unattached architects' – those outside the membership of the Institute.

Certainly the working methods employed by Prior and Wells in Kelling owed little to the conventional contractual procedures then in use within the building industry. The building of Voewood from scratch on a seven-acre turnip field is described in a contemporary account:

> the scheme began with gardeners' lodges and a walled vegetable garden ... In 1904 orchards were planted and a sunk flower garden was begun with terraces and garden houses and at the same time the house, the dairy and stables were put in hand, and the whole was ready for occupation in under two years from the start. These works have not been carried out in the ordinary way by a general contractor ... The general building was done under the superintendance of Mr Randall Wells and Mr Blower,[4] who employed men and purchased materials as

[4] Similarities between the names of Blower and Detmar Blow are coincidental but were responsible for previously published connections (Alastair Service, *Edwardian Architecture* [London: Thomas & Hudson, 1977], p. 92), linking Blow with Kelling. Mr Blower was a local bricklayer who started the work on site for Prior before the

> required ... The material for the walls was in the ground, and how far and in what way it would prove serviceable could only be ascertained by making extended excavations. An acre in extent and six foot in depth was therefore designed to be dug out as a sunk flower garden ... there were obtained by the digging pebble facings for the wall, and ballast for all kinds of concrete, as well as a good deal of building sand and material for road-making and garden paths. In addition the surface earth was used for terraces, and there remained several loads of ballast which were sold to the local authorities.[5]

Another pupil of Norman Shaw's and one of the most radical architects amongst the founder-members of the Art Workers Guild, Edward Prior (1852–1932) believed passionately that craftsmanship and the simple necessities of building must replace style.[6] At Kelling Place it was his aim to achieve an indigenous building in an area with scarce availability of materials and his adherence to true Arts & Crafts principles under such adverse conditions is reflected in the otherwise perverse procedure of excavating and sorting for re-use several thousand tonnes of turnip field. Something of Wells's own character may also be behind such a process. A colleague later described him as: 'Full of drive and enthusiasm'[7] and certainly Wells was a man of innovative and resourceful disposition. Come what may, the result of this collective and eccentrically ingenious way of working exactly reflects the means employed. Pevsner describes its originality as fanatic and in some ways considers it to be like the work of Gaudi. Certainly there is an expressionism in the best of the Arts and Crafts free style work, seen perhaps most clearly at Kelling Place, that supports his case.

The continuing contemporary account provides more details of the building methods used:

> the house and garden walls were built as concrete masses without planking, and faced with larger pebbles. The lintels, chimney stacks, and jambs of the upper windows were constructed with tiles made from the Norfolk clay, which burns naturally to buff and pink shades, matching the colour of the pebbles. The roofing was of pantiles of the same local shade... Internally oak was used simply and constructionally; for this use it could be locally obtained at a cost hardly above that

---

arrival of Wells. [Home Place, Holt, anon, *Country Life* (6 Nov 1909), 634–42, see p. 638].

5 Kelling Place, Holt, Norfolk, anon, *Architectural Review*, 19 (1906), 70–82, see p. 70.

6 'Church Building as it is and as it might be', E. S. Prior, *Architectural Review*, 4 (1898), p. 158.

7 According to W. J. Palmer-Jones who in turn served Randall Wells as clerk of works in about 1913 (Pevsner and Radcliffe, 'Randall Wells', p. 367).

> of good deal. The walls and ceilings of the principal rooms have been left ready for a scheme of painted decoration. In these ways and others the work has differed from that ordinarily specified to contractors; but, carried out without contract, the house has been built cheaply, quickly and the best use has been made of the materials to hand. In order to secure such a result experiments had first to be made, and the gardeners' lodges and the garden walls were designed as tests in the use and cost of the materials. Quantities were then taken out for the house itself and priced in accordance with the experience gained. In the result the expenditure on it has been kept to the sum of the estimate, £8,000. No contractor would have taken the work at this price from drawings, for it would have been impossible to have shown him how he was to vary his ordinary methods so as to build in the ways intended.[8]

The Norfolk coast was a fashionable place for seaside houses at the turn of the century. The butterfly plan became fashionable too, not just in north Norfolk, although here its advantages were clear. At Happisburgh the plan was adopted 'to afford some warmed recesses and shelter from blustering winds'[9] and thus it was equally well suited at Kelling Place where cold winds blow in from the North Sea. The evolution of the butterfly plan is an interesting one and stems from Prior's master, Norman Shaw. Shaw remodelled an old house called Chesters in 1891, adding three diagonal wings to make three quarters of an X plan. It was ingenious and like all of Shaw's work had a great influence on the younger architects in his office, including Lethaby and Prior. The Barn, the first entirely new butterfly-planned house, was designed by Prior and built in Exmouth in 1896 with few, if any, working drawings, Prior closely supervising the construction and staying close at hand at his father-in-law's rectory in Bridport.[10] The Barn had only a single pair of butterfly wings and can be seen as a further development of the cranked plans used by Gimson and by Powell at Stoneywell and Long Copse but although Prior exhibited an unbuilt butterfly plan with two pairs of wings at the Royal Academy soon afterwards, Happisburgh was the first double-butterfly or full X plan house built.

8 Kelling Place, Holt, Norfolk, anon, *Architectural Review*, 19 (1906), pp. 70 and 82.

9 Lawrence Weaver, *Small Country Houses of Today*, Second Series (London: Country Life, 1919), p. 24.

10 Both before and after The Barn, Prior presented rough clay models of unexecuted butterfly-plan houses at the Royal Academy. The architectural critics were shocked both by the radical planning and Prior's presentation: 'It is comparatively rough in appearance and revolutionary in its tendancies. We do not like to suggest anything so much below the dignity of "professional" architecture but we strongly suspect Mr Prior of having made the model with his own hands. He is quite capable of it. Most interesting ...' *The Builder*, Vol. 68 (1895), p. 323, quoted by Margaret Richardson, *Architects of the Arts and Crafts Movement* (London, Trefoil, 1983), p. 54.

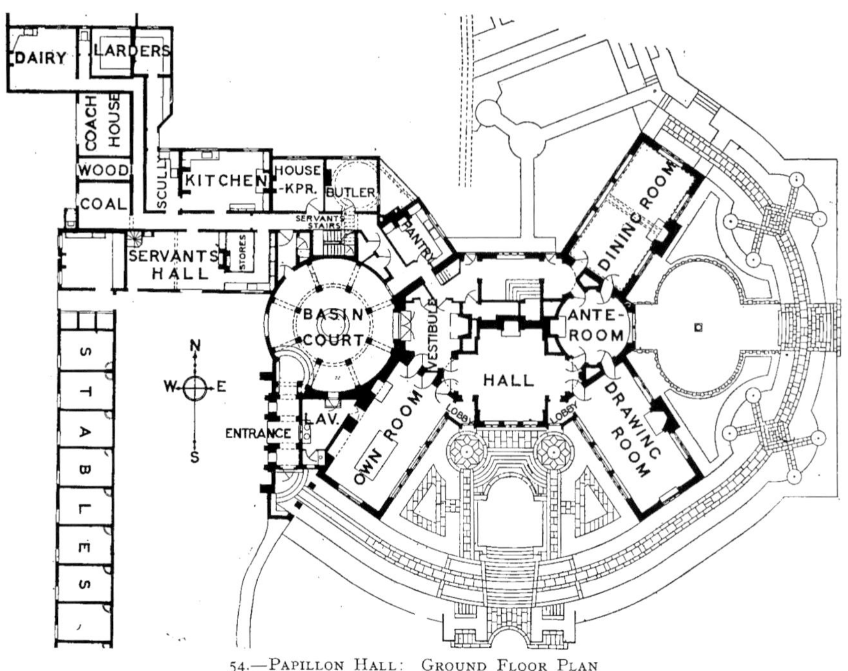

86. Papillon Hall, designed by Edwin Lutyens. The ground floor plan, from *Lutyens Houses and Gardens* by Lawrence Weaver, 1921.

By the time Wells was building Kelling Place in 1904–05 there were already several other butterfly houses including Rosebriers in Llanfairfechan [see (102) and ch. 8] by Herbert North (*c.*1901), Papillon Hall by Lutyens in 1902–04 (86), and How Green House by Robert Weir Schultz in 1904–1905. Schultz also used a butterfly plan for another house near Edenbridge in Kent at about the same time (87). Another of Shaw's pupils, he would have derived inspiration from Shaw's work at Chesters as would Lutyens who had seen that house for the first time only a few weeks before gaining the commission for Papillon Hall in Leicestershire.[11] Papillon was the name of an earlier house on the site, built by David Papillon, jeweller to Charles I and the name, coupled with his chance visit to Chesters, whose planning he considered a masterpiece, was the sort of coincidence that would have made a butterfly plan irresistible to the pun-loving Lutyens. The earlier house was said to have been haunted by a Spanish dancer, the story being that if her shoes left the place it would be destroyed. Lutyens rose to the occassion and designed a safe niche for the shoes in his new house but they were stolen when Papillon Hall was occupied by American troops

[11] Christopher Hussey, *The Life of Sir Edwin Lutyens* (London: Country Life, 1950), p. 121, quoted by Jill Franklin, *The Gentleman's Country House and its Plan 1835–1914* (London, Routledge, 1981), p. 233.

87. 'House near Edenbridge, Kent. Robert Weir Schulz, Architect', 1904.

during World War II. Violent hauntings were said to have followed and the house was pulled down as a consequence.[12]

Kelling Place and Happisburgh share constructional similarities as well as planning. Both made extensive use of concrete; Happisburgh sits on a vast concrete raft and its upper floors are concrete too.[13] As a result it has not suffered the fates of other Arts and Craft thatched houses. Prior's Barn, Gimson's Leasowes, Stoneywell and Blow's Hilles all suffered fires and none today retains its thatch. Kelling was never thatched but the first floor was of 'fine concrete without steel joists ... reinforced with iron chainage.'[14]

Another Arts and Crafts thatch survival is Lethaby's Brockhampton Church (88) and that too exhibits an early and successful use of concrete. Started on site in 1901, soon after Happisburgh was completed, it was to be Lethaby's last new building and Wells's first. Thereafter Lethaby worked as teacher, writer

12 Colonel Pen Lloyd, *The History of the Mysterious Papillon Hall* (Leicestershire Local History Council, 1977), quoted by Gavin Stamp in 'Festival of Destruction', *Building Design* (16 Nov 1984), p. 33.

13 Anon., 'A House at Happisburgh, Norfolk', *Architectural Review*, 15 (1904), 214–19, see p. 214.

14 Anon., 'Kelling Place, Holt, Norfolk', *Architectural Review*, 19 (1906), p. 82.

88. Church of All Saints, Brockhampton, Herefordshire, designed by W. R. Lethaby.

and historian, his building work being confined to the repair and conservation of historic buildings. Brockhampton was the closest he ever came to resolving these difficulties and practising what he was later to teach. As with Morris it was the interface between architecture and practical building that caused him problems and it was Randall Wells who forged the link between Lethaby as architect and the building process on site.

There was no main contractor at Brockhampton and Lethaby deliberately produced few drawings. Avon Tyrrell, Lethaby's first major commission, had been quite the reverse (89). It was built by Albert Estcourt and Son from Gloucester, Webb's trusted contractor at Clouds and there had been 229 sheets of designs and working details.[15] Robert Lorimer, the Scottish Arts and Crafts architect, thought the house a failure and inflexible contract documentation the reason:

> What does the man preach? That modern work fails because it is all done in the office and isn't worked out on the spot as in the old days as afore time! Well if you'd been with me (I wish to God you had been) we'd have agreed a dozen things that failed in this very particular ... The proportions of a lot of it was poor and the staircase I would simply not have owned.[16]

15 Richardson, *Architects of the Arts and Crafts Movement*, p. 32.

16 Quoted by Peter Savage in 'Lorimer and the Edinburgh Craft Designers' (Edinburgh, Harris, 1980).

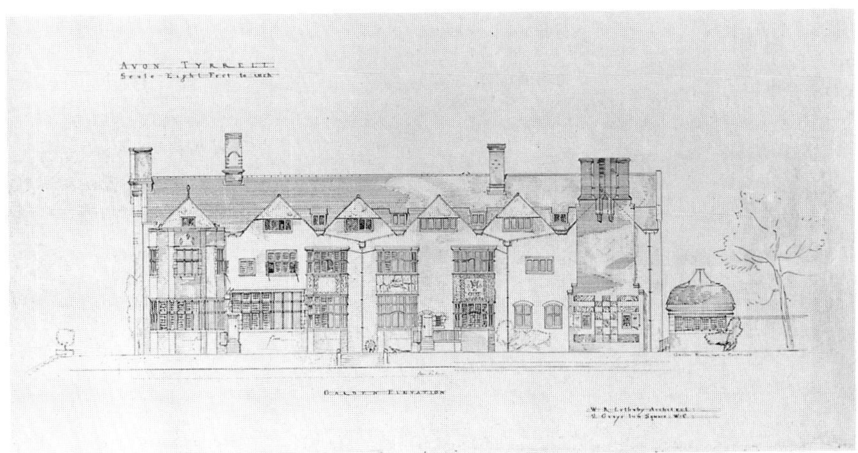

89. Avon Tyrrell, the revised contract design by W. R. Lethaby, 1891. Garden elevation (BAL).

For Brockhampton only eleven drawings survive, Lethaby specifying: 'the whole of the work to be done 'Day Work' under a Clerk of Works and a general foreman appointed by Mr Foster of Brockhampton Court ...'[17] Different methods produce different results: at Avon Tyrell the early signs of a startling talent were constrained by standard working practices but the more intuitive approach exemplified at Brockhampton underlines Lethaby's close association with Powell, Gimson, Blow and the Barnsleys. Lethaby was however eleven years older than Blow and ten years in Shaw's office had taken him a long way down a different road. Such freedom of expression did not come naturally to him but after Avon Tyrrell each new commission was an opportunity for experiment. For Melsetter, a house in the Orkneys on which he was to work extensively, Lethaby set off from London with a scheme already planned but abandoned it on arrival. As a result the original spirit of the place was allowed to survive, Lethaby's final design being that conceived on the spot in 1898. His achievement of such a sense of place is remarkable when it is realised how brief his visits were.[18]

At Brockhampton Lethaby went a step further, achieving a spontaneity that must however be attributed, at least in part, to the contribution made by Wells. The process was by no means painless, with a chain of command that was awkward. In addition to Wells a foreman was appointed by Lethaby's client,

17 Specification for the Building of Brockhampton Church, dated April 1901, in British Architectural Library, quoted by Richardson, *Architects of the Arts and Crafts Movement*, p. 32.

18 Lethaby had lunch with Cockerell at an Aerated Bread Shop before leaving for the Orkneys (Saturday October 22 1898 in the Cockerell Diary). Less than ten days later Cockerell found him home again. Other visits could not have been much longer as Lethaby's attendance at the weekly SPAB committee meetings remained generally regular throughout the Melsetter period (SPAB committee minutes).

90. The church at Abbey Dore, Herefordshire, with its dramatic tower.

Arthur Foster and if anything went wrong Foster, a Halifax mill-owner, was quickly informed. On one occasion Foster contacted Lethaby to ask why he had not been told about a collapse in one of the stone arches supporting the concrete vault; Lethaby had to ask Wells who replied that he was 'putting it up again at once and had not thought it worthwhile to tell him – he had been trying some experiments in mortar which had not succeeded.'[19]

The church was built in memory of Foster's American parents-in-law who had paid for the rebuilding of nearby Brockhampton Court as a wedding present. The Fosters were therefore used to building work but Lethaby's methods were something different, for without a contract much depends on trust. When Wells raised the crossing tower by some ten feet, costs and feelings began to rise too; later the very stability of the building was called into question. Some early settlement cast doubt upon the foundations and Lethaby felt obliged to carry out remedial work at his own expense. Always a man of principle, he

[19] Godfrey Rubens, *William Richard Lethaby* (London, The Architectural Press, 1986), p. 159.

91. The church of St Edward the Confessor, Kempley, Gloucestershire, by Randall Wells.

refused to take his fee. Nevertheless what sounds like a catalogue of disasters resulted in a building of delight and lasting quality. Traditional forms are handled freely with inventive detailing and Pevsner calls it 'one of the most convincing and most impressive churches of its date in any country ... Expressionist in the sense in which Central Europe designed churches about 1920'.[20] The interior is graced with Arts and Crafts treasures, for instance the carved choir stalls with their forty-eight panels of local wild flowers and herbs, a Burne-Jones tapestry and glass by Christopher Whall.

Whilst living at Brockhampton, Randall Wells continued his casework on behalf of the SPAB. Indeed, his idea for raising the crossing tower may have sprung from his involvement on their behalf at Abbey Dore (90) where the relative height of the tower on the truncated church achieves a dramatic effect. 'Wells knows it better than I' replied Alfred Powell when the SPAB wrote to him about a proposed restoration there,[21] indicating another early link between

[20] Nikolaus Pevsner, *Gloucestershire: the Vale and the Forest of Dean*, Buildings of England (Harmondsworth: Penguin Books, 1970), pp. 90–1.

Wells and the other Wandering Architects at this time. The two men made a visit together and letters from Powell at Sapperton and Wells at Brockhampton relating to this visit survive, Wells writing to Powell afterwards hoping he had recovered his bicycle alright.[22]

Whilst Wells was still at Brockhampton, Lord Lygon, the 7th Earl of Beauchamp asked him to design and build a new church at Kempley, five miles away. Beauchamp, back from New South Wales where he had been Governor from 1899 to 1902, was already employing C. R. Ashbee and the Guild of Handicraft at Madresfield Court early in 1902 and later fitted out the library and decorated the chapel, where he created a notable Arts and Crafts interior. Kempley church (91) dates from 1902 too and Wells later described its construction:

> The foundations had been put in under the direction of my client before I started, and I was asked to design a church to fit upon them as nearly as I could, and at the same time fulfil certain requirements of his – that there should be no east window, and that the lighting should be through the roof and from the west end, and that the eaves should be kept low. This necessitated a preliminary sketch, which being accepted, I did not propose to hamper the building with prearranged drawings of details.
>
> The church consists of a nave, a side chapel, a porch and a vestry. We used the nearest local stone, red and grey grit (sandstone), from the Forest of Dean, using, to a certain extent, the piece of stone most suitable for any given work without regard for colour, preferring, however, the grey for wrought work, as it was easier to cut. For the roof we cut down oak trees in a neighbouring wood belonging to my client, and shaped them by saw over a pit, and to cover it, stone slabs from Blakeney, on the estuary of the Severn, having to quarry the bulk for ourselves from a piece of virgin land hired for the purpose. The labour was mainly local, assisted by masons who had worked for me before, with a local builder as foreman. The stonework was set out on the masons bankers – where there is at least a chance of suggestion from the material ... and the roof principals, to suit the available oak, at the saw-pit.
>
> The building was to be inexpensive; this settled the form of construction – rough walling with quoins as little wrought as

21 Unpublished letter from Alfred Powell to Thackeray Turner, 10 May 1902, SPAB Archive: Abbey Dore file.

22 SPAB Archive, Abbey Dore file. Wells and Powell were too late as far as the proposed restoration was concerned, work being already in hand involving the removal of lathe and plaster ceilings, levelling of floors, scraping off of whitewash and rebuilding of the tower parapet.

present-day masons' training will allow – and negatived the cutting of tracery or the free use of arches… . The lighting was to be through the roof, and from the west end. I did not consider that it would be satisfactory from the roof, and so decided to light the whole of the nave from the west and to light the altar from a dormer on the south chancel wall. This meant that the west window had to be as wide and as high as possible if the church was not to be gloomy; this suggested to me the idea of building the west end as a piece of stone trellis work and then glazing it. To take the thrust of these heavy stones – and they were each 2' by 1' by 6" – off the side walls, some of the stout saddlebars were continuous, and pierced the jambs on either side, terminating in iron plates.

For ornament we wanted to limit ourselves to what we could do ourselves. The chapel, being small, gave a chance to carry the finishing a little farther than the church, so the masons crinkled the edges of the stone springers and scooped little hollows for baby shadows to lurk in… . It is the county of cider and perry and oaktrees, and so I cut apples and pears, acorns and oakapples, twisting the stems into a continuous band. The porch I wanted made beautiful, or, at least, interesting, and as the church was to be dedicated to St. Mary, I designed a low relief panel of the mother and child, to go over the church door. For the east end outside, in place of a window, my client wanted a 'crucifixion'. I suggested instead a life-sized figure of Christ, with the cross in the background; however he insisted, so I made a sketch for a 'crucifixion' and this and the Virgin and Child were cut by one of Laurence Turner's men. The figure of Christ I put on the outside of the porch, and cut myself.

Inside there was to be a rood. This I thought should be as gay and bright as possible, glowing with happiness, not for the pleasure of the subtle and cultivated townsmen, but simple and joyous for those of the country. So that it could be painted by a village painter, assisted by my brother, I cut the pattern in with gouges and V tools, then we painted the whole thing black thinly, not much more than staining, and filled the lines in with the most brilliant colours that I could obtain. How to get simple wood figures cut to complete the beam was a problem, but, on consulting Mr Kelly's stupendous work, I found that there was still one ship's figurehead carver in London, a David Gibb, a Scotsman, brought up on the Clyde. He did three rather jolly wooden figures, but, alas, when they were fixed and painted, and all was complete, the Bishop had them pulled down again. But they have since been replaced.

The churchyard was to have the walls covered with crimson ramblers and wild briars, with bright Nasturtiums at the foot, and just inside the wall there is to be a frame of tall forest trees and in the space

92. The interior of the church at Kempley, showing the rood, carved by David Gibb, said to be the last carver of ships' figure heads in London. The rood was immediately taken down by the order of the bishop, but was later reinstated.

> between these and the church wild fruit trees, planted orchard-wise, crabs, cherry and pear trees. The grass is to be allowed to grow like a meadow, and to be filled with daffodils, forget-me-nots, meadowsweet, daisies, buttercups and many other flowers that can be seen in any Gloucestershire hedgerow, and, in their season, crocuses and lillies of the valley growing through the grass at the sides of the paths.[23]

The local builder who acted as foreman was R. James and Linley Wells was the brother who helped with the decorations.[24] The reinstated rood stands today as Wells and his client intended it, lit from the west by the gridded window that

23 'Kempley Church', Randall Wells, *The British Architect* (5 March 1909), pp. 165–6.

24 Linley Wells was killed at Gallipolli, 'saving someone else's life', according to Alfred Powell: unpublished letter from Alfred Powell to Malcolm Powell dated July 1904, in 'Autographed Letters, etc. by Alfred Hoare Powell and Some Others. Written at Home and Abroad, AD MDCCCLXXIX to MDCCCCXII. Bound 1914', p. 363, amongst the Powell papers.

floods the church with light, as if from the mouth of a cave (92). Alfred Powell visited Kempley in June 1903 and his description, in a letter to his sister Emily, makes it clear that the building was in an advanced state if not complete:

> I have just been galavanting - which always does me a lot of good - or I hope it does! with a friend Wells ... he is architecting and building at Kempley near Gloucester and came over to see us last Sat. to Monday and took me back with him on Tuesday. We saw two or three fine churches on Tuesday and his new one - a really admirable and hopefulist [sic] building showing a lot of happy turning thoughts and ingenuity. So refreshing to see stones and other materials made real use of up to their full limits - colour - surface, strength etc. all in real use which you know is the proper basis for all architecture. Wednesday we started off and walked nineteen or twenty miles perhaps into Hereford - stopping and turning aside at all sorts of interesting places and all the walk as jolly as could be with his extraordinary gaiety and enjoyment - and mine too for that matter. We stopped for teas and cider - bread and cheese - and company at all sorts of places he knew and at all sorts of times and finally trod the streets of Hereford at about 11.00 pm and went to a nice clean little place ... in Commercial Road. There we had a two-bedded room and slept like tops until the morning, had a prodigious wash out of a tiny wash tub and then - on the spur of the moment, took a boat and started down the Wye for Ross (28 miles) with jolly weather and a monstrous stream that whipped us along under the willows at a fine pace. We escaped being wrecked on a rock that I caught sight of and called, on the way, at a place where we had tea to see if we could persuade two girlfriends of his to join us, one was out and the other was not allowed to trust herself on such a treacherous stream! So we were rather disappointed as she was a jolly child and would have enjoyed it... . Friday I went to Ledbury with him and on to Stanley Hill to see Clissett, the old chairmaker (87 years old) and found him busy at work and such a dear old man. He gave us quite a glimpse of what the old aristocratic poor used to be. A quiet, homely, hospitable old fellow and so kind looking and ready to talk about his work and show me how to do it.[25] Then back again to Kempley and this morning home again to find a pile of letters to answer! I think Wells one of the most charming creatures I ever came across. I hope you may meet him some day.[26]

25 Clissett was the chair bodger who had taught Gimson the use of the pole lathe to make his ladder-backed, cane-seated chairs. Gimson in turn taught Powell.

26 Unpublished letter from Alfred Powell to Emily Powell dated 20 June 1903, from Gurner's Farm, Oakridge Lynch, Stroud, in 'Autographed Letters, etc. by Alfred Hoare Powell', pp. 336–41.

Alfred Powell visited Wells in Norfolk too, while Wells was working with Prior at Kelling in 1904. Alfred described it in a letter to his brother Malcolm, the furniture maker:

> I had a delicious week at Holt with Wells and Linley who I fell in love with. Also with the Radford girls at Bacton. Hester is another of the hopeful ones; straight as a lath and as springy as walebone. Swims like a fish and one of the jolliest ... we raced and 'roundered' – wheelbarrowed (which I won as barrow, of course!) and otherwise rampaged the sand into unrecognisable heaps. Finished up on Thursday with the Broads. I had determined to take things easy the last day but fate determined otherwise and I began with a puncture which involved running and bicycling about two to three miles in blazing sun to Melton Constable. Then train to North Horsham and eight miles bicycling in half an hour ... Then blessed boats, sailing and rowing till 7.00 ... I took the rowing boat and gently backed myself home nose forward while they laboured after me on the failing breeze. It was very beautiful and we all enjoyed it very much. Then we took and rode to Bacton seven or eight miles and had supper. I slept from 12.00 to 4.00 in the Inn while R and L slept on the shore in a tent. Breakfast at 4.30. Started back to Holt (21 miles) at 5.00 am. Breakfasted again, packed and caught the 8.26 train to Kings Cross ... and feel as fit as a flea![27]

Randall Wells was clearly, like Alfred Powell, a man of enormous energy. His exuberance shows as clearly in the building work at Voewood as it does in Powell's letters and signs of it may be found again at the church of St Andrew's, Roker, near Sunderland. A continuation of his association with Prior, the tender drawings were dated 1905. Wells was at Roker himself by June 1906.[28] St Andrew's is a bigger church than Brockhampton or Kempley and the largely undivided interior, coupled with natural lighting that is more uniform and less dramatic, lacks something of the intimate quality of these buildings. The quality of the architecture is nonetheless assured and its oneness with the fine Arts and Crafts fixtures, fittings and decorations mark it as one of the great achievements of the movement.

Built to satisfy the needs of a rapidly expanding suburb to the north of Sunderland, the major benefactor was John Priestman, a local man, who had started life in the shipyards. Although the church appears stone built inside and

27 Unpublished letter from Alfred Powell to Malcolm Powell dated July 1904, in 'Autographed Letters, etc. by Alfred Hoare Powell', p. 363.

28 Wells wrote to the SPAB from No. 1 Park Gate, Roker about casework at Hexham (SPAB Archive: Hexham file). This address also appears on correspondence from Wells to the SPAB on their Croydon Palace file.

93. Interior perspective of the Church of St Andrew, Roker, Co. Durham; Edward Schroeder Prior, 1905; site architect Randall Wells (BAL).

out, the nave is ribbed with reinforced concrete arches behind the local Marsden stone facings (93). The hidden structure allows the expressionistic virtuosity that is apparant at the foot of each great rib where, on either side, the massive construction is gently brought to earth via relatively delicate paired columns, allowing a tiny passage aisle to burrow through, seemingly almost within the wall thickness. Outside, the church is dominated by its unusually placed east tower, angular and strong, straddling a chancel which only just manages to emerge to the east beyond (94). The tracery too, continuing the free style

94. St Andrew's, Church, Roker; east elevation.

evolution from Brockhampton and Kempley, is simplified and geometrical, the repetition of its small elements building up to make a powerful contribution to the whole. Influences of Wells's earlier work are apparent everywhere.

Internally, the rugged character of the nave contrasts with the richness of the chancel. Here the rough stonework is concealed behind plain panelling by Gimson, the floor is carpeted (by Morris & Co) and below the east window, hanging as a reredos, is a tapestry designed by Burne-Jones. This Arts and Crafts tour de force is completed by further Gimson furnishings below a skyed ceiling by MacDonald Gill. The font was carved by Wells himself, the intricate low relief carving to the legs picking up where he left off at Kempley.

Contemporary with St Andrew's Roker is a new wing designed by Wells, on his own, for the Kelling Sanitorium in Norfolk, near Kelling Place. And not long after Wells was working for Lord Beauchamp again too, designing a new hall at Madresfield. Unrealised, it was to have had triple tiered galleries and a partly glazed roof. Beauchamp again wanted roof-lighting, as originally requested at Kempley but this time it was to be in Prior's patent glass with white doves etched into the colour.[29] The walls of close-studded timber framework rising from a stone base would, with its great height, have made a dramatic room.

Busy as Wells seems to have been, his career appears to have lost its way at about this point. For someone who undertook only one job at a time, this was a risk that had to be taken, for to dove-tail one job's completion with the commencement of the next needs luck as well as continuing patronage. The climate within the building industry was changing too. Social change throughout the Edwardian era saw a growing disassociation between traditional clients and their money. Lloyd George's budget of 1909, together with the General Election that he successfully fought to defend it immediately afterwards, dealt a further blow to declining agricultural land values. The country-house market atrophied and wealthy clients, like those who funded the three churches Wells had built, had less money to spend. The swing of architectural fashion towards neo-classicism, especially within an urban context, was also leaving Arts and Crafts exponents isolated. By nature gothicists, they were forced to change with the times or find work harder to come by. The careers of some adapted naturally. Lutyens, with his lively, flexible approach and constantly evolving stylistic development moved easily with the fashion; Detmar Blow too. Carefully considered historicism as exemplified at Little Ridge and Breccles Hall was well appreciated at this time. His chapel of 1906 for Lord Manners at Avon Tyrrell (85) is of the same date as the work at Roker by Prior and Wells but Blow's chapel reflects the changing taste and exemplifies the neo-baroque or Wrenaissance then fashionable.

Others moved less easily and Randall Wells was not a man to bend to the whims of fashion. This does not mean that his architecture did not develop but that the development was tuned to its own evolutionary process rather than to outside pressures. He designed housing in Letchworth, Hampstead Garden Suburb, Gidea Park and elsewhere and this continued, although it was at best sporadic after 1907, as was his involvement in projects instigated by the SPAB. His housing included an award-winning design in the Cheap Cottages Exhibition at Letchworth held in 1905 and by 1907 he had designed two more nearby along similar lines. A visitor to the Letchworth Exhibition met Wells by chance, finding him at work on the cottage he had designed and the article that the visitor subsequently wrote gives the best of insights into Wells' thinking:

[29] The work had in fact been put in hand in August 1912 but a halt was called soon after. It seems there was concern about accommodation lost elsewhere and doubt about the practicality of the construction had been cast by a timid builder (unpublished letter from Wells to Lord Beauchamp, 7 November 1912, Wells/Beauchamp correspondence, Madresfield Archive).

On going over one of the cottages at the Garden City Exhibition, which later on gained a £10 prize, I turned to ask for some information from a man who was standing on a barrel.

He was sprinkled with brick dust and bits of brick, for he was at work, with cold chisel and heavy, stumpy bricklayer's hammer, rounding off the sharp edge of the bricks forming the corner of the lobby. To my surprise, this labourer, who was so modestly correcting the mistakes of a bricklayer, proved to be the architect!

Though one cannot doubt that architects sometimes get their clothes spoilt in going over half-finished buildings, I had never before seen an architect actually engaged in building work ...

I asked him the name of his builder. He said he was his own builder! It is hardly necessary to say that I was greatly interested. Here was an architect who clearly knew something of building. Naturally I wanted to know how the architect-builder managed. He was frankness itself. To this young man with the flushed face, the voice of breeding and alert intelligence, building was, without doubt, one of the noble careers ...

It might be imagined that a difficulty in the way of an architect buying his own materials and employing the builder merely as a foreman ... would be that an architect could not buy as well as a man in the trade. I believe this is an erroneous impression ... Mr Randall Wells was inclined to think that a man of ordinary education and ability could very soon learn all that was required. 'Do you not remember,' he asked, 'that William Morris in his "News from Nowhere" puts all the shops in the hands of children?'...

Where does the architect who is his own builder gain his technical experience? It is hardly possible to believe that the conventional training of the average architect's office will give it him. The building of which the young men there have experience has been done with ink, a ruler, and washes. In Mr Randall Wells' case, I believe that he set out to be an architect - his father is an architect - by way of the joiner's bench and the foundry. Since then he has worked on buildings as well as in offices - at one time as a carpenter at 6*d* an hour. Now he works, as far as possible, for himself or other architects on 'buildings without a builder.'...

I suppose that to the group of which Morris was the central figure, and to the few who have a right understanding of the teaching of Ruskin, we owe largely what is best in modern building. We certainly owe to them the movement for a new race of master builders, to which I am putting my humble shoulder. Morris and Ruskin are gone, but to some extent the mantles of both have fallen on one man, Professor W. R. Lethaby, a man truly practical and without fads who adds to the finer ideas of Ruskin and the craft knowledge of Morris ...

> The names of such well known architects as Mr Ernest Prior, Mr F. W. Troup, Mr A. H. Powell, Mr Ernest Gimson, Mr R. W. Schultz and a few others occur to one as those who are working on sympathetic lines ...
>
> It might be thought, perhaps, that the title A.R.I.B.A. is a guarantee of an architect's abilities. But can it be said that this has been so? ... To pass the examination means from three to five years' study, during which a man need never be in touch with materials. From a pecuniary point of view it is worth passing, of course, for he who obtains the title is at least certain to get a post as architect's assistant. But is this the proper training of the young architect? Should there not be a time, wanderjahren, when he could actually be working on buildings, not only studying materials and the placing and joining of them, but learning the management of men?[30]

As for Wells's work on behalf of the SPAB, his first involvement on site had come before his time at Roker. The project was the repair of Croydon Palace, for which Detmar Blow had prepared a report for the society in 1904. Wells agreed to help Mr Dickie, the architect already appointed by the school who owned the building and was resident on site from May 1905.[31] Together they strengthened the building where necessary and Thackeray Turner thought it 'a good piece of work and quite wonderful considering it was Wells's "first shot".'[32] In 1912 Wells was involved in another SPAB case at Thaxted in Essex, repairing the church and using his own masons.[33] Some of his proposals were contrary to the society's own views, as represented by William Weir, but an agreement was reached and the SPAB endorsed the appeal the church set up. A huge and ingenious counterbalanced iron stella, designed by Wells, was made to hold candles and light the crossing.

Although Wells went from Croydon Palace to Roker in 1906 and stayed there until the completion of Prior's church in the following year, there is little else known of any of his work built between then and 1912. This is doubly surprising for such an obviously energetic man, as he suddenly seems so busy again in that year with Thaxted, an extension to a house in Cheshire and a much

30 'Building Without A Builder', an article found by Lynne Walker among the papers of E. S. Prior and brought to the author's attention by Charles Keighley, author of 'Randall Wells and the Ruskinian Tradition', an unpublished thesis for the Royal Holloway College, 1994. The publication in which the article originally appeared has not yet been identified.

31 SPAB Archive: Croydon Palace file.

32 Thackeray Turner had in fact suggested the repair technique, using steel rather than oak to repair the roof supports, contrary to Wells' better judgement (SPAB Archive: Croydon Palace file).

33 SPAB Archive: Thaxted Church file.

larger one at Besford Court, near Pershore in the Vale of Evesham. The SPAB files show his address for at least part of this period as being Hastings, his home town,[34] but this may not mean he was resident there. Other Wandering Architects used the parental home as a forwarding address when they were away on site and Wells may have done likewise.

The Besford Court commission came through his old client Lord Beauchamp who recommended Wells when he sold the house. The commission was a significant one for the new owners wanted to increase its size dramatically. As a result the late medieval timber-framed house now stands in startling contrast to Wells's large scale additions. These go far beyond the seamless extensions of the type for which Blow became renowned at this time; neither do they make an artful articulation of old and new such as Lutyens might have created. Instead Wells is, as ever, bold and uncompromising, even forceful. Built in 1913–14, there is a cloistered court with a simplified plate tracery. The hall echoes Brockhampton but the architecture is more fluid and in the staircase there appears the most flowing and sinuous of forms that sets Besford Court apart (95).

The staircase at Besford Court indicates the uniquely innovative nature of its architect but the most significant designs produced by Wells at this time remained unrealized. Dominion House (96), to be built on the site of Bush House in London and designed in 1913, was described by Pevsner as 'one of the most adventurous contributions to office architecture of that moment in Europe.'[35] In 1942 Pevsner summarised the pre-1914 predecessors of Modern Movement architecture in Britain in an article entitled 'Nine Swallows – No Summer'[36] but it contains nothing like Dominion House and had it been built, Wells would have been flying off on his own well ahead of Pevsner's swallows. 1915 saw Wells's competition design for new Board of Trade offices with elements similar to the Dominion House scheme, although massive chimneys and pitched roofs pin down its date more obviously. Another projected office building for the 'All People's Association' (97), an organisation set up by Sir Evelyn Wrench, editor of *The Spectator*, was designed much later but is in its way as far in advance of its time as the Dominion House drawings. Produced in 1931 it looks, as Pevsner observed in 1964, 'strikingly similar to what architects are doing in England at this very moment.'[37]

95 (opposite). The flowing staircase at Besford Court, Worcestershire.

[34] SPAB Archive: Pevensey Castle file.

[35] Pevsner and Radcliffe, 'Randall Wells', p. 337.

[36] Nikolaus Pevsner, 'Nine Swallows – No Summer', *Architectural Review*, 91 (May, 1942), pp. 109–12.

[37] Pevsner and Radcliffe, 'Randall Wells', p. 337.

96 (above). Proposed design for Dominion House, to be built on the site of Bush House, London; Randall Wells, 1913 (BAL).

97 (opposite). Proposed office building for the 'All People's Association', 1931.

Wells had turned his attentions towards London after his work at Besford Court. His clients, Sir George and Lady Noble, divorced and in 1917 Wells married Lady Noble, becoming involved in a joint London venture with her, a craft guild called St Veronica's Workshops, in Victoria. Lady Noble's house in Vincent Square was a showpiece for the organisation, and a typical interior included wall painting, furnishings and fireplace richly decorated in a jungle of naturalistic leaf and bird pattern. There is at first sight a contradiction between the guild's output, by then rather old-fashioned in its Morrisian derivation, and Wells's fiercely futuristic office designs of the same period. But to a man like Wells, steeped in the ways of Lethaby and Prior, the decorative arts of William Morris and the innovative use of modern materials preached by Lethaby and the Central School of Arts and Crafts would not have seemed in any way contradictory. His office designs, so firmly set in the ways of the emerging Modern Movement, spring naturally from such a background and such designs, when considered together with the decorative arts of St Veronica's Workshops do not render each other irrelevant. They are part of the same school of thought and can stand side by side. The work of the St Veronica's Workshop may be found in Wells's alterations to Wardington Manor, near Banbury in Oxfordshire, dating from about 1919. It is possible that the dynamic plasterwork decoration, credited by Pevsner to Mrs Randall Wells, is by Wells himself.[38] He certainly extended the house further at a later date.

[38] J. Sherwood and N. Pevsner, *Oxfordshire*, Buildings of England (Harmondsworth,

98. St Wilfrid's Church at Halton, Leeds; Randall Wells, 1938.

After three fine churches one more was to come from this talented architect. St Wilfrid's at Halton, near Leeds, was built between 1937 and 1939 and is another distinctive building (98). The low tower over the crossing has an octagonal gabled drum above, capped in turn by a spire over a higher and smaller octagonal stage. The apsidal end sets a sweeping and almost uninterrupted curve of stonework against the great cubes of the transepts and chancel; the block of the low tower and the simple triangles and octagons of porches and spire all stand starkly unadorned by buttresses, string courses, plinths or weatherings. The forms are all geometrical and there is something cubist in the juxtaposed massing of boldly defined elements. Only the windows break the unadorned surfaces, imposing their own dominant discipline internally as well as externally, just as the huge grid of the west window did at

Penguin Books, 1974), p. 824.

99. Lloyds Bank, Teddington, Randall Wells.

Kempley some thirty-five years before. A statue of St Wilfrid outside the church was carved by Eric Gill.

After St Wilfrid's, Wells's work is almost done. He had undertaken other relatively small commissions in the preceding years including a house in Chiswick with a bold convex bow window and a bank in Teddington with an even more dominant concavity (99) to its entrance elevation. The focus of this concave façade is the porch, set to a reverse curve with a hemispherical top combining symbolism and purity of form reminiscent of the underground stations designed by Charles Holden.[39] Wells's interior is simple and dignified. The sweep of the vaults and the simple arcs of his arches hark back to the Besford Court staircase and look forward to his work at Halton. The seemingly diverse elements of Wells's career in fact show a continuity of development from first to last.

Wells died in 1942 having suffered much in his private life. His daughter was killed in a train crash and his wife was said to have never recovered from the shock. Wells looked after her on his own in her declining years. His own passing did not go unnoticed:

> By the death at Oban on March 3lst of A. Randall Wells, the architectural profession loses one of the last representatives of that interesting school of practitioners who were content to work on almost Mediaeval principles – as a sort of Master Workman resident on the building under erection and in close personal control, ordering material, engaging workmen, and even doing some of the work with their own hands. Under such conditions the bulk of work produced during a liftetimes activity cannot be large, but the practice is so obvious a mark of sincerity that any building resulting from it is bound to bear the stamp of character.[40]

39 Pevsner draws our attention to Lutyens's use of a similar device in the later Reuters Building of 1935 (Pevsner and Radcliffe, 'Randall Wells', p. 367).

40 Anon., 'The Late Randall Wells', *The Architect & Building News* (10 April 1942), p. 18.

Chapter 8
THREE BUILDER-ARCHITECTS
Herbert North, Geoffrey Lupton & Harold Falkner

> Excursions into handicraft broaden the outlook of an architect and quicken his sense of the right use of material.
>
> Lawrence Weaver, *Small Country Houses of Today*, 2nd Series, 1919

An itinerant lifestyle was symptomatic of an adherence to true Arts and Crafts architectural principles rather than a pre-requisite. After all it is possible for an architect to work on site with his own hands without leaving the comfort of his own home for longer than the working day; all it needs is a sympathetic client offering continuity of work in the immediate vicinity. Achieving such continuity was the problem for the home-loving Arts and Crafts purist but the careers of three architects show how a sympathetic client could be guaranteed if the architect and client were the same person.

Herbert Luck North (1871–1941) worked on his own behalf at Llanfairfechan in North Wales from 1900. Another life-long admirer of William Morris, North had assisted Detmar Blow at the Old Post Office in Tintagel. He was there, lodging at Sea View Cottage, when Morris died in 1896, enabling Blow to help out at Morris's bedside. At Tintagel North learned at first hand that which Morris taught about the intrinsic importance of the ancient stones themselves: 'We have been unearthing all kinds of interesting squints, corbels and things that remind people of the beautiful simplicity of the life of their ancestors.'[1]

With the Old Post Office saved, North went home to Wales for Christmas, his family having moved to Llanfairfechan on Conwy Bay in 1881. After a degree at Cambridge, North had been articled to Henry Wilson in Sedding's old office from 1892. In 1895, the year before North's work at Tintagel, Wilson had been commissioned to build a church in Merioneth and North's Welsh connections made him an obvious choice for its supervision. Wilson's client was the widow of the Rev. Charles Tooth, chaplain and founder of a church in Florence and the new church at Brithdir was to take the same dedication to St

[1] Unpublished letter from Herbert North to Thackeray Turner, May 1896, SPAB Archive: The Old Post Office, Tintagel file.

100. St Mark's, Brithdir, Merioneth; Henry Wilson, 1895, site architects Charles Quennell and Herbert North; and 101 (opposite), the altar by Wilson in raised and beaten copper.

Mark and be designed after the style of a North Italian country church.[2] Herbert North supervised the masonry which was executed by a local man, William Jones, and built from locally quarried stone. The carpentry was the responsibility of Charles Quennell,[3] another of Wilson's assistants.

An Italian church in Wales by an Arts and Crafts advocate like Wilson, who believed that a building should be raised from the soil on which it stood, sounds like a contradiction in terms. These contradictions have been mollified externally by a simple use of forms in stone and slate, hidden in woodland and now hemmed about by rhododendrons (100). But the interior is a rich surprise with an apsidal east end pierced by openings through the curved planes of its thick walls, making a strong sculpted setting for Wilson's breath-taking altar. In raised and beaten copper, its burnished surfaces glow richly amidst the dark red ochre of the painted wall surfaces. The pulpit is similarly sheathed and the reredos is a panel of raised copper too, decorated with a vine springing from a chalice, flanked by bluebells: like the church itself, a little piece of Italy set amongst Welsh flowers (101).

2 Wilson's church was to be built on the proceeds of the sale of Charles Tooth's worldly possessions on land his widow had inherited from an earlier marriage.

3 C. H. B. Quennell wrote a series of books on social history, starting with his memorable *History of Everyday Things in England* (London, Batsford, 1918). He left Wilson's office in 1896 to set up his own practice, producing some very capable and substantial houses around Hampstead Garden Suburb and elsewhere.

Tintagel followed Brithdir and in the new year North went to see Lutyens for an interview, hoping for a job that would give him the security he needed to get married. Lutyens took one look at his heavy working boots and took him on.[4] Such boots were worn off site as well as on, a sign of membership of the school of practical building that Morris and Webb had advocated at the SPAB, and to whose theories Lutyens was also committed. Gimson wore them and rather liked it when they attracted attention on London visits: 'How are the crops?' he used to be asked. To be singled out as a working man from the country reflected a whole range of values he held dear. Both North and Lutyens were planning their weddings in 1897,[5] North marrying Ida Davies just before he started work at Lutyens's office.[6] They settled in Cricklewood. Lutyens

4 From Ian Allan in a letter to the author, 12 April 1985.

5 Lutyens wrote wistfully to Lady Emily Lytton on 9 April 1897, just before the Norths married on April 28th: 'The duties of the day shall be heralded by the striking hour, and we shall rise - but how difficult! Breakfast - simply and prettily placed upon an oak table. Breads and fruits and flowers ... crisp curling bacon in its casserole, on occasions of great state a sausage! hams, and eggs to boil at our own pleasure, and tempting toast upon a bright iron grid before the fire - of wood! The smell of papery pot-pourri by Bumps and the blue cloth with Lavendar's fresh presence there. So we shall eat and read the other's letters each to the other.' Quoted by Christopher Hussey, *The Life of Sir Edwin Lutyens* (London: Country Life, 1950), p. 65.

6 Lutyens Family Papers, 9 April 1897: Reference to North as office boy in Lutyens office. Ida Davies was the daughter of an architect neighbour, G. B. Davies, who had moved to Llanfairfechan from Dudley.

102. 'Rosebriers', Llanfairfechan, Gwynedd; Herbert North, *c.*1901, garden front.

married Lady Emily Lytton on August 4th. In 1898 North left to set up on his own in Bedford Square, freelancing in his spare time for W. A. Pite while saving to start work on his own house in Llanfairfechan. While it was being built he returned to the Lutyens office, perhaps for the steady income, but once his house was finished he opened an office in Conwy and never moved again.

Despite North's own experience on site elsewhere, he chose to use a local contractor, Even Humphreys, to build at Llanfairfechan. Called Rosebriers (102), his house is highly individualistic in its planning. North used a small, tight butterfly plan with a single pair of wings set back to front, presenting a faceted arrangement of rooms, convex on plan, looking out over the panoramic views to Anglesea. These rooms can be used individually or opened up to form a twisting sequence, wrapped around a partially double height entrance hall, clasped between the wings of the butterfly on the northern side. The front door faces the mountains behind. As in the sanctuary at Brithdir the composition is one of intersecting angled planes pierced by unadorned openings, a short step from the thought processes that typified the Modern Movement.

103. Northcot, Llanfairfechan, by Herbert North.

Rosebriers is innovative enough to deserve a place as a pioneer work of 20th century architecture but local materials soften its impact. Re-named Wern Isaf, Rosebriers became an outlier to a group of picturesquely developed houses that North built later, winding along the contours behind Llanfairfechan. Amongst the earliest were Northcot, Bolnhurst, Woodcote and Wylome (103), all built for friends. The little garden suburb grew slowly over a long period and continued to do so into the twenties, after which North practised with his son-in-law as North & Padmore: 'Houses Built to Suit Purchasers' read their sign at the approach. Despite the time-span the Close, as it is still known, is entirely homogeneous, characterised by the quality of the local materials and the adroit handling of simple domestic forms (104).

Herbert North built other houses, both in Llanfairfechan and elsewhere and between the wars was responsible for some outstanding churches and private chapels. He immersed himself in the history as well as the construction of the regional tradition and wrote two books: *The Old Cottages of Snowdonia* and *The Old Churches of Snowdonia*. A house near Lake Windermere, built immediately

104. A typical house by Herbert North in The Close, Llanfairfechan; (opposite) 105 (a) and (b): two views of Keldwith, Windermere, by Herbert North, *c.*1913.

before the First World War, was one of only a handful of projects he undertook further afield. Like Rosebriers, Keldwith (105) as it was called, uses the butterfly plan, by then not uncommon. Later to evolve into the sunlight-seeking configurations of the 1920s and '30s, the Arts and Crafts butterfly became known as the sun-trap plan and enjoyed a vogue especially for sea-side and holiday homes. Keldwith, however, has Gothic qualities that make direct reference to the birth of the Arts and Crafts rather than to its demise. Although Modern Movement sun-trap planners became single-minded in their pursuit of light and airy interiors, it should not be forgotten that such plans evolved from a neo-Gothic lineage where the wide-spread wings had been devised to embrace warm and sheltered enclaves outside rather than to provide sunlight indoors. The late Victorians and Edwardians had a penchant for outdoor living, admittedly, but the loggia, often used as an outdoor dining room, together with the balcony bedroom for sleeping in the open air, were a foil to the enclosing inglenook and deep window embrasures, not a replacement. Either way North's Gothic at Keldwith and elsewhere expresses the elemental, well suited to the grandeur of the scenery in Snowdonia and the Lake District. Quite rightly

Lawrence Weaver said of Keldwith's architect in *Country Life*: 'Ruskin would have felt justified in Mr North as one of his children'.[7]

* * * * * * * * *

[7] Lawrence Weaver, *Small Country Houses of Today*, Second Series (London: Country Life, 1919), p. 47.

Geoffrey Henry Lupton (1882–1949) was another who managed to arrange the majority of his building work within easy reach of home. Educated at Bedales School, he was there in 1900 when it moved to Steep, near Petersfield in Hampshire and became head boy in 1901. Bedales attracted the children of Arts and Crafts exponents whose values it reflected, upholding, it has been said, 'co-education, the simple life, disciplinary rigours, the open air, hygiene, Ruskin and Morris, Arts and Crafts, Liberty dresses, folk dancing, vegetarianism, teetotalism, pacifism, intellectual liberalism, pink middle class socialism, votes for women and moral ernestness.'[8] Lupton left to join his family's engineering firm in Leeds but perhaps the rich mixture poured into him at Bedales left him unsuited to such work for he left in 1905 to work with Ernest Gimson in Sapperton and eventually returned to Steep.

The connections between Sapperton and Bedales were strong and centred on the Powells. Oswald Powell was second master there and his house, Little Hawstead, just outside the school gates, was designed by Alfred Powell [see (31) & Chapter 3].[9] The Gimsons were closely associated with Bedales too, Ernest's nephews Humphrey and Basil both being educated there. When Basil later joined the teaching staff at Bedales, Humphrey in turn designed him a house called Five Oaks nearby. The house, Basil's wedding present, was built in 1912 and paid for by their father Sydney, for whom Ernest had designed Stoneywell. Humphrey Gimson was a pupil of Lutyens and the easy balance of the asymmetrical entrance elevation at Five Oaks (106) betrays the fact. Lupton was the builder and is revealed at once as an uncompromising character: when asked by the Gimsons if they could have deal floors instead of oak, to reduce costs, Lupton replied 'Yes, but you would have to change builders.'[10]

Lupton had returned to Hampshire in 1906, primarily as a furniture maker and the first buildings he put up on his return were his own simple house and workshop at Froxfield, on a steep slope at the top of the east Hampshire hangers above Steep. Although not in its original form, the little house gives some insights into the unconventional character of its builder: in front of its inglenook fireplace is a trap hatch in the floor, folding back to reveal a concrete bathtub, its occupant being able to enjoy the fire whilst bathing. Roger Powell,

8 W. M. Whiteman, *The Edward Thomas Country* (Southampton: Paul Cave Publications, 1978), p. 23.

9 Malcolm, another of Alfred's brothers, spent a year in Sidney Barnsley's workshop before setting up as a furniture maker in Reading. A fourth brother, Edgar, became a bookbinder, as did Roger Powell, Oswald's son; Roger Powell's studio in Froxfield, near Lupton's, was internationally known.

10 Quoted in an unpublished letter from R. J. Holder to the Department of the Environment to support the spot listing of Five Oaks.

106. Five Oaks, Steep, near Petersfield, Hampshire, designed by Humphrey Gimson and built by Geoffrey Lupton in 1912 for Basil Gimson.

Alfred's bookbinder nephew, remembered the concrete surface being rather rough[11] but this didn't surprise him, knowing of Lupton's rather spartan lifestyle.

From the start Lupton worked as a builder as well as a joiner[12] although others, like Powell, helped him with house designs as Lupton had no formal training in architecture. The house next door to Lupton's was a product of their teamwork. Called Red House (107), like the one Webb had designed for Morris fifty years earlier, it was built in 1909, its builder and designer travelling together in Ireland the year after on a camping holiday.[13] Lupton built the house to let to the poet Edward Thomas who had also moved to the area in 1906,

11 Roger Powell, recalled in conversation with the author, 22 March 1989.

12 In about 1908 Lupton is credited with a fine oak staircase in a house attributed to W. F. & O. Unsworth called The Platts in Petersfield (David Ottewill, *Arts & Crafts in the Petersfield & Steep Area*, unpublished typescript (1980), pp. 1–6, see p. 1.

13 Unpublished letter from Alfred Powell to his brother, Malcolm Powell, 11 June 1910, from Oakridge Lynch, Stroud, in 'Autographed Letters, etc. by Alfred Hoare Powell and Some Others', pp. 378–9, amongst the Powell papers.

107. The Red House, Froxfield, Hampshire, built by Lupton in 1909 to a design by Alfred Powell; and (opposite) 108. Red House from across Lutcombe, the gorge of the Ashford Stream above Steep. Lupton built the house to let to the poet Edward Thomas.

becoming a friend while renting a cottage at the foot of Lutcombe, the gorge of the Ashford Stream. Thomas' wife Helen describes how they met Lupton when they sent their children to Bedales:

> Among those whom I had met at the school was a young man who had been a pupil there. He was now settled in the neighbourhood, and occupied himself making furniture. He had means of his own, but being a disciple of Ruskin and Morris he determined to live a simple and useful life, making strong and beautiful things. At the time I met him he was building a workshop at the top of the wooded hill to the left of our cottage and he intended later to build himself a house there.
>
> This young man, though uncouth and brusque, attracted me by his sincerity, and I expect by his good looks too. He was magnificently built; tall and straight with a large well-shaped head covered with fair hair made fairer by constant exposure to the weather. His eyes were bright blue and very clear, his skin was tanned, and he had a reddish beard. He was like a Viking or a young demi-god... . I think the genuine simplicity of our life, enforced by our means, and its rather happy-go-lucky ways, contrasted for him favourably with the thought-out simplicity of the school people. Whatever it was, he

became very friendly with us in his queer abrupt way. He was very clever with his hands. He could build a house, fashion a beam out of an oak tree, bake a loaf of bread or darn a stocking as well as it could be done, and he was very critical of similar work by other people ...

He made [an offer] to build us a house. He had bought a long strip of land at the edge of the plateau up to which we looked ... and here on the edge of this great plateau 400 feet above the sea – which on a clear day you could see like a grey mist below the horizon – our house was built. It rose slowly, for Sinclair [Helen Thomas used an alias for Lupton in her book, to conceal his identity] himself built it to his own design.[14] In his workshop great oaks – which he himself years ago had chosen as they grew – and which he had seasoned and sawn and planed – were transformed into beams, doors and window frames. Everything for the house that could be made locally was so made: the bricks, the tiles, even the glass were made under [Lupton's] direction. The great nails that studded the doors, the hinges and the hasps, were forged by our landlord, and he taught us how to make the oaken pegs which held the tiles in their place. The children and I used to go up every day

14 Nonetheless the cruck-derived mansard roof, if nothing else, puts the design firmly in the Powell genre.

> to see the gradual development of the house which was to be our home. We saw the great oak arches to support the roof shaped and hauled into their place, and the children walked on the rising walls which were to keep the fury of those hill-top storms from us ...
>
> The land sloped so steeply away from the house towards the south that from the windows there was no foreground for the eye to rest on – nothing until the downs seven miles away; and when the downs were hidden by the mists that sometimes filled the combe we felt as if we were on a ship at sea.[15]

The house Lupton built at the top of Lutcombe made the most of its position but Edward Thomas felt ambivalent about it. He loved the countryside but although the wind that howled around the house in its exposed position struck an elemental chord within him, these winds became somehow integral with Thomas's darker moods. His dialogue poem 'Wind and Mist', written after leaving for the war, described the inter-relation between himself, the house and its surroundings:

> ... But the eye watching from those windows saw,
> Many a day, day after day, mist – mist
> Like chaos surging back – and felt itself
> Alone in all the world, marooned alone.
> We lived in clouds, on a cliff's edge almost ...
>
> I might as well be talking to wind and mist.
> ... But one word. I want to admit
> That I would try the house once more, if I could;
> As I should like to try being young again.[16]

For Thomas, associations between the house, the mist, the wind and his own melancholia became almost obsessive but it is no mere nuance that the poet is responding to. The Red House, on its lofty perch (108), strikes even the most prosaic observer as startling and somehow otherworldly. But Thomas, killed at Arras in 1917, had also appreciated its solid qualities. Hand-made brick and tile, massive oak roof construction and wide tapering oak floorboards, many over thirty inches broad and all two inches thick, made for a resolute defence against the elements that Thomas found so all-pervading. Indeed Lupton had tried hard to tailor the house to the needs of the site and of his tenants. There is a built-up terrace above the tumbling garden and Lupton made Helen an alcoved seat here for the view. For Edward's writing there was a remote study with a thatched

15 Helen Thomas, *As it Was ... World Without End* (London: Heinemann, 1935), pp. 213–7.

16 Edward Thomas, 'Wind and Mist', *Collected Poems* (London: Faber & Faber, 1936), pp. 130–2.

roof, a big fireplace and a long window. Actually, only half of this separate building was for the poet; on the other side of the central chimney Lupton kept his bee equipment. Known as the Bee House, this outbuilding later became a house in its own right.

109. The Hall, Bedales School, designed by Ernest Gimson, built by Geoffrey Lupton.

Further down the lane another pair of cottages, now named after Lupton, date from soon after the war and in 1924–25 he built Wood End opposite, to one of Ernest Gimson's last designs.[17] But before Wood End he worked with Gimson on greater things at Bedales School itself. The Hall (109), dating from 1910, is a result of their collaboration and is built on a cruck frame like the Red House. Internally its spacial characteristics are reminiscent of Randall Wells's church at Kempley, which Gimson would have known. Indeed the simple pew seating, the lofty truss frames and the positioning of the big gable dormers in an almost transeptual position make the Bedales Hall the closest thing to a church Gimson ever designed. The fine carpentry makes an effective interior although it lacks the great drama of Kempley's cave-like lighting. Externally an under-

[17] David Ottewill, *Arts & Crafts in the Petersfield & Steep Area*, p. 5.

110. The Library, Bedales School, designed by Ernest Gimson and built by Geoffrey Lupton, 1920–1 after Gimson's death. Lupton's wide floorboards often taper, as here.

111 (opposite). Lupton at work on Bedales Library.

croft raises the building high, diminishing the sweep of the plain clay tiled roof and partly because of this, the overall result lacks the close affinity with its environs that Gimson's more ground-hugging buildings usually achieved.

It was Lupton again who was the driving force behind the later construction of the Bedales library (110). Again designed by Gimson, it was not built until 1920–21, after he died. Sidney Barnsley supervised construction and Lupton was assisted in the building work by Barnsley's son, Edward, who lodged with Oswald Powell at Little Hawstead. Edward Barnsley had been a pupil at Bedales from 1911 and worked in his father's workshop from 1919 before coming to Froxfield to work with Lupton on Alfred Powell's advice. Later Edward went on to study at Lethaby's Central School of Arts and Crafts, returning to Froxfield in 1923 to take over the workshop when Lupton eventually gave it up.

The Bedales library is a grander conception than the hall. Crucks are forsaken here for a fully aisled barn frame and the configuration is well suited to

its purpose. The aisles have an inserted upper level making a gallery either side of the central full-height space and the book stacks that mark the divisions between bays fit naturally into the framework of the aisles, between the arcade posts and the outer wall. The oak floorboards came from Sapperton and the ironwork was made at Froxfield by Stevie Mustoe, one of the Sapperton smiths. The structural timbers are Hampshire grown and the furniture, all designed by Gimson or Sidney Barnsley, mostly came from Lupton's workshops too. The original pole-lathed chairs were made by Edward Gardiner who resumed his chair making for the purpose. As for the building work, Lupton did as much as he could on site rather than off (111), many of the timbers being cut in a sawpit in the centre of the building. Edward Barnsley described the construction:

> The main posts were set out on the concrete floor, marked out as to positions of joints, the joints cut and the pairs of posts fitted to beams in the three dimensions. Then starting at the Hall end, the woodwork was raised and fitted, bay by bay. It was here, especially when at the main tie beam level, that Lupton's knowledge and intelligence was so remarkable to watch.[18]

The library was Lupton's finest and last major work in this country. It was a singular achievement but after Gimson's death there was nothing left to stretch his abilities locally. In 1926 he emigrated to farm in South Africa where he designed and built a considerable house. After his wife died in 1930 he married again, although this ended in divorce not long after and in about 1936 he moved on to farm in Southern Rhodesia, building a similar but smaller house. In 1937 he married for the third time. He died tragically in 1949, gored to death by a bull, having already started the construction of yet another house.

Lupton had spent six years at Froxfield before the Great War and another eight after it. Throughout this period the workshop was the centre of his world. Independent means allowed it to remain so, the majority of his building work being self financed and within a few miles of home. In fact part of the pleasure to be derived from Lupton's work is due to its geographical containment. In the best Arts and Crafts tradition it now seems a part, like the poetry of Edward Thomas, of the beech hangers and leafy lanes of East Hampshire.

Lupton sold his house and workshop at Froxfield in 1925, together with the Bee House and a pair of cottages, to Sidney Barnsley. Edward took them over and stayed for sixty years. On his death in 1987 the Edward Barnsley Educational Trust was set up to continue the tradition. Though neither Ernest Gimson nor Sidney Barnsley had ever written about their art, its tradition, as

[18] Unpublished letter from Edward Barnsley to H. Irwin, 15 August 1972, in the archive of the Edward Barnsley Educational Trust at Froxfield.

handed down through Geoffrey Lupton and Edward Barnsley, is continued through the work of the Trust today.

* * * * * *

Harold Falkner (1875–1963) designed and built a remarkable group of houses at Dippenhall, near Farnham in Surrey, working in much the same way as Lupton had around Steep. Falkner went to school in Farnham and through W. H. Allen, the master of Farnham School of Art, came to appreciate the quality of

112. House at Lodge Hill, Farnham, Surrey, by Niven, Wigglesworth and Falkner, drawn by Harold Falkner.

its eighteenth-century architecture. 'Strangers Corner' in Farnham designed for Allen immediately after Falkner finished his articles in Reginald Blomfield's office, was Falkner's first commission to be built in 1897. He had wanted to train with Norman Shaw but in 1893, when he decided on an architectural career, there was a waiting list of eighty for a place.[19] Instead, he versed himself in Blomfield's neo-Georgian, to the later benefit of Farnham. The Blomfield office was a very formal one and this was reflected in the dress expected of the articled pupils: 'Morning coats and pin-striped trousers were essential, top hats not discouraged; that's the way I began but I developed into a hat and coat

19 *Harold Falkner, Architect, 1875–1963,* Margaret Brandon-Jones, thesis held at West Surrey College of Art and Design, Farnham, 1971.

something like Sandeman's Port Wine poster before I left.'[20] The more radical side of Falkner was beginning to show itself.

From about 1902 Falkner was in partnership with Niven and Wigglesworth, a practice best remembered as one of the few in this country to properly understand Art Nouveau. Nonetheless Falkner's contribution remained firmly within the Arts and Crafts tradition. An accomplished perspectivist, he exhibited regularly at the Royal Academy (112), his drawings usually being entered under the name of Niven, Wigglesworth & Falkner although he became increasingly independent after 1903. Already, much of his own work was in Farnham, sometimes in conjunction with Ernest Borelli, a local landowner. Through him Falkner was able not only to look after some of the best of the eighteenth-century buildings that graced that town but to add to them too, starting with the public swimming baths he had designed, at the age of twenty-one.

From the beginning Falkner had had another string to his bow. In his teens he had been apprenticed to Thomas Birch, a local builder, who had worked for Voysey and Norman Shaw[21] and between 1903 and 1906 Falkner built speculative houses in Great Austins, Farnham, some of which contain examples of his own handicraft. Falkner liked to use what today would be termed architectural salvage and at 'Ilona' (113) the front door is an old French one with enriched panelling. Around it Falkner built a stone doorcase, later described by Lawrence Weaver in *Country Life*:

> This afforded Mr Falkner pleasant scope for his talent as well in handwork as in design. The capitals, shield and swags he carved himself; and the ornament in the curved pediment on the south front is also to his credit.
>
> Mr Falkner's carving was not done because of any idea that it would be better than if carried out by a skilled carver, but for two good reasons. The first was that the narrow limits of cost within which he was working would have allowed only an inferior craftsman. The second is to be sought in Mr Falkner's belief that excursions into handicraft broaden the outlook of an architect and quicken his sense of the right uses of material.[22]

20 Harold Falkner, 'Harold Falkner Speaking', *Architects Journal*, 87 (23 June, 1938), pp. 1055–6.

21 Roderick Gradidge, 'Farnham & the Hogs Back', Victorian Society Study Tour Notes (unpublished, 1975), pp. 1–8, p. 3.

22 Lawrence Weaver, *Small Country Houses of Today*, Second Series (London: Country Life, 1919), pp. 157–64.

113. Ilona, Great Austins, Farnham, Surrey, designed by Harold Falkner with a doorcase carved by the architect.

He furthered his own abilities in this direction by spending time when he could in the joinery shop of Maddon and Ball, a local builder who worked for him from time to time before 1914. He learned the art of lead-casting too and at 'Bourne Corner', built before 1909,[23] he made the lead rainwater heads and gutters.[24] After the Great War Falkner became increasingly involved in building for himself and with his own hands but he continued to work with local contractors too, such as Maddon's former partner John Mills. Alternatively he acted as master of the works on a client's behalf, as with the project he undertook for Borelli in about 1920 when he stripped the old Goat's Head pub in Farnham back to its original form. Despite his precocious talent as a perspectivist, the more Falkner worked on site, the less he drew. In fact Maxwell Aylwin, who later became his partner,[25] recalled his working drawings as rarely more than scrappy sketches when he knew him.

23 Attributed to Niven, Wigglesworth & Falkner.

24 'Current Architecture: Bourne Corner, Farnham, Surrey', *Architectural Review*, XXVI (1909), 294–7.

25 Nicholas Taylor, 'The Private World of Dippenhall', *Architectural Review*, Vol. 143 (1968), 158–60, p. 159.

Falkner escaped from the conformity into which his more formal architectural commissions led him by building nine houses at Dippenhall on his own account. As Aylwin explained: 'What he was doing was building – the thing he always wanted to do. He cut out all the things he hated: drawing, office work, documentation, very nearly the Public Health Act and its officers – and most of all clients.'[26] Built over a period of forty years, the houses became progressively more unconventional. By the 1960s Falkner's eccentricities were already local folklore, but it was not only Falkner that had changed. The authorities were by then no longer prepared to tolerate the cavalier attitude that he took to structural conventions, the showdown between Falkner's freedom of expression and the inflexibility of building legislation coming when the local authority condemned the last of the nine, the Black Barn, for non-compliance. In order to ensure the rapid removal of the offending structure, a fine of £10 a week was imposed but Falkner preferred to pay and thus ensured its survival until his death in 1963. Poor Falkner – without him the Black Barn had little chance and finally met its demise a year later.

To understand why the local authority took such exception to Falkner's work one has to look no further than the surviving houses at Dippenhall. From the building legislation viewpoint one is forced to the conclusion that the loss of the Black Barn is not so much of a surprise as the fact that some of the others managed to avoid a similar fate. Time is the final judge, however, and although the condition of the Dippenhall houses reached a dilapidated nadir after Falkner's death, none actually collapsed and they now enjoy a belated local recognition, metaphorically thumbing their noses at the town hall, which ironically Falkner also designed, albeit in his more conventional mode.

The Dippenhall story started in 1921 when Falkner, whose family already owned land there, bought Deans Farm, a Georgian house with a shell hooded doorcase, and extended its parapeted gable elevation to create a new south front. The house is now known as Dippenhall Grange but a cottage in the garden grew, half-timbered, under Falkner's hands to take the old name of Deans. Another, Barn Cottage, had a hole knocked through its centre to form a gatehouse behind which Falkner re-erected the frames of a large barn and a stable from elsewhere on the site to form another house, called The Barn (114), not to be confused with the Black Barn of forty years later. Here Falkner's emergent expressionism becomes apparent. Approached from the north, the roof comes low to either side of the central entrance door. Inside steps fall to a circular, double height, central space paved in broken marble. Beyond is the garden and to either side rise winding stairs to upper balustraded landings and

[26] Maxwell Aylwin, quoted by Charles Blyth, 'Dippenhall', unpublished thesis for the West Surrey College of Art and Design (Farnham, 1979), p. 5.

114. The Barn, Dippenhall, Farnham. The garden front.

passages at different levels, one of which emerges as a bridge across the back of the drawing room.[27] There is a massive central chimney stack from which these inventive structural conceits are hung but although the stack proved a durable support, the surrounding timber framed walls moved differentially and daylight appeared all around. Maxwell Aylwin remembers an architectural colleague, after surveying one of the houses, remarking that 'if a mouse jumps through a crack in the wall, one can forget it; but what can be said when the cat jumps through after it?'[28]

Despite the ebullient interior, the house externally is a restful composition below a long uninterrupted roofline. The garden to the south is a masterly arrangement in its own right, flanked by gazebos to east and west and structured by formal water channels parallel to the house running from a wellhead on its

27 Beyond the open plan drawing room a more private sitting room boasts a fabulous salvaged plaster ceiling, adapted to fit.

28 Quoted by Nicholas Taylor, 'The Private World of Dippenhall', p. 160.

115. Overdeans Court, from a photograph taken in 1968. The herringbone brickwork between the timber frame was, contrary to Falkner's original intentions, being rendered and painted.

central axis. Falkner's gardens are often unexpectedly good, their design carefully considered and often as ingeniously planned as his interiors. Gertrude Jekyll was his godmother and he is said to have visited her once a week for thirty years.[29] Certainly Falkner's garden designs owe something to her but his time with Blomfield, who himself did much to revive interest in the formal garden, give a strong underlying geometry to his seemingly informal Jekyllesque planting.

The Barn really got Falkner started. Here his love of old and disused building components developed into the re-use of complete structures, and such was his enjoyment he longed to repeat it. In 1925 he bought land nearby from his brother and with Alfred and Bert Hack and another helper, Algie Bass he re-erected another two barn frames end to end, slightly bending the axis at their junction.[30] The house so formed was named Haberdums, after the field on

[29] Jane Brown, *Gardens of a Golden Afternoon* (Harmondsworth: Penguin Books, 1982), p. 196.

[30] The barn frames came from nearby Runwick, according to Nicholas Taylor, 'The Private World of Dippenhall', p. 158.

116. Meads, Dippenhall, Farnham. The open arcade referred to in the text may be seen in the foreground, facing onto the water tank with the bridge beyond.

which it stood but is now known as Overdeans Court. Falkner did not build to sell, so the tenanted houses remained part of his estate until he died, after which the by then delapidated Overdeans Court was rescued by an American who left it a little neater and tidier than Falkner would have liked (115). Something of the garden survived, looser in its structure to that at The Barn but again with interlocking geometrical compartments, this time circular, to tie the composition together.

Overdeans Court, completed in the late 'twenties, was followed in 1930 by Meads (116), again formed from two old barn frames,[31] this time butting to form a 'T'. Falkner was forced to plan ingeniously because his brother, who now owned the family land, would only sell him a small plot. As a result the house and garden almost merge. The south front is an open loggia, broken by a bracketed roof over the garden doors from the linenfold-panelled sitting room. These doors open onto a bridge over an abutting pool and further on the arcade changes form to become the windows to a billiard room which look straight

[31] Rescued from Alton in Hampshire (Nicholas Taylor, 'The Private World of Dippenhall', p. 158).

into the water. On the western side is more water, in circular and interlocking basins, with another bracketed wagon roof hanging above.

Moving on, Falkner and his team next built nearby Halfway House. It is said to contain bits and pieces left over from the construction of Meads but outside the style seems less wilfully perverse, reflecting something of his earlier work, as exhibited at the Royal Academy before the Great War. Inside an Expressionist plan is based on angled inter-relationships giving a strong dynamic quality to the spatial arrangement. At about this time Falkner found two more barns, this time in Gloucestershire and now working to a well-tried formula he re-erected them to form the structure of Burles, perhaps the best of the group, completed in 1937. The house, unlike the three that preceded it, is on a sloping site and it is this additional dimension that makes it outstanding. Falkner made the drive snake round the hill on which Burles stands and jettied out a triple-gabled timber frame towards the approaching visitor. A forecourt is cut out of the hill behind, further perforated with recesses and caverns for storage and parking and with this all to one side and the triple gables standing Stokesay-like above, on a heavily modelled brick base, the feeling of dramatic enclosure is terrific. Steps lead out and upwards towards the front door, set amidst a confusion of roofs sweeping to low eaves, a huge chimney and varied dormers. The jettied garden side is no less impressive, Falkner claiming it, perhaps improbably, to be the longest continuous overhang in England. The western gable elevation owes something to that at Overdeans but with more variation and even greater panache (117).

Burles was the last of the big barn houses. It shows not only the culmination of Falkner's freehand design skills but also the virtuosity of constructional and craft techniques developed by the builder/architect and his team. After Burles, Bert Hack and Algie Bass left but Falkner carried on. In 1949 his housekeeper and her husband, who had been with Falkner since 1926, left too. Alfred Hack, the last of his trusted fellow builders moved in to look after him. They built Burles Lodge when Falkner was over eighty, H. Dalton Clifford visiting him there in 1958 when writing for *Country Life*. Clifford's article was turned down by his editor, Christopher Hussey, on the grounds that the Dippenhall houses were not serious architecture,[32] but ten years later Nicholas Taylor described the building process at Burles Lodge in the *Architectural Review*: 'By now he was right out of his period – or any period: and the local authority, armed with the battery of post-war byelaws, succeeded in stopping work by alleging that the breeze block foundations were faulty; but the story goes that one of the breeze

32 Unpublished letter from Christopher Hussey to H. Dalton Clifford, 5 September 1958, in the author's possession.

117. Burles House, Dippenhall, Farnham. The entrance court is overlooked by three gables seen here on the left.

blocks broke the testing machine and anyway work went on.'[33]

Falkner's eyesight was failing; some of his tenants fell behind with their rents but if bureaucracy could not stop him, nor could old age and recalcitrant tenants. In 1958 he bought Grovers Farm, aquired from a neighbour whom he had outlived. Walking on crutches, Falkner employed his tenants as building labour in lieu of rent, and the interior of the farmhouse was opened up to incorporate an adjoining oast-house. Outside he built a neo-Georgian facade, a style he defended to the end; in 1961 in the Farnham Branch Newsletter of the National Association of Local Government Officers (entitled 'Bumbledom', no doubt to Falkner's approval) he wrote: 'Finally, as for your 'mock Georgian', do you, when making an apple pie, Mock Cook it? Architects must follow a

[33] Nicholas Taylor, 'The Private World of Dippenhall', p. 159.

traditional style that has proved its worth, whether it be Georgian or the second Elizabethan.'

Exhausted by his labours, Falkner spent much of his time at Grovers Farm asleep and his press-ganged workforce took advantage of the situation, sitting around and playing cards as he dozed. Falkner died in 1963, ignored by the architectural press. He had, however managed to complete both Grovers Farm, after a fashion, and the ill fated Black Barn at Ridgway, near Dippenhall. During the conversion of the Black Barn, which had belonged to Falkner since the 1920s, Alfred Hack, ninety years old and Falkner's last faithful co-worker, fell from the scaffold and died. Falkner had Hack's masonry trowel gold plated and initialled. But the Black Barn itself, which should have made a more lasting monument to Hack, did not outlive him by long[34] and the rest of the Dippenhall houses, tenanted but without pride of ownership as a spur, fell into decay, quickly forgotten until their relatively recent and well deserved re-emergence.

34 The Black Barn that stands on the site today is a less interesting rebuilding.

Chapter 9
THE FAR WEST
Philip Tilden

> On journeying through the shires, as I used to do in the leisurely days, and coming to my journey's end, I remember a hundred sun-sets over the outline of the next village which was to be my resting place.
>
> Philip Tilden, *True Remembrances*, 1954.

Philip Tilden (1887–1956) was at Bedales School in the 1890s at about the same time as Basil Gimson. Two of Alfred Powell's brothers were then teaching there: Oswald the second master, and Malcolm[1] who taught Tilden to draw. Tilden, like Geoffrey Lupton when he left Bedales, was also attracted to the Cotswolds, but for him the magnet was not Sapperton but Chipping Campden. Tilden first visited in 1906, by which time C. R. Ashbee had made the place an established centre for those prepared to commit themselves to the more radical aspects of the Arts and Crafts movement. As Goodhart-Rendel said of Ashbee: 'If you had taken him up, you really were in with the revolutionaries.'[2]

Ashbee's wife Janet was under no illusion as to the degree of commitment that taking up with him required. Honeymooning at The Clergy House, Alfriston in 1898,[3] they swam in the Cuckmere river nearby. Janet took off her stays by the river's edge and never wore them again, her symbolic commitment to a life with Ashbee and his unfettered ways. She must have known even then that her marriage was likely to be neither romantically idyllic nor commonplace but by the time they moved with the Guild of Handicraft to Campden in 1902, she had also come to realise that her husband was homosexual. Janet looked upon their relationship as worthwhile in many ways nonetheless and compensated for, at least in part, by a liaison with Gerald Bishop, an early

1 Malcolm Powell had spent a year in Sidney Barnsley's workshop himself and later set up as a furniture maker in Reading. He took great interest in building work too and organised architectural expeditions for the Bedales boys.

2 Nikolaus Pevsner, 'Goodhart-Rendel's Roll Call', *Architectural Review*, Vol. 138 (October 1965), 259–64, p. 263.

3 Rangeing red apples along the beams (see the end of Chapter 3).

proponent of the Garden City movement who introduced Tilden to the Campden circle. Ashbee noticed him immediately: 'Gerald [is here] and that fascinating youth Philip Tilden ... Of course I lost my heart to him in five minutes.'[4] Tilden, articled to Thomas E. Collcutt and studying at the Architectural Association, visited frequently, enjoying Campden's literary company as well as that of its artists and its crafts exponents. While back in London he met regularly for lunch at the Mont Blanc in Gerrard Street with Edward Thomas (who had just moved to Steep), Joseph Conrad, Ford Maddox Ford, Charles Ricketts, Wyndham Lewis, W. H. Hudson and others.[5] In the country his youth proved no obstacle to a friendly association with Ernest Gimson, Laurence Housman, John Masefield, F. L. Griggs and Dr Coomaraswamy. All knew or were part of the Chipping Campden circle by the time Tilden first visited. F. L. Griggs, for example, had arrived two years earlier (on an unreliable and noisy Rex motortricycle)[6] to make the drawings for the Cotswold volume in Macmillan's 'Highways & Byways' series. He had never moved on but the flame which had drawn such moths was already guttering by the time Tilden arrived. Although much of its energy dissipated with the financial failure of the Guild in 1908, many of the Guildsmen remained and it was with one of these, Jim Pyment, that Tilden lodged.

Jim Pyment was a cabinet maker and one of the old stalwarts of the Guild of Handicraft, having been elected on 13 July 1894.[7] He had led the village band that Ashbee had taken over as part of his attempt to integrate the Guild into the local community. Ashbee's Guild plays, summer swimming sports, football, hockey, cricket, bicycling and gardening were all intended to foster such links. In many way he succeeded and the village band, with townspeople and Guildsmen playing together, must have seemed to Ashbee a fine example of the proper use of leisure as it marched down Campden High Street with Pyment at its head. The church, however, in the form of Parson Carrington, held out against Ashbee, setting up a school treat and sale of work as a counter-attraction to the exposure of male physique at Ashbee's swimming sports and hiring Pyment's band for two guineas to add colour to their cause. But the band rather overdid it, leading the parson down the high street in a grand cavalcade, while

4 Unpublished letter from C. R. Ashbee to his wife, 15 December 1906. I am grateful to Alan Crawford for his notes on the Ashbee Journals, in which this letter appears.

5 James Bettley, *Lush & Luxurious – the Life and Work of Philip Tilden*, published by the RIBA to accompany the exhibition of the same name at the Heinz Gallery in 1987, p. 6.

6 Alan Crawford, *C. R. Ashbee, Architect, Designer and Romantic Socialist* (New Haven and London: Yale University Press, 1985), pp. 129–30.

7 Ibid., p. 449, note 12.

the watching Guildsmen laughed. Charley Downer, the blacksmith, led the band that day with Arthur Bunten, cabinet maker. Pyment himself spent the afternoon quietly chuckling in his workshop and later wandered down to the sports to smoke his pipe.[8]

When the Guild of Handicraft went into liquidation in 1908, Pyment bought the old Silk Mill that had housed the majority of the craft activities. He started his own building and joinery business and, together with Ashbee and ten other active loyal members, carried the Guild on by signing a Deed of Trust, setting up a less formal company of independent guildsmen. They met regularly with Ashbee still taking the chair. When, in 1919, seven guildsmen met for its last meeting, Jim Pyment was amongst them. Ashbee had left Campden long before but he returned from time to time, and in 1924, on one of his visits, he found Jim Pyment still in business. Indeed his firm still trades today.

From Ashbee, Tilden learned the virtues of a direct involvement in the building process: 'The architect must take off his top hat ... he must set to work in an apron with the other workmen.'[9] For Ashbee it was not the architect that was to benefit from such co-operation but the craftsmen themselves: 'Co-operation will inevitably approximate to the medieval guild system, in which the workman was enabled to put his own individuality into his work'.[10] Ashbee built up a work force for building projects both in Campden and Chelsea and maintained the continuity of work required to employ his tradesmen on a permanent basis. He registered as a builder with the London County Council District Surveyor six times at Cheyne Walk between 1896 and 1898,[11] the period when Blow was beginning to get his own itinerant work force on the road. Ashbee described his own experience: 'I engaged my own foreman and workmen, entered into direct relations with tradesmen and Local

8 Fiona MacCarthy, *The Simple Life – The Ashbees in the Cotswolds* (London: Lund Humphries, 1981), p. 138.

9 Quoted in Crawford, *C. R. Ashbee, Architect, Designer and Romantic Socialist*, p. 236, note 9.

10 Crawford, *C. R. Ashbee, Architect, Designer and Romantic Socialist*, p. 236, note 11.

11 Direct labour was later investigated enthusiastically by the London County Council Works Department themselves, as an alternative to the highly developed late Victorian contracting system. Indeed, direct labour was a topical subject among Ashbee's associates at this time. He knew some of the forward-thinking young men in the LCC including Lionel Curtis, private secretary to its chairman. Owen Fleming, chief architect to the LCC's 'Housing of the Working Classes' Branch', shared a flat with Curtis and it was Fleming who had been involved in the repair work on the Old Clergy House at Alfriston prior to its acquisition by the National Trust. Curtis in turn was one of the Trust's earliest tenants there (Crawford, *C. R. Ashbee, Architect, Designer and Romantic Socialist*, p. 118, note 50).

Authorities, payed my own wages and took up contracts for the execution of works.'[12] The advantages of direct labour to Ashbee were its simplicity, its fairness to the craftsmen themselves and its known standards. His requirements were: 'A group of conscientious workmen, say a joiner or two, a few masons and a couple of blacksmiths, all of whom were intimate with me, knew my ways and worked in my spirit.'[13]

Such was Ashbee's way of working. Tilden followed his lead, signing his drawings as builder as well as architect up to 1911 at least. After completing his articles with Collcutt and Hamp, Tilden joined them in partnership while working independently on occasions also. This freelance work was sometimes undertaken in conjunction with Harold Thomerson who also had previous connections with Collcutt's office. Unlike Ashbee, whose architectural work was mainly restricted to his own locality, Tilden had to travel further afield for his commissions. He built a small house in Hindhead and undertook other work, perhaps through Collcutt and Hamp, in Buckinghamshire. He had friends in Herefordshire where he visited and designed choir stalls in Sollershope Church. But it was in the far west of Cornwall that Tilden was encouraged to take Ashbee's doctrine one step further

The opportunity came about as a result of friendships made on family holidays among academic friends of Sir William Augustus Tilden, Philip's father. The friends in question came from Birmingham where Sir William had been Professor of Chemistry at Mason College. The family moved to London in 1894 when he took up a similar position at the Royal College of Science. Knighted in 1909 he was one of the most distinguished chemists of his generation. Well-connected, his early morning tricycle ride from the family home at 9, Ladbroke Gardens sometimes took him to Downing Street and breakfast with Arthur Balfour. Philip Tilden described how these family connections led to other things:

> When I paid my first visit to the far west of Cornwall, there was a small hut on the high land behind Mullion, ticking with mysterious secrets, whilst high to the sky, great skeletons of masts seemed preposterously assertive in the loneliness; but Marconi was a nine days wonder then and whilst half of the world applauded, the other half hated his doings.

[12] Crawford, *C. R. Ashbee, Architect, Designer and Romantic Socialist*, p. 236, note 13.

[13] C. R. Ashbee, *Craftsmanship in Competitive Industry* (Campden: Essex House Press, 1908), p. 142.

I stayed at Landewednack with the Sonnenschein family from Birmingham, and in the evening we sat in penetrating mist and listened to the Professor reading Carlyle's French Revolution, backed by a Greek Chorus of fog-horn, that rose and fell with a sort of muffled horror. In the long autumn days we stumbled amongst the heather and groped for hut circles.

Every expedition, 40 years ago and more, was an affair and as I call them back to mind they each one stand out as isolated and important; there was no hurry to start, to get there, nor to return in those days, and from afar we could see from the rising smoke of dust along the roads, the single carts or donkey drays performing miracles of speed at five miles an hour.

... [One] expedition took us to Prussia Cove, where John Carter, the King of Prussia self-styled, the most notorious smuggler of the west, reigned from 1777 to 1807. [Carter assumed the title of his hero, the King of Prussia, in boyhood exploits and the name stuck not only to him but to the Cove too.] Tucked in a rocky bay behind Cudden Point, his little cottage then laid crouching against the hillside, embattled against a high walled enclosure against the storms, and fed by rough tracks up the valley and over the cliffs.

But this old story could not be left alone, and when I next visited Cornwall in 1908, it was to live in the new house which replaced the humble thick walled cottage and flaunted its gaunt, hard hideousness to the world. I little knew that it would be my lot in a few years to spend a year and more in destroying as much of this new usurper as I could, and hiding what I could not destroy.

But what a place to live in those days!

My first architectural work in Cornwall was, however, inland some four miles or so at Buckshead, Townshend (118), where old Dr Vyvian, a great and rather crazy character, had built himself up a strange long house, mysterious, damp and intimate, along the edge of the dusty road, and constructed out of bits of Breage Church, an ancient Inn, and timber rescued from the sea; it gazed with half shut eyes over a south slope of old orchard and a garden lit by red hot pokers under the Cornish elms. My dear friends, Dr & Mrs Chown, let me convert it for their home, and with a mixed crew of artisans from up country, William Harris from Chipping Campden, Fred Pearson from Chesham, and a sprinkling of men from the countryside, I tried to make it gay, comfortable, and indigenous. Those were the years to build in, that was the time when we could do what we liked with what we liked, to create those little eccentricities arising from exigencies which makes a design grow. Every atom of old wood, the

118. Buckshead, Townshend, Cornwall, by Philip Tilden, 1911: the garden front.

little granite windows of a former age, enormous granite quoins from deserted mines, and granite slabs upon the floor. I seem to remember that we started at 7.30 in the morning and went on as long as we cared to. But the evenings I had to myself and I used to wander down to Godolphin House, sitting blue bloomed from wood smoke in the midst of its gnarled trees, whilst near at hand the ever lasting stamps[14] thudded out their modern rhythm. The pillared entrance, and lamentable court of cold grey granite filled me with melancholy, yet when I turned from rotted Elizabethan grandeur, I could see the gay fresh whitewash of cottages through the trees, and the thumping of the stamps changed from a death watch to the tempo of modern men.[15]

14 Stamp mills were used in tin mining in Cornwall and elsewhere in the West Country until well after the Great War.

15 Philip Tilden, notes for an unpublished talk on Architectural Reminiscences in the West Country, amongst the Tilden Papers, British Architectural Library, ref 3/3/7, TiP/2/2/9.

119. 'Additions to a Cornish Manor House', a drawing showing suggested alterations to Godolphin House, near Townshend, Cornwall, by Philip Tilden, February 1913. Hung at the Royal Academy that year (BAL).

The evenings that Tilden had to himself whilst working on Buckshead resulted in the submission of a drawing for the Royal Academy Exhibition (119). Entitled 'Additions to a Cornish Manor House' and dated February 1913 it was, in fact, a scheme for a new long gallery to close the courtyard at Godolphin House. This entrance range was to be flanked by circular towers with conical roofs but it seems that Tilden had no commission for the work, it was just a way to while away the winter evenings.[16]

Buckshead, called after the Buckshead Inn, from which part of Dr Vyvian's house had grown, still stands today. The road, against and below which the house straggles, is less dusty but the roadside elevation was never preposessing. The majority of Tilden's work is on the garden side and here the composition is more serene, the outlook rural. The old orchard and the Cornish elms have been replaced by a mature, sheltered and tranquil garden but in 1986 the house was still occupied by the doctor who fifty years before had taken over from Dr Chown, Tilden's client.

16 By the time the drawing was published, Tilden had moved on and his address is given as Porth-en-Alls, Marazion, Cornwall (*The Building News*, 16 May 1913, p. 677).

120. 'A hillside entrance cottage in Cornwall', Royal Academy drawing by Philip Tilden in 1912 for a cottage, curved in plan, facing the entrance to Porth-en-alls across a small circular forecourt that straddles the coast path (BAL).

Tilden's drawings for Buckshead are dated May 1911 and he signed them as 'architect and builder, Northwood R.S.O. Middlesex.'[17] His father was living at Northwood at the time, having re-married in 1907 after the death of Philip's mother. The work cost £800 and out of his fees Tilden bought a gold watch for each of Dr Chown's two children. One, Dr Dorothy Chown, recalled Tilden living with the family when Buckshead was in hand; she told how he used to work with the men and how, his clothing suffering as a consequence, he sewed braiding around the bottom of his trousers to stop them fraying.[18] Tilden's own narrative continues:

> Upon the completion of Buckshead, and with many thanks and regrets, I took my things one day, and journeyed over those four miles along the edge of the clear leat below Tregonning Hill, along the main road by the moor to the Falmouth Packet and then down to Prussia Cove. [The Inn, the Falmouth Packet, still marks the head of the lane that winds down to the Cove.]
>
> The first thing to build was a curved cottage on the hillside, in which we could live during the construction of the large house, and where I could draw and plan (120). I seem to remember, during those brilliant years just before the 1914 war only the intense heat of spring and summer, the endless tapping of granite on the roadside below, and the pleasant feeling of when, after the day's work, the men and boys scrambled amongst the gorse on the cliffs to get their donkeys. Up the various tracks they struggled slowly, until one by one they silhouetted against the bare sky line and left the cove in loneliness.
>
> It wasn't all beer and skittles, for in the evenings I had to draw, and with the help of an adding up machine, work out the wages and accounts. Those were the days when we payed the labourers 4½*d* or 5*d* an hour and they were happy with it, the skilled masons even up to 7*d* and 8*d* an hour, and they were happy with it - cement was 25*s* a ton delivered and I paid £19 for a whole ruined mine house as a quarry for quoins and ashlar.
>
> Brian Behrens [the younger brother of Tilden's client, Tankred Behrens] and I lived on lobsters and asparagus and hock and there was a little vineyard in the valley behind that led up to the high land.
>
> Had I ever been able to complete that house, called Porth-en-Alls, it would have stuck out on to the sea-sprayed rocks and towered up high and assertive (121). But I had to content myself with half a dream come true, the rest lies only on paper as I sent it to the Academy.
>
> I wish now that I had kept to the Cornish tradition more closely than I did, but I had been impregnated with the Cotswold tradition,

[17] In the posession of Dr Stanley Jones at Buckshead in 1986.

[18] Recalled by Dr Dorothy Chown in a letter to the author dated 15 July 1988.

121. Royal Academy drawing of Porth-en-alls, from the sea, by Philip Tilden, exhibited in 1912. The tall gabled block in the forground, with its battered lower walls beyond the water gate, would have stood in the sea at high tide had it ever been completed (BAL).

> and the mullioned windows, chimneys and doors and stonework were almost too fine in texture, whilst the windows were of bronze to withstand the corrosion of the sea spray and air.
>
> Inland, a few miles away, lay St Hilary and Goldsithney, and I used to treck over in the evenings to play on a clanking piano for the village to dance to, whilst the Chapel folk prayed next door for our souls, until they joined in and danced as well.

Ashbee saw the house and wrote to his wife about it in January 1913 from St Mawes:

> ... yesterday I took a day off and joined Philip Tilden at Falmouth. He brought his client Mr Behrens and we motored over to Marazion where that lovely house of his is abuilding. That's the way to do it, with a full purse... . Philip's arrangement is that he has to give six months of the year to the work and live there superintending it. It will be three years or so building. Thats the way to build. He is paid £500 a year for his time. I don't think we shall get proper building or building conditions unless we devise some system like that to work under.[19]

Tilden's design for Porth-en-alls was exhibited at the Royal Academy in 1912, and it is indeed a pity that he never had the opportunity to complete it. A distant relative of the Behrens, Tilden retained the shell of the earlier house but extended it inland to the west, burrowing into the side of the hill. Its eastward extension, on the seaward side,

> was to contain a noble staircase, a great hall with elaborate oak framed roof and a minstrels' gallery, a balcony jutting out over the sea, a subterranean boat house and other wonders. Building operations began in 1912, the work being done entirely by direct labour. Craftsmen were collected – four stonecutters and a foreman from Penzance, a mason and a master carpenter from Gloucestershire and so on – and accommodated in a vacant house which the foreman's wife ran as a hostel. The younger brother supervised the job for the three years that it lasted, paying the wages, ordering the materials, organising transport and often working alongside the tradesmen. The granite quarry at Tregonning Hill was taken over, complete with an aged quarryman, and farm horses hauled the roughly shaped stones down to the cove ... the piping, pumps and tanks were installed by the family chauffeur, who subsequently did all the plumbing in the house.[20]

One of the workmen Tilden took with him, a joiner called Henry Fitton from Tewkesbury, married the daughter of a local fisherman and settled in the cove. He was killed in the Great War.

Despite its non-completion the house is, as Tilden claims, still half a dream come true (122). The forecourt is a circular platform cut into the tumbling rocky hillside at the point where it has fallen almost to the foreshore. This forecourt straddles the coastal footpath on one axis and is closed on the landward side by Tilden's earlier curved cottage. To seaward is the echoing

[19] Later that year, according to another letter from Charles Ashbee to Janet, dated 8 May 1913, Tilden planned to join Ashbee on a trip to Northern France (unpublished letter from C. R. Ashbee to his wife dated 8 May 1913, in the possession of Felicity Ashbee). I am grateful to Alan Crawford for this information.

[20] H. Dalton Clifford, 'A House at a Smuggler's Haunt', *Country Life* (1 May 1958), pp. 955–6.

122 (opposite, top). Porth-en-alls, the entrance elevation seen from above the cottage.

123 (opposite, below). Porth-en-alls, from the garden. The house was left incomplete, its toothed masonry facing the sea to accept the unbuilt final stages of construction.

curve of the embracing entrance walls of the house and this entrance, due to the sharp fall in levels from the forecourt down to the sea below, is at that which in an ordinary house would be the attic (123). Beyond, the house itself juts like a promontory out into the sea.

The tapping of granite on the roadside, recalled by Tilden, must indeed have been endless. Tilden's mouldings are unusually delicate for this intractable material. Nonetheless there is at Porth-en-alls something of the gaunt character of Lutyens's granite fastness at Castle Drogo (building from 1910 onwards). The terraced shoreside garden is still embattled by the same high walled enclosures against the storms that previously protected Carter's smuggling hideout and a first glimpse across them to the incomplete house beyond suggests that the truncated building with its toothed masonry, still open-jawed and jutting seaward, has been shattered by storms rather than left unfinished.

On 30 July 1914, just before the outbreak of hostilities, Tilden married the mother of Robert de Rustafjaell, a young mining engineer and friend, who had died tragically only six weeks earlier after a motorcycle accident. Forsaking her previous married name, Tilden's wife called herself Amalia Caroline Brodin on the marriage certificate. She had led a highly colourful life. Twelve years older than Tilden and a member of the Vasa family which ruled Sweden in the sixteenth century, she had married a Swedish Count and honeymooned on her grandfather's yacht. Having sailed to Finland they were attacked by Bolsheviks when out riding and he was never seen again. While recovering from her own injuries she gave birth to her son Robert. Between then and Penzance, where mother and son were operating a tin mine at Gurnards Head, there were art studies in Rome, medical studies in Edinburgh and a crossing of the Ghobi Desert, not to mention a meeting with Lord Kitchener in Egypt.[21]

Although Tilden had little to do after the outbreak of war, he did not enlist. The mental crisis that followed may be attributed in part to his lack of work and in part to the guilt he was made to feel by his father for his continued refusal to join up. But there is no doubt that much of his anxiety was caused by marital problems too. For a time, in 1917, he and his wife went separate ways; she to Sweden and he to Sollershope where he lived, for part of this period at least, with a Belgian refugee painter. Tilden's recovery was slow but he, like his marriage, survived and it was the story of his chequered past that eventually

[21] As related to H. Dalton Clifford by Philip and Mrs Tilden and described in an unpublished description by Clifford, dated 15 Feb 1985, in the author's possession.

captivated his next client, leading him back from chicken farming on Dartmoor. Considerable success as a society architect eventually followed: by 1922 he had a chauffeured car on permanent loan from Harrod's to carry him and his picnic hamper to Chartwell where he was working for Winston Churchill. But before all this there was one more excursion that had echoes of his earlier footloose life-style – to Allington Castle on the Medway to work for Sir Martin Conway, later Lord Conway of Allington, and his wife Katrina:

> I spent my days making a survey of the Castle, and for some weeks walked to and fro between Allington and Aylesford, a little over a mile down stream, where I lodged with Mrs Joy in a timbered house at the end of the old bridge. My daily walk took me along the bank of the river below Preston Hall, where then stood a fringe of the most immense elm trees ... fishermen sat all day and the boys and girls walked in the evening, so that on every journey I had changing pictures of the riverside that made me dawdle. My track took me aslant the hopfields, then skirted sand-pits, and rag quarries, a bit of hazel copse and, along the brilliant-flowered quayside of old Allington Lock, at length to a flat lush meadow across which the castle was set.
>
> ... All through the autumn I pursued this delightful duty, but when the November fogs came, I went to live in the Castle itself, occupying two rooms one above the other in the red-capped tower overlooking the privy garden ... alone ... I heard the owls, the gurgling and slashing of the water from the shoots of the roof, dropping sheer to the cobbles below, and much of my time I spent reading and stoking the insatiable fire place.[22]

Tilden worked at Allington (124) over a period of more than fifteen years, carrying on the work that Conway had started with W. D. Caröe before the war. At first Tilden could do no more than make plans and lay out a garden as the war was not yet over. Later he was able to continue the building process, starting with the north-east tower and finishing in 1933 with the Great Hall. It all stemmed from Prussia Cove. In April 1916 Agnes Conway, Sir Martin's daughter, was on holiday there and met Tilden who was presumably staying at Porth-en-alls. 'He is a most attractive person' she wrote. 'His life has been most astounding, I have never heard anything more strange than his wife's story and his story and the strange way in which they lived.'[23]

Tilden charmed Agnes' mother too. He visited Allington and the Conways visited Prussia Cove again before, at the end of 1917, Martin Conway engaged Tilden, armed at last with a certificate of total exemption from war service, to work at the Castle. But Allington almost concludes Tilden's itinerant

[22] Philip Tilden, *True Remembrances* (London: Country Life, 1954), pp. 15–16.

[23] Bettley, *Lush & Luxurious*, p. 9.

124 (top). Allington Castle, from the NW, showing Tilden's new work on the left (*Remembrances...*).

125 (left). Unbuilt scheme by Tilden for a great tower over Selfridge's in Oxford St (BAL).

126 (below). Unbuilt scheme for Selfridge's Castle, Hengistbury Head (BAL).

excursions. Perhaps such a life-style seemed irrelevant as his career blossomed via contacts made through the Conways. They led to work for Gordon Selfridge (125 & 126), Sir Philip Sassoon, Lord Beaverbrook, Lloyd George, Winston Churchill and King George V. But Tilden never gave up his on site work completely. He painted in tempera on bare plasterwork at Allington and at 'Wardes', Otham, the other side of Maidstone, he used the same medium. His painted plaster panelling there included an allegorical scene depicting the unsuspecting stag (or payer of income tax) pursued by the hunter (or collector) and tiger (or inspector). He did *trompe l'oeil* work at Watlington, Oxon and a floral frieze at Long Crendon (127) nearby.

127 (right). Long Crendon, Buckinghamshire.

128 (opposite). Philip Tilden's design for a church that led to the commission for the church of St John Bosco (both from *Remembrances...*).

After great things in the 1920s, the 1930s were for Tilden comparatively lean. Forays into commercial architecture were unsuccessful but Martin Conway stayed loyal to him. Conway's second wife was the widow of Reginald Lawson of Saltwood Castle where Tilden was employed to restore the great audience chamber, spending many months there: 'I stood on scaffolds in the east wind and carved some of the corbels in the great hall that I built.'[24]

Tilden had no trouble finding time for this return to a slower tempo of work. He had little else to do and his financial affairs were at such a low ebb he was obliged to accept financial help from Alfonso Crivelli, whom he had employed to help run his office. Crivelli helped him spiritually too and Tilden, coming close to joining the Roman Catholic church, gained solace from a commission to build a church for the Salesian Order – the chapel of the Salesian Missionary College at Shrigley Hall, Cheshire (128):

[24] Philip Tilden, *True Remembrances*, p. 113.

> No site I have ever dealt with has better subscribed towards a satisfactory creation. Here, as I watched the boys of the order cutting the sods and wheeling earth, heard the clanging of hammers and bars in the quarry in the hillside, and saw the thick stone walls arise, reminiscences, very deep and clearly felt, came rushing back to me of the first work that I ever did.

> I was able again to work with my own hands and in the biting wind carved the stone. The Reverend Father Hall, a genius with his hands if ever there was one, had helped me to design the ironwork, hinges, rails and great candle-sticks, and in the forge above the church it was made on the spot.[25]

Work started on the church at Shrigley in 1933, building between 1935 and 1938 (129). Apart from the restoration work at Saltwood, Tilden did practically no other work during this period but although his workload dwindled to a trickle at the outbreak of the Second World War, his enforced retirement was a happier one than that brought about in 1914.

[25] Philip Tilden, 'Architectural Reminiscences', *The Builder* (2 March 1945), p. 169.

129. The Shrine of St John Bosco, Salesian Missionary Church, Shrigley Hall, Cheshire.

His career had a final third flowering in the post war period. He was much sought-after to adapt old houses and to remove Victorian extensions to suit the austerity of the times. In old age the Tildens returned to Devon where H. Dalton (Tony) Clifford and his wife met them in 1953:

> They were living in this vast isolated ruin of a house without any domestic help, and with no central heating ... In 1949 Tilden had been asked by the Devon County Planning Authority to report on the condition of Dunsland House. He found that it needed urgent attention. Parts of what he called the Plantaganet wing had gone too far to be saved, but the main part of the house was deteriorating rapidly owing to the fact that whenever it rained all the rainwater was conducted into a huge slate tank above the main staircase - and the bottom of the tank had fallen out. Also the fine plaster ceiling in the drawing-room was on the point of collapse owing to a rotting beam above it. Impatient at the slow reactions of the authority to his most urgent report, the Tildens had bought the house themselves selling their comfortable home, Wortham Manor.[26]

Only emergency repairs had been carried out before Philip Tilden's health collapsed:

> The only help they had was a farm labourer called Hurd who arrived every morning on a tractor towing a load of logs, and got fires going in three of the huge fireplaces. He must have spent the rest of the day felling trees and cutting them up into logs, but now and then he was

[26] As related to H. Dalton Clifford by Philip and Mrs Tilden and described in an unpublished description by Clifford dated 15 Feb 1985, op. cit. in the author's possession.

called in to lift Philip out of bed so that he could be washed and the bed made ... We slept upstairs in 'The Kings Room' which was comfortable but bitterly cold. It was furnished with a splendid four poster bed on a raised platform and a portrait of Charles I hung over the fireplace.

There were two resident dogs, a large and very fierce Pyrenean shepherd dog which lived in the dungeons and appeared in the central courtyard now and then to bay at the moon, or to be fed. No one ever went near it but it was fed regularly with hunks of meat tossed out of a window, and dishes of cream pushed under a door. The other dog, Toto, was a Pekinese puppy, full of good humour in spite of spending most of its life shut up in a lavatory off the main stairs.

Meals were at odd times, but the food was good. Lavish quantities of meat and groceries were delivered regularly, and a gallon of milk appeared every morning. Neither of them drank much milk so it was poured into preserving pans and set on the cooker to make clotted cream – most of which was eaten by the dogs. About fifteen feet of corridor had been separated off to make a larder, and in one corner of this was a pile of sides of bacon. A new one arrived from the grocer every other week and was put on top of the pile. We asked Mrs Tilden why she did not cancel the order and she replied 'The grocer was so good to us during the war, we don't want to upset him now'.

Philip was always good tempered and friendly but he lived in the past, in a world very remote from anything we had experienced, so it was a surprise to all of us when, one morning, he put forward the notion of selling Dunsland and building a cottage near the walled garden. Mrs Tilden ridiculed the idea but the next day she announced that she had ordered Noon (a farming contractor she employed to plough and sow the fields of the 100 acre estate) to come with a lorry and cart all the loose stone from the crumbling Plantaganet wing down to the site. We went to inspect the place after lunch and found a small sloping swampy piece of ground with a spring at the top. I questioned its suitability as a building site and Mrs Tilden promptly rang Noon and told him to level the ground and block off the spring. My suggestion that it might be wise to design the cottage first was ignored.

One morning Mrs Tilden went off in a taxi to Shute Barton. She must have been up all night packing trunks with rugs and knitting wool, making sandwiches and filling a hamper with thermos flask and tins full of cake and biscuits. As usual she disappeared that morning just when breakfast was ready and emerged half an hour later from one of the upstairs bedrooms with a pair of antique silver slippers with long pointed toes and waisted heels, which she presented to my wife. When the car came she was still flapping about in the corridor/kitchen wearing stout brown shoes and many waistcoats, one of leopard skin,

> one quilted and one knitted in pale blue wool. She topped this off with a long grey tweed overcoat trimmed with fur, and got away about 10.30 with Toto under her arm.
>
> It was later that we learned that this was one of a series of visits made with the object of testing the 'ambience' of a cottage on the Shute Barton estate, near Axminster which had been offered the Tildens by Sir John Carew Pole. She was afraid the cottage would be too small and claustrophobic, and she would sit there for an hour or so eating her lunch and knitting to see if she could stand it. On her return about 4.30 she tipped Albert, the driver, with a £1 note, but she was never able to pay the taxi fare. Months later she gave the local garage who owned the taxi her grand piano in payment.[27]

Tony Clifford had been helping Tilden prepare his autobiography for publication and he and Mary, his wife, returned to Dunsland House once or twice after this, the last time to read Philip the proofs. In August 1954 the National Trust bought Dunsland House and in September the Tildens moved to the cottage at Shute Barton. Philip Tilden died there in February 1956. In his book he recalled his wandering days:

> On journeying through the shires, as I used to do in the leisurely days, and coming to my journeys end, I remember a hundred sun-sets over the outline of the next village which was to be my resting place. There was hardly one that did not thrill me with its warmth and welcome, even from afar, and which I recognised from its very outline of church and roofs, of clumps of trees, barns and fields, of walled gardens and the open village green. These pictures I have always held close to my heart when designing, and I pray that the time may come when we once more revert to this form of colonising our countryside, thus leaving large tracts of real country in between, instead of the never ending ribbons of populated highways.[28]

The Cliffords persuaded Mrs Tilden to come and stay and in 1959 she moved down to Penzance permanently, occupying a flat over the antique shop adjoining the Clifford's Abbey Hotel. She lived there until her death in February 1964. Dunsland House was restored by the National Trust and filled with appropriate furniture and pictures but was destroyed by fire on 18 November 1967.

[27] Ibid.

[28] Philip Tilden, *True Remembrances*, p. 125.

Chapter 10
FAR AND WIDE
William Weir and the SPAB

> The only way in which the crafts can again be made harmonious by beauty is for men with a sense of architectural fitness ... to take up the actual workmanship and practice it themselves.
>
> W. R. Lethaby, *Leadwork*, 1893.

William Weir (1865–1950) put in more time on the road than any other of the Wandering Architects. But although the archive of the SPAB is full of his letters and reports, their absolute professionalism, complete detachment and lack of personal reference, through file after file of minute constructional detail, frustrate an enquiry into the man himself. A contemporary of Detmar Blow and Alfred Powell, Weir shared the early SPAB repairs with them, as Thackeray Turner confirmed in 1900:

> As you know my Committee is very anxious to extend the new custom which it has started, of architects undertaking the personal and continual supervision of the repair of ancient buildings. At the present time Mr. Detmar Blow, Mr. A. H. Powell and Mr. Weir are all willing to undertake the repair of buildings in this way, and they are practically now all engaged.[1]

In the early days of the twentieth century the SPAB's techniques were at last being seen as capable of achieving the results that their long-admired philosophy demanded. To the experience already gained by Blow and Powell had been added the personal dedication and single-mindedness of William Weir. Like Blow and Powell, Weir was a craftsman as well as an architect; he could turn his hand with a similar degree of proficiency to carpentry, stonemasonry, plastering

[1] A letter from Thackeray Turner to Sidney Barnsley, persuading him to take on the repair of North Wyke House, Devon. Barnsley acted on an initial report prepared by William Weir, repairing wooden panelling. See the exhibition catalogue for 'A School of Rational Builders (the History of The Society for the Protection of Ancient Buildings)', published by the RIBA and held at the Heinz Gallery, London, in 1982, p. 14.

and leadwork and in the end it was he who, consistently and thoroughly, maintained the Society's reputation and brought its manifesto to bear on a wide cross-section of ancient buildings. 'Do not let us talk then of restoration. The thing is a lie from beginning to end', insisted Ruskin in 1849,[2] but it was not until the height of Weir's career that the Society could at last support its fulminations against 'restoration', or the vain attempts to return a building, often conjecturally, to its original state. His comprehensive case-book of conservative repair methods provided the alternatives needed for so long.

Today William Weir's achievement has long been recognised by those who appreciate the importance of building conservation work:

> The total number of buildings on which Weir worked during his life is impossible to assess with any accuracy; it is probably something between 300 and 350. A number of these, certainly, were small scale projects; but 50 of the 275 documented ones were two year jobs, a further 40 lasted three years and a few even took seven or eight years to complete. We may need to remind ourselves that throughout a career that spanned well over half a century, William Weir never employed a professional assistant of any kind... . He would often consult Charles Winmill and George Jack during his early years, but the work, once begun, was done by himself. He never had a partner, not even an office boy but dealt with every architectural project entirely on his own – for many years, to the extent of recruiting and personally directing the labour, buying the materials and himself taking part in the work on site.[3]

The importance of the structures with which Weir was involved varied from an old signpost or a dovecot to monastic buildings, colleges, castles, country houses and churches but, rather surprisingly, only one cathedral (Peterborough). He did much to conserve the finest of our parish churches, one hundred of those on which he worked appearing in John Betjeman's selected favourites – each one, in Betjeman's opinion, 'worth bicycling 12 miles against the wind to see.'[4]

William Weir was born in Edinburgh in 1865. At the age of sixteen he was articled to Archibald MacPherson, leaving for London in about 1883 to work in Leonard Stokes' office. In 1888 he was joined by Charles Canning Winmill[5]

2 John Ruskin, *The Seven Lamps of Architecture* (1849), Chapter 6, para 19. See Ch. 1, ref. 4.

3 Reginald Snell, *William Weir and Dartington Hall* (Dartington: The Dartington Hall Trust, 1986), p. 78.

4 John Betjeman, *Collins Guide to Parish Churches of England and Wales* (London: Collins, 1958), p. 14.

5 Winmill studied in the evenings with Blow at the Architectural Association at this

130. William Weir and his penny-farthing in about 1890.

(1865–1945) and although Weir accepted a position with Philip Webb in the following year, he and Winmill remained firm friends, taking the first of many holidays together in 1890:

> They cycled from London to Walsingham, sketching as they went – Essex churches, Cambridge colleges, Norfolk manor houses. On their high bicycles (130) they were above the level of the hedges. They made a point of dashing through every stream and water splash. Overhead was the great windy expanse of East Anglian sky. They made their headquarters at Walsingham, and sketched the old churches within a ten mile radius ... Weir and C.C.W. [Winmill] stayed with a Mrs Codman in the High Street at Walsingham. One morning they saw the postman going from house to house, showing an envelope, which was always greeted with laughter and surprise. Arriving at Mrs Codman's he handed it to C. C. W. whose name was shown by an excellent drawing of a windmill by an architect friend.[6]

time.

6 Joyce M. Winmill, *Charles Canning Winmill. By His Daughter* (London: Dent, 1946), p. 24.

When Weir started at Webb's in 1889 he was paid £117 a year. Payments indicate that he was only employed full time until about 1895; thereafter he received only small amounts indicating perhaps temporary or site work, including a job as clerk of works at Newmarket where Webb had designed a substantial extension to Exning Hall. Weir finally left Webb in about 1897 and spent a year with J. T. Micklethwaite, Surveyor to the Fabric at Westminster Abbey. Thereafter he was in practice on his own.

Weir did not become an SPAB committee member until 1902 although he claimed (and records of anything relating to his work were always meticulous) to have supervised three SPAB repair jobs during one year soon after joining Leonard Stokes, perhaps more than fifteen years previously. As most SPAB projects enjoyed practical input from Webb, if only from his advice at committee meetings, these and other early works by Weir may account for George Jack's comment that 'William Weir came to give occasional help to Webb before joining him 'altogether'.'[7] In any event they clearly show that Weir's interest in the repair of ancient buildings had developed at least to some degree before his association with Webb.

Weir and Winmill went different ways but shared much throughout their careers. Winmill was another SPAB stalwart and later recalled the Gatti's suppers that made such a deep impression on all the young men that attended them: 'It all comes back to me – the "after meetings" of Anti-Scrape when we went over to Gatti's. Lethaby, who generally had a cruet of red wine with his food, Webb a half bottle of Graves. Emery Walker, who seemed to eat the whole of a fish, skin, bones and all. I think it was Sydney Cockerell who now and again had his chocolate made with milk instead of water.'[8] Winmill attended SPAB meetings as early as 1894, and like Weir, saw a lot of Cockerell, Gimson and Webb. Knowing Winmill wanted to see Kelmscott Manor, Webb arranged a visit and Winmill came away with a copy of 'News from Nowhere', inscribed by Mrs Morris. He kept it by his bedside and added his own note: 'Given to me by Mrs William Morris in the room "hung with old tapestry" mentioned on page 228.'[9]

From 1892 to 1923, Winmill worked in the Housing Section and then the Fire Brigade Section of the Architects Department at the London County Council (131). Although fundamentally a loner, Weir turned to his friends for a second opinion when he felt the need, Winmill being one and George Jack (1855–1931) another. Although Philip Webb helped many young architects like

7 W. R. Lethaby, *Philip Webb, His Life and Work* (Oxford, 1935), p. 117.

8 Joyce M. Winmill, *Charles Canning Winmill. By His Daughter*, p. 28.

9 Undated letter from Charles Winmill to Sydney Cockerell quoted by Joyce M. Winmill, *Charles Canning Winmill. By His Daughter*, p. 30.

131. Belsize Fire Station, Eton Avenue, London NW3, by L.C.C. Architects Dept., Fire Brigade Section, built 1914–15.

Blow, Powell, Sidney Barnsley and Ernest Gimson, only William Weir and George Jack worked with him for any length of time. The lasting influence of this experience shows in the careers of both men. Jack, born of British parents in the USA, had worked for Webb since 1882 and stayed nearly twenty years in his employ, continuing the practice after Webb retired in 1901 (132). Jack designed furniture for Morris & Co. and later taught under Lethaby at the Central School of Arts and Crafts. He worked with his own hands too, mainly as a woodcarver but in clay also. Thackeray Turner's brother, the sculptor Laurence Turner who worked with Wells at Kempley, was associated with this side of his career. George Jack worked on site for Webb and much later for Weir as well when he repaired Rievaulx Abbey in 1907, writing to the SPAB: 'I had some difficulty in arranging for constant supervision, but I am glad to say Lord Feversham has agreed to pay 3 guineas per week, which will just cover the supervision cost. I hope to get Jack there next week to make a start.'[10]

10 The work in hand involved considerable repairs to stabilise the walls, chiefly in the south transept. Work was completed under Jack's supervision by May 1909 [exhibition catalogue, 'A School of Rational Builders (the History of The Society for the Protection of Ancient Buildings)', p. 19].

132. Faire-na-sgurr, Arisaig, Highland, designed and drawn by George Jack, 1903 (BAL).

William Weir worked for the SPAB through Webb on church repairs in Herefordshire, Oxfordshire, Cambridgeshire and Buckinghamshire in the late 1890s[11] but Webb did not consider him fully fledged in conservation work until his involvement in the rescue of Eglwys Brewis, a little church in Carmarthenshire, in 1900. Weir spent much of that year there, aided by Webb's constant written advice and encouragement:

> That you will be wanted before long to undertake reasonable church mending I have no doubt, any more than I have of your capability in that way. The Brewis will, I think, be a test for you as to doing the necessary repairs to the walls, which will require cautious handling; but I am satisfied it can be done soundly on the principles advocated by our Society.[12]

11 Snell, *William Weir and Dartington Hall*, pp. 29–30.

12 Undated letter from Philip Webb to William Weir quoted by Snell, *William Weir*

Weir lived in the neighbourhood throughout the work and adopted the technique for wall reconstitution, developed by Webb and Blow at East Knoyle and Clare. Indeed Webb first considered Blow for the work at Eglwys Brewis but found him busy at Happisburgh. Weir repaired the chancel arch by bonding courses of stone between concrete bands. He called the system 'Webb's sandwiches' and when they reached the roof timbers Webb suggested another of his simple and honest repairs: 'I would not chamfer the new – let the thing tell its own tale as well it may.'[13]

As with Randall Wells in Gloucestershire, Weir moved from one church to another nearby. The church of St Margaret Marlos, Eglwys Cummin had been the subject of another of Webb's reports and Weir was the obvious choice for the supervision of its repair. A steepened roof pitch had resulted in the raising of the west gable in an insecure fashion and work started in July 1900 on strengthening it: 'Weir discovered moulded stones indicating that the gable had originally been curved. Webb wanted Weir to reveal these stones on the outside, explaining: "I am not for a moment proposing to repair the church in any supposed earlier form of roof or vault, but only as the work now is".'[14] Weir attended to the roof and in May 1901, after the interior plastering was completed, Mr Treherne, the local member who had brought the case to the SPAB's attention, wrote to the Secretary: 'The Society through Mr Webb, under the supervision of Mr Weir, have advised as to certain works of repair to this ancient church with great success and much economy.' The repairs had cost £450. On receiving Weir's photographs of the church in November 1901 Webb eulogised: 'Truly it looks more "ancient" than before you laid hands on it... The continuous looking solid stone ridge is more than worth the money it cost. The pointing too – now, looks really workmanlike.'[15]

Weir's next project at All Saints, Wilby in Norfolk was the first in his own name, Webb's involvement through the SPAB being advisory only. Weir had first visited in February 1900 but could not start until spring 1901 when, with Eglwys Cummin completed, he strengthened, repaired and retiled the roof, rectified the bulging north wall, stitched its cracks and rebuilt a buttress. When reinforcing the north-east portion of the nave, he discovered the remains of a staircase to the rood loft and Webb advised on its repair: 'All we can do is to strengthen, and hide as little of the present untouched work as possible.' The repairs were completed in the Spring of 1902, Weir returning to the church in 1912 and again in 1933 to give further advice on its upkeep.[16]

---

and Dartington Hall, p. 29.

13 'A School of Rational Builders', p. 11.

14 'A School of Rational Builders', pp. 11–12.

15 'A School of Rational Builders', p. 12.

133 (opposite). The church tower, Coln St Denys, Gloucestershire. Its venerable and misshapen form survives, repaired according to the conservative techniques of the SPAB by William Weir and his itinerant masons.

Later in 1902 Weir was on site in Nottinghamshire, at All Saints, Sutton on Trent. Local workmen were employed between September that year and June 1903, repairing the tower in the same fashion as Knoyle or Clare:

> The south wall had suffered most severely from the weather ... towards the west angle a bad crack ... [ran] up to the belfry floor. The inside core of the wall was completely disintegrating ... as to necessitate its being wholly rebuilt up to the back of the stone facing on the outside. Concrete was largely used for its core and the outside face was well bonded into the new work by means of long stones, built in at intervals.[17]

And so the momentum of Weir's career developed. Before becoming involved in repairs to the church at Coln St Denys (now more commonly spelt Coln St Dennis), just north-east of Cirencester in 1905, he was able to quote a list of a dozen buildings already undertaken using direct labour. By so doing he persuaded the incumbent to spare the tower (133), whose rebuilding had been recommended by the church's own architect in 1903. Fortunately the SPAB had been aware of this tower, buckled, bulged and bowed, since being alerted to threats to its future survival by Ernest Gimson as early as 1894. That the tower survives today is a tribute to them all and especially to Weir who strengthened it from inside in the now well-tried way, with concrete and hard materials: stone and brick in this instance. Such methods may be contrary to those used in present-day conservation but the tower's survival is a telling tribute also to the influence of the SPAB itself. Ten years previously others in better condition were pulled down as a matter of course. The society had at last made such misshapen indicators of a building's history not just acceptable but venerable, and something worthy of great effort to retain. 'The weathered and timeworn surface of an ancient building' was, as Morris had earlier hoped[18] 'at last the proper recipient of the due care and attention that it truly deserved.'

Weir spent two and a half months on site at Coln St Denys, fairly typical of his method of working on a project of this scale at the time, all significant projects enjoying his personal supervision, sometimes for a considerable period.

16 'A School of Rational Builders', p. 12.

17 William Weir, his description of the repairs written in 1903 and quoted in 'A School of Rational Builders', p. 12.

18 Society for the Protection of Ancient Buildings, Paper to the Annual General Meeting, July 1884. In the 'Report of the General Meeting' published in the Committee Report of that year.

He used a motorcycle to travel from site to site, at one stage a New Enfield, travelling light and never arriving with drawings prepared previously. All measurements and therefore all drawings were undertaken on the spot if possible although later in his career his vast experience allowed him to pre-judge to a certain extent, drawing at home on the kitchen table.[19] His success was very much dependent on the methods he used:

> Most important among the factors which go to make the system notable is his practice of employing direct labour and of obtaining materials at first hand. He does not work from a city office as most architects do. He relies on the men he has trained and upon unremitting personal supervision for his success. Most architects employ men who have been accustomed to their methods by always engaging a builder of their choice. But this does not always prove successful, for builders are at the disposal of many different architects, both those who restore and those who repair, and their men, more or less bewildered by the contrary instructions of different firms, are hesitant and fearful when they are not actively ignorant and thoughtless. On the other hand the men employed by Mr Weir know no other master, and when they are not directly trained by him they learn their special craft from others of older standing who have had that benefit. Thus tradition in repairs true and right as the great building tradition of the middle ages itself is being evolved. Mr Weir's work has not been confined to the tradesmen alone, for he has from time to time taught younger architects, and through them has helped to establish a school of repair which must have a lasting effect on the architectural learning of our country.[20]

Often one of these younger architects would be left on site so Weir himself could move on to something new. Two such men were Norman Jewson and Walter Gissing, Gimson's assistants, who he spared from time to time to improve their experience under Weir's supervision. Jewson's honeymoon, spent supervising work at the church in Salle, Norfolk (see Chapter 5), was preceded by three months there before the wedding: 'No builder was employed, the men having been trained for the work by Weir, so I gained valuable experience by watching them at work.'[21]

Another who learned from Weir in this way was Albert R. Powys (1881–1936), appointed successor to Turner as Secretary of the Society from 1911. 'A.R.P.', as he was known, carried the SPAB flag until his death in 1936

19 Snell, *William Weir and Dartington Hall* , p. 32.

20 Snell, *William Weir and Dartington Hall*, p. 31.

21 Norman Jewson, *By Chance I Did Rove* (privately published, 1951; republished, Barnsley, Nr Cirencester: Gryffon, 1986), pp. 92–3.

and his *Notes on the Repair of Ancient Buildings*, one of the Society's pivotal texts, originated from notes made when he worked under William Weir and Walter Cave between 1902 and 1904.[22] Under Weir he supervised repairs to churches at Denton in Oxfordshire and Onisbury in Shropshire.[23] Powys joined Turner's practice and was allowed to work almost full-time for the society. He was eventually succeeded as Secretary in the mid 1930s by John MacGregor, by then his partner and another of Weir's proteges. MacGregor had worked with Weir at Tattershall Castle in Lincolnshire, shortly after leaving the Architectural Association where he trained until 1912. Their client was Lord Curzon and later the National Trust:

> The castle was then a veritable ruin; the double surrounding moats had been filled and some 50 or 60 labourers were digging them out again. The building was roofless and floorless except for the vaulted basement. There were two or three masons and three or four bricklayers (brothers). For a couple of months I shared digs with Weir, simply observing and trying my hand in the various crafts on the castle.
>
> Twice I spent a fortnight working a shapeless lump of stone without a flat surface into a piece of medieval window tracery or chimney cap and also learning to use the adze on the oak timbers, or run a concrete floor. So derelict had the castle become that it, with an acre or so of filled in moats and the tilt-yard were sold for £500. The wily speculator carefully removed the splendid stone fire openings, packed them carefully in timber cases, and carted them up to London. He then raised the alarm that they were being sold to transfer to America.[24]

Lord Curzon bought the ruin, paid some £15,000 to buy back the fireplaces and called in Weir. Initially asked to rebuild much of the castle, Weir managed to dissuade Curzon from restoration and concentrated instead on reinstating the timber floors, repairing the window tracery, battlements and gatehouse and providing the necessary bridges over the moats.

Weir had Ernest Gimson make the bridges in oak (134), a commission readily accepted as Gimson later explained: 'I am very pleased that Lord Curzon and yourself think we have done some good carpentery and joinery. The men who did the work are now taking in hand the most delicate and expensive inlaid and veneered cabinetmaking and I shall find they will do it all the better for

22 'A School of Rational Builders', p. 20.

23 The careful repairs at Onisbury have previously been mistakenly attributed to Blow (as in John Betjeman, *Collins Guide to Parish Churches*, p. 319).

24 J. E. M. MacGregor, 'Recollections of William Weir, November 1975', unpublished MS, quoted in Snell, *William Weir and Dartington Hall*, p. 33.

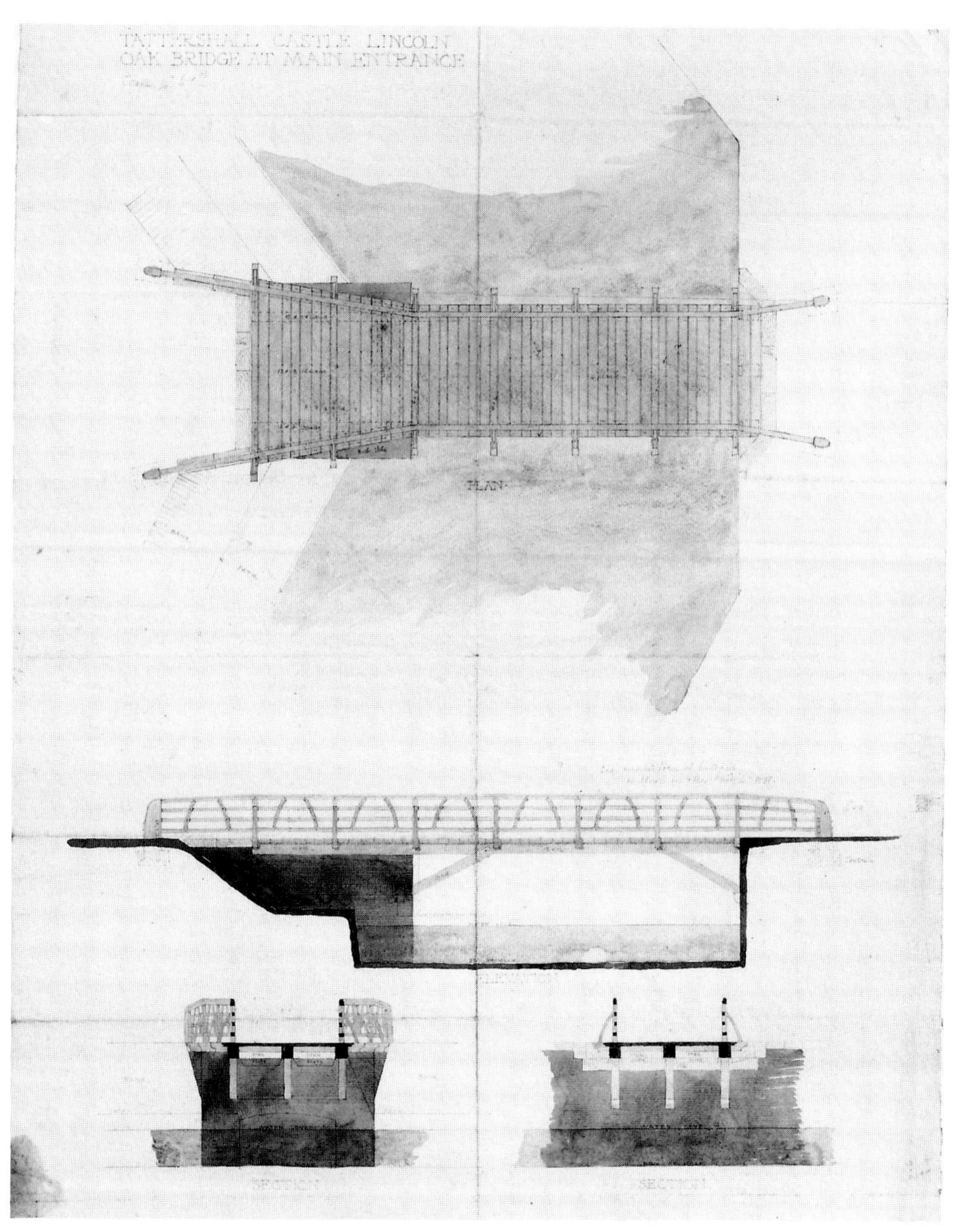

134. 'Tattershall Castle, Lincoln, Oak Bridge at Main Entrance', by Ernest Gimson, *c.*1914 (Cheltenham Art Gallery and Museums).

their six months bridge building.'[25] Lord Curzon threw himself enthusiastically into the proceedings too, returning triumphantly, seated on top of the rescued fireplaces on their final cart journey to the castle.

From Tattershall Weir sent MacGregor to Norton Church in Norfolk to repair the church walls and install new pews, again made by Gimson. More churchwork followed at Orston, south of Nottingham, MacGregor helping contain the outward leaning walls and learning to recast and re-lay lead roofing. At Compton in Surrey, where the magnificent Saxon Tower had been badly cracked by the action of the bells, he learned the technique of repair from within and noted that it took some fifty tons of material. The outbreak of hostilities in 1914 marked the end of MacGregor's time with Weir:

> The work was virtually finished and I went sailing in a homemade boat out of Rochester across to Southend. I had retired from the Territorials shortly before and as we approached the pier we saw one of the first boats taking our troops to France. I felt I had to rejoin ... At the end of the war I got in touch with Weir again and we were lunching in an ABC (Weir, my wife and I) when the sirens sounded the end of the war. I explained that as I was now married I would not be returning to the nomadic life ...[26]

MacGregor continued his architectural career nonetheless, working into his old age and dying at ninety three.

Weir's own career had been at its height at the outbreak of the Great War. Between 1906 and 1914 he averaged twenty-six jobs a year; in 1914 there were thirty-two. But hostilities brought such impressive achievements to a halt: 'The war deprived him forever of the valuable help of a number of his skilled assistants whose pride and enthusiasm for the work upon which they were engaged had, in many cases, equalled that of their employer.'[27] In the twenties craftsmen of a high standard were still at Weir's disposal nonetheless, and he trained successors to those he had lost. Charles Winmill occasionally borrowed such people, describing how, without a workforce under his own direct control, it was difficult to get the quality of work he was after:

> The trouble is that there is a space between words and deeds. In that space things occur which are most difficult, if not impossible, to alter – unless the man in charge is really anxious as to the work, and wants to

[25] Letter from Ernest Gimson to William Weir dated 11 Feb 1914, quoted by Clive Aslet, *The Last Country Houses* (New Haven and London: Yale University Press, 1982), p. 214.

[26] From the unpublished 'Recollections of William Weir, November 1975' by J. E. M. MacGregor. I am grateful to Reginald Snell for this information.

[27] Obituary in *The Builder* (11 August 1950), p. 194.

> do it as the SPAB holds right, one gets a 'gobble-de-oh', as Philip Webb used to say. When you have a master mind at work, with a master man to do the actual work, be thankful.[28]

Weir himself spent part of the war in a West End contractor's office. After a long engagement he had married and then lived in north London, near Winchmore Hill, in a house he originally bought to accommodate his father who had since died. Weir's wife died there too, after only a few years of marriage and his sister came from Welwyn Garden City to share the house with him. In fact, although he spent most of his time away, his base had usually been in or close to London from the time he left Scotland. Sydney Street was an address of greater duration than most, although three years were spent in both Melton Mowbray and Attleborough – curious locations as neither seem to have obvious connections with known major works, although they may have proved convenient for his wide ranging activities.

In 1917 Weir's old client Lord Curzon bought another castle, Bodiam in Sussex. At the outset Curzon thought of living there, a fact clearly unknown to Philip Tilden who later praised Curzon's altruism: 'He was the one owner who never intended living in the buildings he rescued.'[29] Discouraged from so doing by Weir amongst others, Curzon did little for two years, until:

> In the summer of 1919 I commenced the work ... placing the supervision of the undertaking in the capable hands of Mr William Weir who had already assisted me at Tattershall ... For more than a year a staff of more than 25 men were employed on the work firstly of exploration, secondly of strengthening and repairing the foundations and superstructure of the castle.[30]

Curzon, Viceroy of India from 1888 to 1905, frequent visitor to Clouds, friend and admirer of the Tennant sisters and himself a key member of the Souls, died in 1925. The castle was bequeathed to the National Trust and Weir was appointed architect to the Management Committee. His association with Bodiam lasted twenty years, the castle being one of eight Trust properties with which he was involved – two of the others being the Old Post Office, Tintagel and Joiners' Hall, Salisbury where he carried on from where Blow and Powell left off.

28 Joyce M. Winmill, *Charles Canning Winmill. By His Daughter*, p. 88. The brothers Clare and James Sargeant were loaned by Weir to Winmill on more than one occasion.

29 Philip Tilden, *True Remembrances* (London: Country Life, 1954), p. 27.

30 The Marquis Curzon of Kedleston, *Bodiam Castle Sussex – A Historical and Descriptive Survey* (London: Jonathan Cape, 1926), p. xiv.

The work of a man who, despite many hundreds of projects, left no major building to stand clearly and identifiably as his own design can only be illustrated by looking at those buildings that survive as a result of his intervention. A close examination of his repairs reveals that Weir never attempted to deceive history by pretending his work was part of the original. Inherent in his philosophy was an insistance that repairs must stand on their own merit, without being stylistically imitative, but so deeply was he imbued with the spirit of ancient work that the mantle of traditional craftmanship now cloaks his repairs and the old alike.

There is though a place where one can stand and look, knowing confidently that the entire structure in question is Weir's doing. That structure is the hammerbeam roof of the Great Hall at Dartington (135). To attract such attention would probably have met with the disapproval of its architect; it was, after all, not what his life's work was all about. Nonetheless, it is clearly indicative of his ability and, like Lupton's library at Bedales, it represents a fine piece of craftsmanship in the medieval timber-framed tradition. When Weir first saw Dartington in September 1926 the Hall had been roofless for more than fifty years. Everywhere was ruinous and in a state of collapse. The court was a farmyard, part of the entrance block a stable and part of the lower range of the courtyard a cowhouse. Weir was recommended to Dartington's new owner, Leonard Elmhirst, by Oliver Baker, an SPAB west country contact of long standing. Baker, initially retained in a supervisory capacity with Weir as a technical adviser, had been concerned about the possibility of re-roofing the Great Hall in oak. He had insufficient knowledge of the problems presented in terms of technique and thought it unlikely that adequate timber could be procured. Weir was under no such delusions and soon after his appointment wrote to his client:

> If the trees are felled this winter it would be time enough in the spring for sawing. The best age to fell oaks is considered at about 100 years ... it would be safe enough to have some trees sawn into planks 4" and 6" in thickness, and carefully stacked to allow for a free circulation of air between the planks.[31]

When Weir took on Dartington he was in his early sixties and his days of long stays in temporary lodgings were over. He would visit regularly and stay overnight, usually as a guest of his clients but occasionally at the Seymour Hotel in Totnes:

> Leonard always made the most of Weir's short visits, and would accompany him as he trudged through the Dartington woodlands to choose oak branches of the right curved shape for the making of roof

[31] Snell, *William Weir and Dartington Hall* , p. 38.

135. The hammerbeam roof of the great hall, Dartington, Devon, during construction.

> trusses. The two men were absolutely of one mind that, if it was at all possible, the roof should be built entirely with timber from the estate; Dartington was in fact one of the few estates in the country where oak trees suitable for the work were still to be found. Weir's design demanded, apart from the smaller lengths of timber which would pose no problems, 22 principals each of them 29 feet long ... Even more difficult to obtain, in the event, were the large curved collars tying each pair of principals. Leonard never missed a minute of his search for the right trees; and later, when the roof was actually being built, he would stand by Weir's side as he chatted to the tradesmen on the site and demonstrated with his own hands how their forefathers half a thousand years ago had used the spoke shave to finish off the chamfers of an oak beam. Admiration – indeed affection – is written into every line of a description of Weir at work that he wrote many years later, wishing that today's discerning visitor to Dartington 'could have seen the diminutive Scot in action, his catlike figure moving up ladders and over scaffolding, as he applied his broad grasp of medieval design and gave intimate attention to the smallest detail; how his keen eye would often twinkle with appreciation of honest and solid craftmanship...'[32]

There was no perceived contradiction between Weir's work to the Great Hall and Elmhirst's commitment to Modern Movement architecture elsewhere on the estate. He described Weir's principles as

> so eminently suitable that we subscribe to them absolutely; there would be no attempt to fake any repair or construction, so that whether by the use of materials or of modern methods all new work should be recognisable as such by visiting experts; and if any old building were needed for some new use, it should boldly be adapted for that purpose, if possible without disturbance of any ancient stonework or timber.[33]

Weir had faith in his stonemason, Jimmy Eales and also, most importantly for the roof, in Jack Goode his foreman carpenter. His leading plumber was Tommy Nicholson who made the lead rainwater goods. The site manager was Alfred Fincham, a skilled worker in his own right. At one stage it had been thought that one of Weir's own masons would be brought in but by the time work started on the Hall in 1931, Weir had built up a good rapport with the Dartington men through earlier work around the courtyard and was happy to put Eales in charge. Between the spring of 1931 and the Hall's completion in 1933, Weir visited more than twenty times. He continued to work for Elmhirst elsewhere at Dartington until 1938 but his contribution, as always, is not

[32] Snell, *William Weir and Dartington Hall*, p. 41.

[33] Snell, *William Weir and Dartington Hall*, p. 40.

assertive – the Great Hall is Weir's great visible achievement. Baker had initially pondered the use of concrete but although the old roof was gone, its original materials were never in doubt and Weir's roof is an honest expression of oak roof construction in its own right. It may be new and its pattern conjectural but its simplicity and Weir's refusal to incorporate pseudo-medieval detail reflect the assimilated knowledge of a lifetime, and as such it is a real continuation of the medieval tradition – as it had been learned by succeeding generations from their forefathers and adapted to each new situation accordingly.

Although Weir began to wind down after Dartington, he worked on into his eighties. John MacGregor took on more and more of the SPAB workload but Weir was still active after the Second World War when, as his eyesight failed him, he would prevail upon the then Secretary of the SPAB, Monica Dance, to check timbers for beetle holes for him. He died, like Webb, just before his 85th birthday.

Chapter 11
THE END OF THE ROAD
Detmar Blow's Career, 1906–1939, Conclusions

A minor revolution in the history of British Architecture.
Alfred Powell's obituary, *The Times*, 1 June 1960

Despite the continuing dedication of William Weir and his disciples, and the later isolated individualism of architects like Harold Falkner, there is no doubt that the Wandering Architects reached a crossroads towards the end of the first decade of the twentieth century. The latter part of Detmar Blow's career epitomises the changing times. By 1900 his itinerant way of working was well developed, but at the same time he was becoming established as a society architect. Blow loved to build but his widening clientele no longer allowed him to devote long periods of time to a single job. Demand outstripped his personal ability to supply. As a consequence Wilsford Manor and Little Ridge were almost the last of Detmar Blow's hand-built houses and in 1906 he entered into a partnership with Fernand Billerey (1878–1951), forming the basis of a country house practice that was to accelerate rapidly to a success in the five years before the Great War rivalled only by Lutyens.

Billerey was a very capable architect indeed. As a result opinion on who was responsible for the meteoric success of the partnership has always tended towards polarities. Romantics blame Billerey for turning Blow from his Arts and Crafts roots and fail to admire Billerey's highly professional stylistic sophistication. Classicists on the other hand favour Billerey's discipline and denigrate Blow's less rigorous approach.[1]

1 Goodhart-Rendel (1887–1959) said: 'The really architectural work is by Billerey who was a very, very good architect.' See Nikolaus Pevsner, 'Goodhart-Rendel's Roll-Call', *Architectural Review*, 138 (October 1965), p. 263. Pevsner put this comment in context, pointing out that Goodhart-Rendel was inspired more by Parisian classicism than by English trends. Goodhart-Rendel had a vested interest in Billerey's reputation too. In 1938 Goodhart-Rendel, then President of the RIBA, was director of the Architectural Association School, in turmoil over a campaign for a socially committed architecture. He appointed Billerey in a reactionary

136. Horwood House, Winslow, Buckinghamshire. The garden front.
A latter-day Wilsford Manor by Blow and Billerey in 1912 (CL).

Christopher Hussey took a more balanced view when he wrote up Horwood House (136), built by the partnership in 1911 and typical of the literally hundreds of significant commisions, both in London and the country that they received.[2] He ascribed its success to the combination of 'The genial

---

attempt to reform the school. See Gavin Stamp, 'Centenary Decorations', *Building Design* (19 June 1987), p. 20. Such an appointment was doomed to failure and must have been something of a gesture on Goodhart-Rendel's part – a reaffirmation of his belief in the disciplines of architecture as portrayed in the teaching of the Ecole des Beaux-Arts.

2 The drawings from the Blow and Billerey partnership are now lodged in the British Architectural Library, Drawings Collection, following a campaign in 1987 to ensure their survival when under threat of sale and dispersal. Still in a largely uncatalogued state, the collection may comprise over 5,000 drawings. The size of the practice's output is confirmed by an index prepared by Billerey which numbers 85 significant projects undertaken with Blow up to 1920. Few relate to Blow's work prior to the formation of the partnership in 1906.

personality of Mr Blow and the comprehensive ability of Mr Billerey'.[3] Horwood is a latter day version of Wilsford, with multi-gabled elevations and a thatched stable block, but Blow's reasons for the partnership become apparent on closer analysis of this house. His contribution was his love of materials, Early English Renaissance styles and the picturesque; Billerey added organisational skills and impeccable planning and together they produced a product that must have been ideally suited to their clientele at this date. Hussey dwells particularly on Blow's contribution:

> The surface ... and this applies to the whole exterior – is of a brownish red brick, the edges of which are softened by the overlapping mortar and is of a richness peculiar to these architects. It is to be seen in London in Lord Glenconner's house for example [34 Queen Anne's Gate, extended by the partnership in 1912]. The front, though it has ... undeniable shortcomings, yet acquires distinction from the material, and aptly illustrates a remark by Mr Roger Fry made lately on the subject of Mr Blow's work. After dwelling on some of the 'dives' that used to be, and still are, made by architects into old styles, whence they 'bring up innumerable architectural fragments which are carefully glued on to their houses', Mr Fry goes on to say: 'the search has flagged of late, people know it is useless, and here and there architects have set to work merely to build so well and with such a fine sense of the material employed that the result should satisfy the desire for comeliness without the use of style. I am thinking of some of Mr Blow's earlier works where a peculiar charm resulted from the unstinting care with which every piece of material had been chosen and the whole fitted together, almost as if the stones had been precious stones and not flint or bricks'.[4]

Horwood exemplifies the partnership's output in the years before the First World War. While others were feeling the chill in the rapidly changing social and economic climate, Blow and Billerey went from strength to strength. In 1914 Charles Ashbee agreed that: 'during the last few years all the best work, and there was little enough of that, had been collared by Lutyens and Detmar Blow,'[5] adding uncharitably that 'their genius had helped them but their women helped them more.'

3 Christopher Hussey, 'Horwood House, Winslow, Bucks.', *Country Life* (10 November 1923), pp. 644–51, p. 644.

4 Hussey, 'Horwood House', p. 648. The quote from Roger Fry is from *Vision and Design* (Harmondsworth, 1920), pp. 214–15. Hussey draws attention to other carefully contrived elements at Horwood: 'The staircase is of unstained oak, the colour of latten, sand-blasted so that the softer parts of the surface are removed and the whole then beeswaxed.'

5 C. R. Ashbee, journal entry, 26 November 1914. (The Ashbee Journals, 44 vols,

The difference that Lutyens's marriage made to his career has been considered before now and generally, with hindsight, judged not to be as critical as Ashbee suggests. To the success of a society architect, a society marriage is unlikely to be insignificant nonetheless, and so it was with Blow. Marrying into the Tollemache family in 1910, in St Pauls Cathedral, strengthened his association with those still in a position to put work his way. It is easy to conclude that Blow's career changed course with his partnership in 1906 and accelerated after his marriage in 1910 but such a conclusion would be superficial. Both partnership and marriage were contributory rather than fundamental to his success. Blow and Billerey had been working together for four years before their partnership was formed in 1906, and on closer examination it can be seen that although a change in Blow's style seems to coincide with its formation, the change was neither as sudden nor as radical as it might at first appear.

The two men met through their mutual friend, the sculptor John Tweed. Billerey and Tweed studied in Paris at the Ecole des Beaux Arts and both knew Auguste Rodin.[6] In 1902 a dinner was held in Rodin's honour at the Cafe Royale and Tweed introduced Blow and Cockerell to the great man beforehand.[7] Through Tweed, Blow met Billerey at the same time and a week later Blow in turn introduced him to Cockerell. By July Billerey was working in Blow's office.[8] George Wyndham, who had inherited Clouds, presided over the Rodin dinner. Cockerell had to leave early but next morning Blow called to tell him how it ended: '[Blow] went back in a cab with Rodin and Tweed soon after 2.00 am and sat talking and smoking for about an hour. They then walked along the Embankment to see the dawn and tapped on Sargent's windows in Tite Street but without any result. And then they went back to bed. Detmar very brisk in spite of it all, but Rodin reported to have a headache!'[9]

If Billerey seems a more appropriate partner for someone with an eye to increasingly fashionable French neo-Classicism than for a man rooted in the

---

King's College Library, Cambridge). Ashbee was talking over the difficulties of architectural practice with fellow architect Francis Inigo Thomas. I am grateful to Alan Crawford for sharing the findings from his research into the Ashbee journals, of which this is one.

6 A. Stuart Gray, *Edwardian Architecture* (London: Duckworth, 1985), p. 358.

7 Sydney Cockerell, diary entry, Wednesday 14 May 1902, amongst the Cockerell Papers in the British Museum Manuscripts Collection.

8 Sydney Cockerell, diary entry, Monday 14 July 1902.

9 Sydney Cockerell, diary entry, Friday 16 May 1902. The dinner supported a public subscription, organised by Tweed, to commission Rodin to sculpt a St John the Baptist for the nation (see also the Tweed papers, Reading Borough Council: Leisure Services, Museum & Art Gallery for Rodin's correspondence to Tweed between 1898 and 1917).

teachings of Ruskin, it should be understood that in fact Billerey's Beaux Arts training and the ideals of the Arts and Crafts Movement were far from incompatible. A member of the SPAB, he was introduced to Cockerell as 'a young French architect who is an admirer of Morris'.[10] Blow was impressed from the start. A sketchbook from 1902 includes a note, perhaps a rough draft of a letter: 'I am much drawn to our friend Billerey. We want ... to persuade him to remain with us for we must try to work harder and get something attempted, done. I feel as if new life had been poured into me. Let us try soon to get a good work...'[11] The major commissions that followed at Wilsford and Little Ridge show no Beaux Arts influence despite Billerey's presence in the office. Even the chapel of 1906 for Lord Manners at Avon Tyrrell (Lethaby's house of 1891), credited by Blow to a collaboration with Billerey,[12] is English Wrenaissance rather than fashionably French (137). Their country work continued in Early English Classical styles until the war, as at Horwood.

In London things were different and they followed a different path. Edward VII had visited Paris in 1904 and put the royal stamp of approval on the Louis Quinze revival, which had been imported to London as early as 1900 with the interior of the Carlton Hotel by another Anglo-French architectural partnership, Mewes and Davis. The Ritz, with its Rue de Rivoli pavement arcade and light French interiors, was by the same firm but although Blow and Billerey's Wrenaissance chapel for Lord Manners is directly contemporaneous, their London work was as advanced in taste in its own way as that of Mewes and Davis. Their interior at No. 10 Carlton House Terrace for Viscount Ridley, started at the same time as the Ritz, was certainly highly sophisticated. Again, Blow attributes the design to a collaboration with Billerey. Its immaculately dressed stonework (to a state of the art known in the terminology of the day as stereotomy) and the solid black marble staircase typify the approach one might expect from a fashionable French architect but Blow's influence may be detected in the simplicity of the design. Painswick stone as well as Caen, and the patination of the gilt decoration to give the appearance of old work suggests the

10 Sydney Cockerell, diary entry, Saturday 24 May 1902. Soon after, Billerey was spreading the gospel of the SPAB in France: in September 1902 Blow, involved in casework relating to St Thomas's Church, Salisbury, wrote to the SPAB for nomination papers to enable another French architect to join: 'He had heard of the Society through my friend Mr Billerey' (unpublished letter from Detmar Blow to Thackeray Turner, 20 Sept 1902, SPAB Archives: St. Thomas's Church file, Salisbury).

11 Detmar Blow, Sketchbook No. 3, 1902, Ref 1987.55, p. 40, British Architectural Library, Drawings Collection.

12 Detmar Blow, Fellowship Nomination Papers RIBA, 30 September 1906, British Architectural Library.

137. The chapel at Avon Tyrrell, Hampshire, built in 1906. The painting in the apse by Phoebe Traquair depicts the *Te Deum* and among the throng stands a man dressed in traditional masons' attire, possibly depicting Detmar Blow.

restraint and careful choice of materials that exemplified Blow's methods.

This stylistic split between town and country exemplified by the work of Blow and Billerey at Avon Tyrrell on one hand and at Carlton House Terrace on the other, was widespread. Stanley Ramsey of Ramsey and Adshead, another fashionable architectural partnership of the time, summed it up:

> Georgian in the country,
> Neo-Grec in town,
> That's the stuff to give 'em,
> If you want renown.[13]

Neo-Grec, a Greek Revival style resuscitated with added (and always fashionable) French chic marked the position on the classical evolutionary scale that London society architecture had reached at the outset of the Great War. But in the country English-looking houses like Horwood were still much sought after, even though society clients increasingly demanded sophistication inside. Blow and Billerey obliged.

Throughout, when working on pre-existing buildings, Blow and Billerey's partnership set great store by archaeological exactitude. In 1907 Blow, working with Stallybrass at Breccles Hall in Norfolk, traced previous foundations to give the lead for the reconstruction of the entrance. Another Norfolk doorcase, this time from Raynham, was copied around 1910 to adorn the entrance to the much extended and altered Heale House, near Wilsford in the Avon Valley, where Frank Green was to work with Blow, once more ending his career as Clerk of Works to the estate.[14] At Heale, as at Breccles and Wilsford, there was an attempt to define the extent of an earlier, larger house archaeologically. The garden front to the west was 'completed' to match the surviving seventeenth-century fragment, following the lines of the sub-structures they uncovered.[15]

13 Quoted by Gavin Stamp in 'London 1900', *Architectural Design*, 48 (5 June 1978), 305–94, on p. 310. Ramsey's partner, Stanley Adshead was the site architect for William Flockhart during the construction of Rosehaugh House in Ross and Cromarty between 1893 and 1903, and married the local school teacher.

14 This doorcase was illustrated in John Belcher, *Essentials in Architecture* (London: Batsford, 1907), p. 59. Frank Green's presence at Heale was recalled during a conversation with the author in 1999, and confirmed by entries in Kelly's Directory.

15 Lawrence Weaver's description of the house tells how Blow's client, Mr Louis Greville, had searched for documentary evidence: 'Mr Greville has made a vigorous search for an old view of the house before its reduction in size, but so far without success. Probably one exists somewhere, buried in a scrapbook in some private library ... If such a picture should turn up, Mr Greville will be glad to know of it.' (Lawrence Weaver, 'Heale House, Wiltshire', *Country Life* (27 Feb 1915), 272–7, p. 276.) Sure enough a plan, dated 1810, did turn up in the British Museum and was

138. Heale House, Woodford, Wiltshire, 1910. From the south. The original house is to the left, its sash windows in the process of replacement with mullions and transomes. Detmar Blow's new wing is to the right.

Simultaneously, and with some charm, a later classical style was used for a new wing. Knowing that here he was transgressing the bounds of the slender archaeological evidence, Blow acknowledged the fact. For, although he reintroduced historically correct mullions and transoms to the windows of the original seventeenth-century house, he used sashes in his new wing of the type that the mullioned and transomed windows replaced in the old (139), thus indicating a later addition.

As their reputation grew so did the size of their projects. Blow and Billerey exhibited the enormous Wallingford Court – 'an entirely new mansion in Berkshire' – at the Royal Academy Exhibition in 1913 (140). They intended 'that this house should be in complete harmony with its environment, and typical of an Englishman's country residence, quite free from foreign influence.'[16] The design is a scholarly attempt to recreate the seventeenth-century classicism of John Thorpe but although 'foreign influence' may not

---

traced by Blow. It is to be found amongst documents relating to Heale House in the National Monuments Record and shows how accurately Blow's new work on the west front reproduced the old.

16 Wallingford Court, Berkshire, unattributed article in *Building News* (11 July 1913), p. 46.

139. Heale House, Woodford, Wiltshire. Detmar Blow's new wing from the north on completion in 1910 (National Monuments Record).

appear stylistically either inside or out, the impeccable planning, the symmetry, the precision and the attention to detail would have made it a most acceptable piece of society architecture for its time.

Even amongst Blow's wealthy patrons there were not many who could afford the scale of a Wallingford Court. The Second Duke of Westminster, known as Bend'or (after a racehorse), was the wealthiest of them all. Bend'or was the stepson of George Wyndham and Blow had known him since early days in Wiltshire (141). After the death of the First Duke in 1899, Eustace Balfour, his Grosvenor Estate Surveyor,[17] continued to undertake the majority of Bend'or's architectural work in London. But following overtures from others, including Lutyens, the new Duke later allowed his tenants to employ an

17 Eustace Balfour was Thackeray Turner's partner and Arthur Balfour's brother. He held the post as Grosvenor Estate Surveyor until 1909 when he fell ill and was replaced by Edmund Wimperis.

140 (above). Wallingford Court, Berkshire. Royal Academy Drawing, 1913.

141 (right). A christening group at Stockton House, Stockton, Wiltshire, 1897. Edward and Pamela Tennant are seated in the centre, flanked by Mrs Tennant's parents, the Hon. Percy and Mrs Wyndham. Detmar Blow stands behind and to the right of Pamela Tennant, next to George Wyndham. On the far right is Bend'or Grosvenor, later the Second Duke of Westminster (Simon Blow).

architect of his approval for their own work. A new house to Blow's design at 28 South Street in 1902 [see (64)] ensured Blow's favour in such matters from an early date.[18] In 1911 Blow, by then a close friend, designed and acted as master of the works for Bend'or's hunting lodge, The Woolsack, in Mimizan near Bordeaux[19] (142). Westminster was also instrumental at this time in Blow's

18 Leslie Field, *Bend'or the Golden Duke of Westminster* (London: Wiedenfeld & Nicholson, 1983), p. 106.

19 'When Mr Blow went to Mimizan to see what materials were available, he found

142. The Courtyard, Mimizan, from a watercolour by Detmar Blow.

men ... busy with the building of a blacksmith's shop. A team of bricklayers and carpenters was soon gathered. Materials were brought by a continuous procession of mules to a sandy promontory at the foot of a hill which juts out into one of the great lakes of South Western France. How great is the influence of materials and local craftsmanship is seen from the fact that this classical type of plan developed naturally into a building which looks almost medieval.' See anon., 'The Work of Mr Detmar Blow and Mr Fernand Billerey', Architectural Supplement to *Country Life* (26 Oct 1912), v–xxxvi, p. vi.

commission for Government House in Salisbury, Rhodesia, where Bend'or had considerable colonial interests. In southern Africa Blow secured other commissions from the British South African Company, working also at Government House, Bulawayo and Government House, Livingstone.

When the war came the Duke of Westminster was one of Blow's main clients. He was also building for himself at last at Hilles (143). An inscription running round the bay window in the best bedroom there read 'STARTED WORK IN 1913, STOPPED AND RESTARTED IN 1914'. The massive Wallingford Court project, amongst many others, came to a more permanent standstill but Blow and Billerey were well established with a programme of work that included alterations at Broome Park in Kent for Lord Kitchener. Kitchener bought the property in 1911, involving Blow from the start,[20] and as with Bend'or, architect and client became close friends. Winifred Blow, replying to a letter from Sydney Cockerell about arrangements for Philip Webb's funeral in 1915, told how her husband was then spending two evenings a week with Kitchener.[21]

Work at Broome was still unfinished when Kitchener died in 1916 and after two years of war Blow's practice was at last feeling the pinch.[22] In August 1917 Lutyens wrote to Lady Emily with glee: 'I met Blow last night. He is doing no work! except a house for himself and living with Westminster running his house, a sort of bailiff and Maitre d'Hotel! as far as I can make out!'[23] Lutyens was not far off the mark. In 1916 Blow had accepted a permanent post as the Duke's private secretary and manager of the Grosvenor Estate. The shortage of work that forced the move was widespread; even Lutyens was a worried man, having come home from Delhi that April with progress on Government House stopped at basement level. Plans for Lutyens' Little White House still lay unrealised in the casket he had given Lady Emily before their engagement; the

[20] Bend'or had met Kitchener in Egypt in 1911 (Leslie Field, *Bend'or the Golden Duke of Westminster*, p. 120). He may have made the introduction.

[21] Unpublished letter from Winifred Blow to Sydney Cockerell dated 10 June 1915 from Little Kimble, Bucks (a rented house in the park at Chequers), amongst the Cockerell Papers in the Manuscripts Collection at the British Museum.

[22] Blow was, however, involved in other work for the war effort. He worked for the War Office in Newcastle on housing for munitions workers and there was other war work too – as a stretcher bearer according to his daughter (Mrs Warre-Cornish in conversation to the author, 10 Jan 1985). This may have been in France for the letter from Winifred Blow to Sydney Cockerell mentioned above continues: 'Detmar has not been back to Dunkirk since the early spring as he has work to do for the War Office'.

[23] Letter from Edwin Lutyens to his wife dated 24 August 1917, quoted by Clayre Percy and Jane Ridley (eds), *Letters of Edwin Lutyens* (London: Collins, 1985), p. 354.

Blows meanwhile were moving into Hilles.[24]

At first Blow, knowing he was no businessman, had declined the Duke's offer of a permanent post. But Bend'or insisted: 'I don't want a businessman I need an artist. Artists have vision.'[25] Blow accepted although his partnership with Billerey continued. There was however considerable truth in Lutyens' assessment of their workload. Bend'or took up an increasing amount of Blow's time and in return for a lump-sum payment, he surrendered his other interests in 1920 to devote himself to estate duties alone.[26] That year Bend'or remarried. Blow was his witness at the register office. A trusted friend, he became far more than the Duke's agent, given power of attorney in the Duke's affairs.[27] Blow's grandson described how complete the trust between the two men had become: 'When Bend'or wanted him aboard the Flying Cloud – the yacht Detmar had designed to resemble a floating Queen Anne country house (144) – Detmar was there. When Bend'or nearly broke off his engagement with his third wife-to-be, Detmar was sent to inform her. And when Bend'or's ex-mistresses had to be paid off, it was Detmar who was asked to take it out of his cash fund. That way the monies never need be recorded since Detmar was under no obligations to show his accounts.'[28] A little more accountability might have been to Blow's advantage for Bend'or's third wife, fighting hard for her emancipation during their brief marriage, sowed the seeds of doubt. Blow's role as go-between in the stormy engagement that had preceded their marriage did not stand him in good stead for, not unnaturally, she saw others close to her husband as a threat, estranging Bend'or from a number of his old friends. Bend'or's hounding of his brother-in-law, Randall Wells' loyal client the Earl of Beauchamp, forcing him to leave the country in 1931 to avoid exposure as a homosexual, indicates the Duke's state of mind at this period. The episode was said to have been immortalised in *Brideshead Revisited*, although Evelyn Waugh later denied it. Come what may, Beauchamp did not return to Madresfield until 1937. A sick man, he died a year later.

24 An unpublished letter from Detmar Blow to Sydney Cockerell, 22 August 1917, confirms the date, amongst the Cockerell Papers in the Manuscripts Collection at the British Museum.

25 Simon Blow, 'A Blow by Blow Account of a Duke's Desertion', *The Spectator* (25 January 1986), pp. 22–3, p. 22.

26 Despite this, the Blow and Billerey partnership name continued in use afterwards, appearing on later drawings.

27 Later observers compared the relationship to that between Cardinal Wolsey and Henry VIII (see The Survey of London, re the Grosvenor Estate, quoted in Simon Blow, 'A Blow by Blow Account of a Duke's Desertion'.)

28 Simon Blow, 'A Blow by Blow Account of a Duke's Desertion'.

143. Hilles House, Painswick, Gloucestershire. The garden front.

Blow was next for the treatment. A showdown came on the 'Flying Cloud', with Bend'or insisting on examining Blow's arrangements concerning Grosvenor Estate leases in front of his new young wife. Part of the Duke's informal arrangements with his friend back in 1916 appears to have been the gift of seven leasehold properties in Mayfair but now, more than fifteen years later, the Duke declared he had not intended Blow to profit from them by sub-leasing.[29] A rift rapidly widened and despite Blow's immediate offer to hand back whatever amount Bend'or requested, he left the Duke in 1933 amidst much malicious gossip. His health suffered and although Bend'or eventually accepted repayment from Blow, allegations of further embezzlement were rumoured. Such persecution wrecked Blow's last years at Hilles and he survived the unfortunate Beauchamp by only a few months.

When Blow helped himself to Billson's postage stamps at Ulverscroft half a lifetime before, his client had asked: 'Why do you trouble to take them one at a time? Why not take a dozen? 'Oh thank you.' replied Detmar and took them.'[30]

[29] Simon Blow, 'A Blow by Blow Account of a Duke's Desertion'.

[30] S. A. Gimson, Random Memories of the Building of Stoneywell, 1938, a manuscript

144. The Flying Cloud. The interior of the Duke of Westminster's yacht, fitted out by Detmar Blow (BAL).

In comparison with the Westminster fortune the Duke's sub-leases were probably worth little more than the postage stamps had been to Billson. The achievement of common goals had always been more important to Blow than the details of his expenses. Blow may have been naive but both men were sometimes childish: 'Benny could, when he wanted to, transform himself into a mischievous little boy. Those blue, blue eyes grew round and appealing and the alarming Duke vanished to be replaced by a sort of Peter Pan character.' Thus, Loelia Ponsonby, the Duke's third wife, described Bend'or.[31] In turn Winifred Blow said of her own husband: 'With all children Detmar is – isn't he – the greatest child?'[32] Perhaps it is not uncommon for wives to see the child in their husbands, but in this instance the observations seem well founded. For Blow it

in a private collection.

31 Loelia, Duchess of Westminster, *Grace and Favour* (London: Weidenfeld & Nicholson, 1961), p. 193.

32 Unpublished letter from Winifred Blow to Sydney Cockerell dated 10 June 1915 from Little Kimble, Bucks, amongst the Cockerell Papers in the Manuscripts Collection at the British Museum.

was that bitterest of all childhood experiences, a fall from the favour of a powerful friend.

The money Blow took from Bend'or, whether it was taken justly or unjustly, was taken for Hilles. At Hilles all were equals and the irony is that the only way Blow could perpetuate such romantic Morrisian socialism was for it to exist in some curious symbiotic relationship with the estates of the richest man in England. Perhaps such irony appealed to Blow – his life is full of such apparent contradictions – but there is no doubt that Hilles was Blow's Kelmscott. Anachronistic when seen alongside the work his practice was producing elsewhere at the time, it was nonetheless a true reflection of his own steadfast underlying values. All about him changed but the spirit of Morris stayed with Blow and appears most readily in his more private moments: his marriage, his subsequent home life and even his death all reflect Morrisian ideals. The grand wedding in St Paul's Cathedral implies acceptance of a new found social status but the presence in the front pews of his itinerant stonemason friends underlines the fundamental beliefs he still held. This gesture was no snub to high society and only seems so now to those with an incomplete understanding of the thinking of the day. To the Souls and to others like them, Blow's actions showed a way forward, towards a social order in which the aristocracy and an enlightened working class peacefully strove together for a common utopia.

Hilles encapsulated all this, being that rare example, an architect's own house built to reflect not just stylistic predilection but a whole way of living and working. Lutyens too had dreamed of such things at the time of Morris' death but poor Emily's disappointment at the unrealised plans locked in her casket must have been aggravated by the fact that her brother, Neville Lytton came to know Blow's dream house so well. Too young to be a 'Soul', although another of his sisters acquired Soul status by marrying Gerald Balfour, Neville Lytton nonetheless was the author of *The English Country Gentleman*, a strange period piece written with hindsight in an attempt to identify the sort of man who might be upheld, from a Soul viewpoint, as 'an example of the modern squirearchy', the sort of man who could carry the landed gentry on into the society that had evolved in the years following the Great War. Lytton was distantly related by marriage to Blow's wife and came to know the couple well at Hilles. Although he did not reveal Blow's identity, it was he who Lytton chose to represent his modern squire in *The English Country Gentleman.*

Hilles was run on what Lytton perceived to be a 'sovietic system', but the image that this conjured up for Lytton is at odds with the one that we might imagine from such a description today. Lytton said of the Blows (without naming them):

> He and his wife have exceptional ideas about property. I really believe that they think that all things belong to God, and that He alone is entitled to the arrogance of possession ... Mr & Mrs regard themselves as the servants of all their dependants; children, domestics, farmers, and labourers.[33]

Lytton thought the kitchen the best room in the house:

> Here, as a rule, the whole house foregathers – monsieur, madame, all the babies and the servants. The servants have a separate table; that is the only distinction. They enjoy the same food and, to a large extent, the same conversation.[34]
>
> The rooms are large and full of light. All is paved with stone, which does not fear the muddiest boots. The long drawing room has a floor of raw elm, which also cannot be injured by large boots with nails in the soles ... there is little furniture, one or two beautiful chests and chests of drawers; three or four tapestries and three or four pictures, a splendidly solid dining room table, a few good chairs, an old organ, and one beautiful frieze carved by the owner.'[35]

Such a description could indeed be mistaken at first glance for a description of Kelmscott. Blow intended Hilles to be so, as we have seen earlier in his attempts to integrate family life with the fellowship he still felt for his mason friends:

> from the first, Detmar determined to put into practice the socialism learned from Morris. During building, the stone masons were to eat at the same table as the family. But it was an instance of false optimism all too frequent in the movement. The builders were embarrassed and the family selfconscious. Once it became clear that the scheme for equality could never work, it was dropped.[36]

Despite such setbacks Blow never gave up,[37] even after his death the Morris tradition was venerated by his wife and family. Detmar Blow, like Morris, was

[33] Neville Lytton, *The English Country Gentleman* (London: Hurst and Blackett, 1925), p. 31. There is no doubt that Lytton is referring to the Blows for despite the anonymity of *The English Country Gentleman*, Lytton repeats aspects of anecdotal Blow family history elsewhere, undisguised. For example, he repeats his description of Blow's early education at Hawtreys and an accident with a cricket ball that led to visits, during his convalescence, to the South Kensington Museum (and a subsequent early interest in the arts), mentioned in 'The Art of Detmar Blow', in *English Life* magazine (June, 1925), p. 58.

[34] Neville Lytton, *The English Country Gentleman*, pp. 35–6.

[35] Neville Lytton, *The English Country Gentleman*, p. 28.

[36] Simon Blow, 'Watching the Sun Set on Our Brave Utopia', *The Times* (9 October 1982).

[37] Blow continued to treat those that worked at Hilles as equals. A 19-year-old

carried to his grave on a farm cart and Oliver Lodge, in his tribute 'To Detmar Blow', made a lyrical reference to the early days:

> Goodbye old friend. Though years and woes,
> Had parted us, yet with you goes,
> One half of all I was. I stand
> Looking across the sunset land
> Like the one tower that time has left,
> A little while, in the dark cleft
> At Llanthony. O dawn at Clare,
> When light and hope possessed the air,
> When the great sun arose to enfold
> The ancient walls in morning gold!
> To work we clome [sic] the old flint tower,
> At play we swam the winding Stour,
> And up the hill at sweet nightfall
> To Belchamp Otton, or Belchamp Paul,
> Or Cavendish or Melford grey,
> We tramped and laughter dogged our way,
> Now on the Cotswold hills you sleep,
> Near all you love. And the good sheep
> Graze quietly by your rural grave
> Such sepulchre as kings might crave.[38]

Winifred carried on. She re-created Hilles, badly burned in a fire in 1951; changing only the roof coverings from thatch to stone slate. Three years after the fire she died in the house she had re-built

> her eyes resting on the Burne-Jones tapestry of the Primavera.[39]

Her grandson described how she was laid to rest near her husband:

> As the bells tolled in the neighbouring villages, we followed the cart along the narrow lane to the grassy hill top. May blossom spilled from hedges and decked the coffin. Standing around Detmar's grave were the choir from Gloucester Cathedral. After the prayers they sang 'There is a Green Hill Far Away' and it was over.[40]

---

plumber, Sydney Wallace, working there for three months in 1929 and paid £3 a week (£1 above the London rate), returned when he was 77 and wrote soon after: 'to work and live for a few months in such luxury and to mix on such equal terms with a family of what is classed as the 'upper' was quite an eye opener. It must have taught me the basis of equality' (unpublished letter from Sydney Wallace to Detmar Blow's grandson, also named Detmar, 7 July 1988; among the Blow family papers at Hilles).

38 Oliver W. F. Lodge, 'To Detmar Blow', *Country Life* (7 Sept 1940), p. 205.

39 Simon Blow, 'Watching the Sun Set on Our Brave Utopia'.

Detmar Blow and the sad tale of the latter phase of his contradictory career has been seen in the past to personify the dilemma in which the Arts and Crafts architects increasingly found themselves during the Edwardian period.[41] Social and economic developments meant a change of fortune for architects generally and especially for those favoured to build large new country houses. But there was an alternative, and one which Blow, had his practice survived the War, might have benefited from. For it was the Wandering Architects, perhaps more so than any others, who were responsible for its introduction. In the latter part of the Edwardian era the small country house, a comparative rarity before the turn of the century, rapidly became a very desirable commodity. The motor car made week-ending easier for the well-off and the triple pressures of a servant problem, a widening middle class and a changing distribution of wealth meant a vogue for the sort of house that, curiously, the Wandering Architects had advocated from the start. When it came to doing without back stairs and ostentation their early houses were market-leaders, and although this all became confused later with sandals and garden-city socialism, the thinking to which their work gave rise produced an inter-war flowering for their kind of architecture. Vernacular styles, a sense of place and local materials were also just what the new week-ender wanted then (and still hunts remorselessly today). *Country Life* magazine, trading on the romance of the rural, first published its collection of *Small Country Houses of Today* in 1911 and there, right at the front, came Ernest Barnsley's Upper Dorvel House in Sapperton (see 38) followed not far behind by Gimson's Leasowes (see 29) and Powell's Long Copse (see 20). None of these houses were then new but by his careful choice of examples Lawrence Weaver, who edited the series, still advocated indigenous styles that were in many respects a direct continuation of the Gothic Revival lineage in which the Arts and Crafts Movement had been nurtured.

That craft-built houses should be chosen to illustrate the genre seems hardly surprising. That these houses were the way they were because of how they were put together was perhaps not always perceived by the buying public. Weaver did not overlook it, indeed as time went by he may have felt that this aspect needed stressing. In any event, when he produced a second collection just before the Great War he went back to the same starting point, this time using Stoneywell and Happisburgh as his opening examples, reinforcing them with later houses by North and Falkner.

40 Simon Blow, 'Watching the Sun Set on Our Brave Utopia'.

41 See, for example, the accounts of Blow's career by Gavin Stamp ['London 1900', *Architectural Design*, 48 (1978), p. 310] and Clive Aslet (*The Last Country Houses*, pp. 244–50).

Lawrence Weaver more than anyone else was the recorder of the works of the wandering architects. His third title in the series, *Small Country Houses – Their Repair and Enlargement* crossed the divide between new build and old, never a barrier to the group of architects under discussion. The dream of the cottage in the country had begun. Further up-market the careful adaptation of old buildings to a new style of living was in full swing as at Breccles Hall, Heale House and Broome Park. Now smaller examples, the more romantic the better, attracted attention. Weaver campaigned for an SPAB approach to such work and his message was taken seriously. After all the SPAB was trying to protect the very things that the new owners of these old places had bought them for – their place in the country was a place in history; their little part of England was built out of little pieces of the England upon which it stood. As Weaver said in his introduction:

> Those who have a feeling for old things find in such work three chief sources of satisfaction. They like to live with work done in traditional ways, and to mark the irregularities and odd devices which show the unaffected workmanship and nimble minds of long dead craftsmen. They are affected by the sense of continuity and enduring usefulness, and join themselves in thought with owners of bygone centuries, though nothing may remain but their names, and often not even such slight knowledge. They please themselves in the endeavour to make the additions to the handiwork of the old men in a spirit of reverence for their achievement, and of a single intent to do nothing unworthy of their example.[42]

Thus Weaver encouraged, even more so than with the earlier companion volumes of new houses, the continuation of the crafts tradition of the Wandering Architects. Amongst the work of better known men like Ernest Newton, Robert Lorimer, Edwin Lutyens, Reginal Blomfield, E. J. May, Edward Prior and Guy Dawber due attention is given in this volume to the advice of the SPAB, The National Trust, Ashbee, Lethaby and Morris. Between the better known names appear the work of Basil Stallybrass at the Old Bell House, Ludford and Quennell House, Plaistow. The lessons of conservative repair and respect for the craftsmanship of the past were, in the years immediately before the Great War, reaching an ever widening public.

Their relevance continued afterwards but there was a shift in attitude. The contrasts between the fields of Flanders and the fields of home were acutely felt by so many and certainly no less so amongst that *Country Life* reading section of society – the families that provided many of the young infantry officers whose

42 Lawrence Weaver, *Small Country Houses – Their Repair and Enlargement* (London: Country Life, 1914), p. xix.

mortality rate was so high. 'When I return from the observing post at dark, after changing from wet muddy things, I get some tea,' wrote Marjorie Noble's twenty-year-old son Marc, who died in France, 'then out comes my pipe, and the latest *Country Life* from England, and I sit down in front of my dug out and read about the old houses.'[43] The post-war tendency was to sentimentalize those things that had been taken for granted in 1914. The village war memorial would take the form of a lych-gate or a market cross. The oak or the stone, its traditional style and the way it was crafted was seen to stand for much of that which the young men died for. At Bedales Lupton, home from the war, built the cruck-framed Memorial Hall with his own hands to commemorate those, like Edward Thomas, who didn't come back. At Long Crendon (see 127), Tilden's work was described as a kind of therapy for his client, Laline Hohler. The Hohlers had bought Long Crendon when Arthur Hohler returned from the front, only to die of pneumonia soon after. The house grew 'from a mere farm of four or five bedrooms and a couple or so of sitting rooms, into a house of five sitting rooms, each of them large and individual, with nearly twenty bedrooms.'[44] To avoid the anachronism of corridors, primitive planning arrangements were retained using independent staircases to the bedrooms. Tilden stayed for long periods at the house, working with a small team of builders from a local firm. During the restoration he and his wife and Mrs Hohler lived in the old house until it became too draughty whereafter they moved into a nearby thatched cottage. Some of the work of stripping stucco from the Tudor beams they did themselves, Tilden remembered, 'when we felt energetic enough'. Bouts of therapeutic activity were interspersed with outings in the surrounding countryside, searching out local buildings of interest: 'A pony, a jingle and a rather decrepit bicycle were our means of progression in those days. Laline and my wife would drive along the country lanes, or rather they would waddle from side to side, fearless in this because there seemed to be no traffic, whilst I would stunt on the bicycle to keep their minds off worse things.'[45]

Tilden's contemporary, Oliver Hill (1887–1968), fought as an officer in the London and Scottish Regiment, returning, as he described later, to the security of his Arts and Crafts roots when he could:

> A Country Life article caused me to go and see Detmar Blow's house in Gloucestershire. Like many other people he [Blow] was attracted to the countryside, acquiring several farms near Painswick Beacon and

[43] Marc Noble, *Marjorie Noble* (London: Country Life, 1918. Published for private circulation), quoted by Clive Aslet, *The Last Country Houses*, pp. 155–6.

[44] Philip Tilden, *True Remembrances* (London: Country Life, 1954), p. 62.

[45] Philip Tilden, *True Remembrances*, p. 62.

> building himself a remarkable house on the edge of the Cotswolds [145]. I returned there for long visits during the war ... It took longer to know Mrs Claude Biddulph, of Rodmarton, where I had been drawn by Arthur Oswald's articles. When I succeeded she would invite me to archery meetings with the village boys. Being no high-flyer, I was startled on one occasion to receive a prize. When I enquired why, she replied: 'For not hitting the target once.'[46]

After the Second World War, Hill settled in Sapperton at Daneway House, still full of memories of Gimson and hand-crafted enterprise. Hill however could equally well turn his talents to neo-Georgian, neo-Grec, Hollywood Spanish or the International Style (his 'Joldwynds' ironically replaced an earlier Webb house of the same name, admired by Gimson and Lethaby on a visit in 1890). To all he applied a Lutyensesque inventiveness to which his society clients succumbed. He went to the same school, Uppingham, as Alfred Powell and Herbert North. Brought up in west Surrey he, like Falkner, knew Gertrude Jekyll. He hero-worshipped Lutyens and described how, like Sydney Blow, he followed Lutyen's advice and obtained a grounding in the building industry. He worked in a builder's yard for over a year as he later described:

> He [Lutyens] recommended an established London firm, J. Simpson & Son, whose proprietor was an old hunting friend of my fathers. Mr Simpson readily allowed me the run of his workshops, I spent a year or more there, working at the bench in the wood working mill, joiner's shop, stonemason's yard, and the painters and polishers shops ... I acquired an appreciation of the nature of building materials and, I think, some knowledge of the men who work them and the way they set about their job. I had to report to Mr Simpson once a week, and well remember sitting in his study, his over-hanging eyebrows and quizzical eyes glinting beneath them as he questioned me about my activities. The workshops extended from the back of the house to the offices in Paddington Street and there were more extensive yards at Kilburn, where I worked, which Mr Simpson visited in his brougham every Friday, to make his weekly inspection. His staff held him in greatest respect and I think, affection; and when he died, he left them the business. I finished my time there watching a large contract through from the beginning under the tutorledge [sic] of Mr Robinson, the general foreman.[47]

Although he never afterwards felt the need to spend much time on site – in fact his inter-war clients were more likely to complain that he spent too little

[46] Oliver Hill, 'An Architect's Debt to Country Life', *Country Life* (12 January 1967), p. 72.

[47] Oliver Hill, 'Architect's Biography – 6', *Building Magazine* (1949), p. 205.

time there – the teaching was ingrained and the handling of materials as self-assured as that of his hero. At 'The Cour' in Argyllshire (146), built in 1921 and one of his most dramatically inventive compositions, the local blue-grey Whin stone was quarried on site as Wells or Prior might have done fifteen or twenty years earlier.

Perhaps it is fitting that it was Hill who sketched the design for the little stone building that stands, incomplete though it is (147), to mark the place where the wandering finally came to an end for Detmar Blow. Part memorial, part lychgate, part wayside shrine and part belvedere, it was erected by Winifred who now lies with her husband beneath the same nearby stone.

Other talented architects of the twenties and thirties with more limited stylistic range than Oliver Hill still returned to the same craft roots but the ideals of the Wandering Architects had become diffused. What had been an attempt to revive a proper understanding of local materials and building methods in a post-industrial society was lost in the all pervading rose-tinted haze of times gone by. Although Harold Falkner's work at Dippenhall was not without parallels when he started in 1921, he was on his own long before Alfred Hack fell from the scaffold at the Black Barn forty years later. In the intervening period fashion had moved on from up-market Stockbroker Tudor to the mass-market by-pass version and all signs of craftsmanship and regional variation had finally disappeared behind the applied surfaces of false timber framework and rendered brick. What Falkner would have made of today's speculative revival of the style, with its joke oak and stick-on leaded lights one can guess but even this sad reflection of an unrequited love affair with the country cottage is still indicative of the lasting impact made by the architects who wandered in the wake of Ruskin and Morris.

The inter-dependence between work and lifestyle within this group exemplified the teaching of their mentors, offering living proof that the teaching of Ruskin, as interpreted by Morris and Webb, could find tangible expression in architectural terms. But although their achievement thus gave credibility to the whole architectural wing of the Arts and Crafts movement, they avoided public recognition. They had no collective manifesto and their output was small. They cared little for publicity, sought no awards and rarely entered significant national competitions. It was left to others to promote their way of working and, as is often the way, history has remembered instead those who were better self-publicists.

Unlike Morris and Ruskin, their commitment to education was largely by example. At the Central School of Art however, Lethaby taught a design philosophy that incorporated their values so effectively that it become an integral part of art education. So deeply did he instil such teaching in the

145. Hilles House, Painswick, Gloucestershire, by Oliver Hill.

national psyche that the passing fashions of the Edwardian era did not displace it. Although society was demanding Beaux-Arts architecture in London by the time the Central School of Art was firmly established, early historians of the Modern Movement, whose all-pervasive flood eventually dominated the central fifty years of this century, argued that the Beaux-Arts excursion into classicism and its own consequent populist manifestation, neo-Georgian, was a historical irrelevance. The British Arts & Crafts were, they thought, the true pathfinders of the International Modern Movement. In 1942 Nikolaus Pevsner identified some of these early forerunners in his article entitled 'Nine Swallows – No Summer', an attempt to find continuity in this country between Morris – the opening character in his seminal *Pioneers of Modern Design* of 1936 – and the Modern Movement's early flowering.[48] In truth the early high fliers of the Modern Movement were only to be found further afield in continental Europe.

48 Nikolaus Pevsner, 'Nine Swallows – No Summer', *Architectural Review*, 91 (May 1942), pp. 109–12.

146. Design for The Cour, Kintyre, Argyllshire, by Oliver Hill, 1921. The entrance front (BAL).

Although Pevsner identified nine brave British swallows, for this country the summer they foreshadowed was hardly a summer at all. The free style achievements of the Wandering Architects may in fact represent the thread Pevsner had been seeking. For whether or not they were the true forerunners of the Modern Movement, they were most certainly the last progressive movement in British architecture to precede it. Their work has a continuing relevance because their influence is fundamentally more than merely stylistic, for theirs was a far broader approach. They understood the relevance of locality and context, both geographic and temporal. They advocated an architecture that explored the complex and complete relationship between man and art and building.

147. The gravestone and memorial building that mark the burial place of Detmar and Winifred Blow near Hilles House on Cud Hill, overlooking Gloucester. The memorial building was from an original design sketched by Oliver Hill.

INDEX

INDEX